JY 22 '16

WITHDRAWN

Agriculture

Library of Congress Classification
2012

Prepared by the Policy and Standards Division
Library Services

LIBRARY OF CONGRESS
Cataloging Distribution Service
Washington, D.C.

This edition cumulates all additions and changes to class S through List 2012/01, dated January 16, 2012. Additions and changes made subsequent to that date are published in weekly lists posted on the World Wide Web at

<http://www.loc.gov/aba/cataloging/classification/weeklylists/>

and are also available in *Classification Web*, the online Web-based edition of the Library of Congress Classification.

Library of Congress Cataloging-in-Publication Data

Library of Congress.
Library of Congress classification. S. Agriculture / prepared by the Policy and Standards Division, Library Services.
pages cm
"This edition cumulates all additions and changes to class S through List 2012/01, dated January 16, 2012. Additions and changes made subsequent to that date are published in weekly lists posted on the World Wide Web ... and are also available in Classification Web, the online Web-based edition of the Library of Congress Classification"--Title page verso.
Includes index.
ISBN 978-0-8444-9540-8
1. Classification, Library of Congress. 2. Classification--Books--Agriculture. I. Library of Congress. Policy and Standards Division. II. Title. III. Title: Agriculture.

Z696.U5S 2012 025.4'663--dc23 2012010230

Copyright ©2012 by the Library of Congress except within the U.S.A.

For sale by the Library of Congress Cataloging Distribution Service,
101 Independence Avenue, S.E., Washington, DC 20541-4912.
Product catalog available on the Web at **www.loc.gov/cds**

PREFACE

The first edition of Class S, *Agriculture*, was published in 1911, the second in 1927, the third in 1948 (reprinted with supplementary pages of additions and changes in 1965), and the fourth in 1982. A 1996 edition cumulated additions and changes that were made during the period 1982-1996. A 2008 edition cumulated additions and changes that were made during the period 1996-2008. This 2012 edition cumulates additions and changes made since the publication of the 2008 edition.

In the Library of Congress Classification schedules, classification numbers or spans of numbers that appear in parentheses are formerly valid numbers that are now obsolete. Numbers or spans that appear in angle brackets are optional numbers that have never been used at the Library of Congress but are provided for other libraries that wish to use them. In most cases, a parenthesized or angle-bracketed number is accompanied by a "see" reference directing the user to the actual number that the Library of Congress currently uses, or a note explaining Library of Congress practice.

Access to the online version of the full Library of Congress Classification is available on the World Wide Web by subscription to Classification Web. Details about ordering and pricing may be obtained from the Cataloging Distribution Service at:

<http://www.loc.gov/cds/>

New or revised numbers and captions are added to the L.C. Classification schedules as a result of development proposals made by the cataloging staff of the Library of Congress and cooperating institutions. Upon approval of these proposals by the editorial meeting of the Policy and Standards Division, new classification records are created or existing records are revised in the master classification database. Lists of newly approved or revised classification numbers and captions are posted on the World Wide Web at:

<http://www.loc.gov/aba/cataloging/classification/weeklylists/>

Libby Dechman, senior subject cataloging policy specialist in the Policy and Standards Division, is responsible for coordinating the overall intellectual and editorial content of class S. Kent Griffiths and Ethel Tillman, assistant editors of classification schedules, are responsible for maintaining the master database and creating index terms for the captions.

Barbara B. Tillett, Chief
Policy and Standards Division

March 2012

OUTLINE

S1-(972)	Agriculture (General)
S21-400.5	Documents and other collections
S403	Agricultural missions, voyages, etc.
S419-482	History
S530-559	Agricultural education
S539.5-542.3	Research. Experimentation
S544-545.53	Agricultural extension work
S548-548.6	Historic farms
S550-559	Exhibitions. Fairs
S560-571.5	Farm economics. Farm management. Agricultural mathematics Including production standards, record keeping, farmwork rates, marketing
S583-587.73	Agricultural chemistry. Agricultural chemicals
S588.4-589.6	Agricultural physics Including radioisotopes in agriculture
S589.7	Agricultural ecology (General)
S589.75-589.76	Agriculture and the environment
S589.8-589.87	Plant growing media. Potting soils
S590-599.9	Soils. Soil science Including soil surveys, soil chemistry, soil structure, soil-plant relationships
S600-600.7	Agricultural meteorology. Crops and climate
S602.5-604.37	Methods and systems of culture. Cropping systems Including fallowing, rotation of crops, plowing
S604.5-604.64	Agricultural conservation
S604.8-621.5	Melioration: Improvement, reclamation, fertilization, irrigation, etc., of lands
S605.5	Organic farming. Organiculture
S606-621.5	Special classes of lands and reclamation methods Including woodlands, burning of lands, deserts, saline environments, moors
S622-627	Soil conservation and protection
S631-667	Fertilizers and improvement of the soil
S671-760.5	Farm machinery and farm engineering
S770-790.3	Agricultural structures. Farm buildings
S900-(972)	Conservation of natural resources Including land conservation
SB1-1110	Plant culture
SB39	Horticultural voyages, etc.
SB71-87	History
SB107-109	Economic botany

	Plant culture - Continued
SB109.7-111	Methods for special areas
	Including cold regions, dry farming, tropical agriculture
SB112	Irrigation farming
SB113.2-118.46	Seeds. Seed technology
SB118.48-118.75	Nurseries. Nursery industry
SB119-124	Propagation
	Including breeding, selection, grafting, air layering
SB125	Training and pruning
SB126	Artificial light gardening
SB126.5-126.57	Hydroponics. Soilless agriculture
SB127	Forcing
SB128	Growth regulators
SB129-130	Harvesting, curing, storage
SB169-172.5	Tree crops
SB175-177	Food crops
SB183-317	Field crops
	Including cereals, forage crops, grasses, legumes, root crops, sugar plants, textile plants, alkaloidal plants, medicinal plants
SB317.5-319.864	Horticulture. Horticultural crops
SB320-353.5	Vegetables
SB354-402	Fruit and fruit culture
SB381-386	Berries and small fruits
SB387-399	Grape culture. Viticulture
SB401	Nuts
SB403-450.87	Flowers and flower culture. Ornamental plants
SB406.7-406.83	Plant propagation
SB409-413	Culture of individual plants
SB414	Forcing
SB414.6-417	Greenhouses and greenhouse culture
SB418-418.4	Container gardening
SB419-419.3	Indoor gardening and houseplants
SB419.5	Roof gardening. Balcony gardening
SB421-439.8	Classes of plants
	Including annuals, climbers, ferns, lawns, perennials, shrubs
SB441-441.75	Flower shows. Exhibitions
SB442.5	Care and preparation of cut flowers and ornamental plants for market
SB442.8-443.4	Marketing. Cut flower industry. Florists
SB446-446.6	Horticultural service industry
SB447	Preservation and reproduction of flowers, fruits, etc.

	Plant culture
	Flowers and flower culture. Ornamental plants - Continued
SB447.5	Bonkei. Tray landscapes
SB449-450.87	Flower arrangement and decoration
SB450.9-467.8	Gardens and gardening
SB469-(476.4)	Landscape gardening. Landscape architecture
SB481-486	Parks and public reservations
	Including theory, management, history
SB599-990.5	Pests and diseases
SB608	Individual or types of plants or trees
SB610-615	Weeds, parasitic plants, etc.
SB617-618	Poisonous plants
SB621-795	Plant pathology
SB818-945	Economic entomology
SB950-990.5	Pest control and treatment of diseases. Plant protection
SB950.9-970.4	Pesticides
SB973-973.5	Soil disinfection
SB974-978	Organic plant protection. Biological control
SB979.5-985	Inspection. Quarantine
SB992-998	Economic zoology applied to crops. Agricultural zoology
	Including animals injurious and beneficial to plants
SD1-669.5	Forestry
SD11-115	Documents
SD119	Voyages, etc.
SD131-247.5	History of forestry. Forest conditions
SD250-363.3	Forestry education
SD388	Forestry machinery and engineering
SD388.5	Tools and implements
SD389	Forest roads
SD390-390.43	Forest soils
SD390.5-390.7	Forest meteorology. Forest microclimatology
SD391-410.9	Sylviculture
SD411-428	Conservation and protection
	Including forest influences, damage by elements, fires, forest reserves
SD430-(559)	Exploitation and utilization
	Including timber trees, fuelwood, logging, transportation, valuation
SD561-669.5	Administration. Policy
SF1-1100	Animal culture
SF41-55	History

OUTLINE

	Animal culture - Continued
SF515-515.5	Reptiles
SF518	Insect rearing
SF521-539.8	Bee culture
SF541-560	Sericulture. Silk culture
SF561	Lac-insects
SF600-1100	Veterinary medicine
SF756.5-769.5	Special preclinical sciences
	Including veterinary genetics, ethology, anatomy, physiology, embryology, pathology
SF780.2-780.7	Veterinary microbiology, bacteriology, virology, mycology
SF780.9	Veterinary epidemiology. Epizootiology
SF781-809	Communicable diseases of animals (General)
SF810	Veterinary parasitology
SF810.5-810.7	Predatory animals and their control
SF811-909	Veterinary medicine of special organs, regions, and systems
SF910	Other diseases and conditions
SF910.5	Veterinary orthopedics
SF911-914.4	Veterinary surgery
SF914.3-914.4	Veterinary traumatology. Veterinary emergencies
SF914.5	Veterinary acupuncture
SF915-919.5	Veterinary pharmacology
SF925	Veterinary physical medicine
SF951-997.5	Diseases of special classes of animals
SH1-691	Aquaculture. Fisheries. Angling
SH20.3-191	Aquaculture
SH33-134.6	By region or country
SH138	Mariculture
SH151-179	Fish culture
SH171-179	Diseases and adverse factors
SH185-191	Frogs, leeches, etc.
SH201-399	Fisheries
SH213-216.55	By oceans and seas
SH219-321	By region or country
SH327.5-327.7	Fishery resources. Fishery conservation
SH328-329	Fishery management. Fishery policy
SH334	Economic aspects. Finance
SH334.5-334.7	Fishery technology
SH334.9-336.5	Fishery processing
SH337	Packing, transportation, and storage
SH337.5	Fishing port facilities

OUTLINE

Agriculture (General)

Periodicals. By language of publication

For works about societies and serial publications of societies see S21+

For general yearbooks see S414

1 English (American)

3 English

5 French

7 German

9 Italian

11 Scandinavian

12 Dutch

13 Slavic

15 Spanish and Portuguese

16.A-Z Other European languages, A-Z

Colonial, English, and American see S1+

18 Polyglot

19 Other languages (not A-Z)

20 History and description of periodicals and societies (General)

Documents and other collections

Including societies and congresses

United States

Federal documents

Commissioner of Patents

21.A19 Agricultural report

Department of Agriculture

21.A2-.A29 Report of the Commissioner or Secretary

21.A3 The official record of the Department of Agriculture

21.A35 Yearbook

21.A37 Agriculture handbook

21.A4-.A49 Circulars

21.A6 Farmers' bulletins

21.A63 Weekly newsletter to crop correspondents

21.A7 Bulletin

21.A74 Agriculture information bulletin

21.A75 Journal of agricultural research

21.A78 Weather, crops, and markets

21.A8-.A99 Other reports

21.A86-.A95 Financial: accounts and disbursements, etc.

21.A86 Estimates of expenditures

21.A87 Expenditures ... Letter from the Secretary of Agriculture

21.A99 Miscellaneous general. By date

21.C8-.C9 History

21.C8 Official

21.C9 Nonofficial

Documents and other collections
United States
Federal documents
Department of Agriculture -- Continued
Administrative documents; appointments; personnel
21.D2-.D39 Serial publications
21.D4-.D7 Monographs
Reports of individual bureaus
Bureau of Agricultural Economics see HD1751
Bureau of Biological Survey see QH104+
Bureau of Chemistry see S585
Bureau of Crop Estimates see HD1751
21.D85-.D859 Crop Reporting Board
Bureau of Entomology
see SB823
Office of Exhibitions see S559.A+
Office of Experiment Stations
21.E2-.E8 Serial publications
21.E9A-.E9Z Monographs
21.F4 Office of Farm Management
21.F6 Foreign Agricultural Service (1953-)
Office of Foreign Markets see HD9000+
Forest Service see SD11
Library see Z733.A+
Bureau of Markets see HD9000.9.A5+
Bureau of Plant Industry see SB19
Division of Pomology see SB19
Office of Public Roads see TE21+
21.R44 Agricultural Research Service
21.S2 Seed Distribution
Class here only departmental publications
Bureau of Soils see S591.A1+
21.S3-.S36 Solicitor
21.S37 States Relations Service
21.S4-.S8 Bureau of Statistics
21.S9 Supply Division
21.T43 Technical Assistance Division
Weather Bureau see QC983
21.Z2-.Z8 Congressional and other documents
22 National societies and conventions
Sections
22.7 Northeastern States
23 New England
24 Middle States
25 Southern States
26 Central States. Upper Mississippi Valley
27 Great Plains

Documents and other collections
United States
Sections -- Continued
28 Mountain States
29 The Southwest
30 Pacific Coast
30.5 Documents concerning States collectively
State documents, etc.
Alabama
31 General
32.A-Z Local, A-Z
Alaska
33 General
34.A-Z Local, A-Z
Arizona
35 General
36.A-Z Local, A-Z
Arkansas
37 General
38.A-Z Local, A-Z
California
39 General
40.A-Z Local, A-Z
Colorado
41 General
42.A-Z Local, A-Z
Connecticut
43 General
44.A-Z Local, A-Z
Delaware
45 General
46.A-Z Local, A-Z
District of Columbia
47 General
48.A-Z Local, A-Z
Florida
49 General
50.A-Z Local, A-Z
Georgia
51 General
52.A-Z Local, A-Z
Hawaii
52.5 General
52.6.A-Z Local, A-Z
Idaho
53 General
54.A-Z Local, A-Z

Documents and other collections
United States
State documents, etc. -- Continued
Illinois
55 General
56.A-Z Local, A-Z
Indian Territory
57 General
58.A-Z Local, A-Z
Indiana
59 General
60.A-Z Local, A-Z
Iowa
61 General
62.A-Z Local, A-Z
Kansas
63 General
64.A-Z Local, A-Z
Kentucky
65 General
66.A-Z Local, A-Z
Louisiana
67 General
68.A-Z Local, A-Z
Maine
69 General
70.A-Z Local, A-Z
Maryland
71 General
72.A-Z Local, A-Z
Massachusetts
73 General
74.A-Z Local, A-Z
Michigan
75 General
76.A-Z Local, A-Z
Minnesota
77 General
78.A-Z Local, A-Z
Mississippi
79 General
80.A-Z Local, A-Z
Missouri
81 General
82.A-Z Local, A-Z
Montana
83 General

	Documents and other collections
	United States
	State documents, etc.
	Montana -- Continued
84.A-Z	Local, A-Z
	Nebraska
85	General
86.A-Z	Local, A-Z
	Nevada
87	General
88.A-Z	Local, A-Z
	New Hampshire
89	General
90.A-Z	Local, A-Z
	New Jersey
91	General
92.A-Z	Local, A-Z
	New Mexico
93	General
94.A-Z	Local, A-Z
	New York
95	General
96.A-Z	Local, A-Z
	North Carolina
97	General
98.A-Z	Local, A-Z
	North Dakota
99	General
100.A-Z	Local, A-Z
	Ohio
101	General
102.A-Z	Local, A-Z
	Oklahoma
103	General
104.A-Z	Local, A-Z
	Oregon
105	General
106.A-Z	Local, A-Z
	Pennsylvania
107	General
108.A-Z	Local, A-Z
	Rhode Island
109	General
110.A-Z	Local, A-Z
	South Carolina
111	General
112.A-Z	Local, A-Z

Documents and other collections
United States
State documents, etc. -- Continued
South Dakota
113 General
114.A-Z Local, A-Z
Tennessee
115 General
116.A-Z Local, A-Z
Texas
117 General
118.A-Z Local, A-Z
Utah
119 General
120.A-Z Local, A-Z
Vermont
121 General
122.A-Z Local, A-Z
Virginia
123 General
124.A-Z Local, A-Z
Washington
125 General
126.A-Z Local, A-Z
West Virginia
127 General
128.A-Z Local, A-Z
Wisconsin
129 General
130.A-Z Local, A-Z
Wyoming
131 General
132.A-Z Local, A-Z
Other countries
Canada and Newfoundland
133 General works
Alberta and Northwest Territories
135 General
136.A-Z Local, A-Z
British Columbia
141 General
142.A-Z Local, A-Z
Manitoba
147 General
148.A-Z Local, A-Z
New Brunswick
149 General

	Documents and other collections
	Other countries
	Canada and Newfoundland
	New Brunswick -- Continued
150.A-Z	Local, A-Z
	Newfoundland
151	General
152.A-Z	Local, A-Z
	Nova Scotia
153	General
154.A-Z	Local, A-Z
	Ontario
155	General
156.A-Z	Local, A-Z
	Prince Edward Island
157	General
158.A-Z	Local, A-Z
	Québec
159	General
160.A-Z	Local, A-Z
	Saskatchewan
161	General
162.A-Z	Local, A-Z
163	Yukon and Mackenzie
164.A-Z	Other (Franklin, Keewatin, Labrador, Ungava, etc.), A-Z
	Mexico
165	General
166.A-Z	Local, A-Z
	Central America
167	General works
168	Belize
169	Costa Rica
170	Guatemala
171	Honduras
172	Nicaragua
173	Panama
174	Salvador
	West Indies
175	General works
176	Bahamas
177	Cuba
179	Haiti
180	Jamaica
181	Puerto Rico
183.A-Z	Other, A-Z
184	Bermuda

Documents and other collections
Other countries -- Continued
South America
Including Latin America (General)
185 General works
Argentina
187 General
188.A-Z Local, A-Z
Bolivia
189 General
190.A-Z Local, A-Z
Brazil
191 General
192.A-Z Local, A-Z
Chile
193 General
194.A-Z Local, A-Z
Colombia
195 General
196.A-Z Local, A-Z
Ecuador
197 General
198.A-Z Local, A-Z
Guyana
199 General
200.A-Z Local, A-Z
Suriname
201 General
202.A-Z Local, A-Z
French Guiana
203 General
204.A-Z Local, A-Z
Paraguay
205 General
206.A-Z Local, A-Z
Peru
207 General
208.A-Z Local, A-Z
Uruguay
209 General
210.A-Z Local, A-Z
Venezuela
211 General
212.A-Z Local, A-Z
Atlantic islands
213 General
214.A-Z Local, A-Z

Documents and other collections
Other countries -- Continued
Europe
215 General works
British Isles
217 Great Britain
England
218 General
218.2.A-Z Local, A-Z
Ireland (Republic or General)
219 General
220.A-Z Local, A-Z
Northern Ireland
220.5 General
220.6.A-Z Local, A-Z
Scotland
221 General
222.A-Z Local, A-Z
Wales
223 General
224.A-Z Local, A-Z
Austria
Including Austria-Hungary
225 General
226.A-Z Local, A-Z
Hungary
227 General
228.A-Z Local, A-Z
France
229 General
230.A-Z Local, A-Z
Germany
231 General
232.A-Z Local, A-Z
East Germany
(232.5) General
(232.6.A-Z) Local, A-Z
Greece
233 General
234.A-Z Local, A-Z
Italy
235 General
236.A-Z Local, A-Z
Low countries
Belgium
237 General
238.A-Z Local, A-Z

Documents and other collections
Other countries
Europe
Low countries -- Continued
Netherlands
239 General
240.A-Z Local, A-Z
241 Russia. Soviet Union. Former Soviet republics (General)
For former Soviet areas of Asia see S309
Russia (Federation)
For Siberia see S313+
241.3 General works
241.4.A-Z Local, A-Z
(242.A-Z) Individual former Soviet republics, A-Z
(242.E8) Estonia
see S269.E75
(242.L3) Latvia
see S269.L35
(242.L35) Lithuania
see S269.L78
(242.M64) Moldova
see S269.M629
(242.U45) Ukraine
see S269.U38
Scandinavia
243 General works
Denmark
245 General
246.A-Z Local, A-Z
Iceland
247 General
248.A-Z Local, A-Z
Norway
249 General
250.A-Z Local, A-Z
Sweden
251 General
252.A-Z Local, A-Z
Spain
253 General
254.A-Z Local, A-Z
Portugal
255 General
256.A-Z Local, A-Z
Switzerland
257 General
258.A-Z Local, A-Z

Documents and other collections
Other countries
Europe -- Continued
Balkan States
259 General
260.A-Z Local, A-Z
Bulgaria
261 General
262.A-Z Local, A-Z
Montenegro see S268.A+
Romania
265 General
266.A-Z Local, A-Z
Yugoslavia
267 General
268.A-Z Local, A-Z
269.A-Z Other European, A-Z
e.g.
269.E75 Estonia
269.F5 Finland
269.L35 Latvia
269.L78 Lithuania
269.M3 Malta
269.M629 Moldova
269.P6 Poland
269.U38 Ukraine
Asia
270 General works
Afghanistan
271 General
272.A-Z Local, A-Z
Baluchistan see S322.P27
China
277 General
278.A-Z Local, A-Z
India
279 General
280.A-Z Local, A-Z
Sri Lanka
281 General
282.A-Z Local, A-Z
Indochina
283 General works
French Indochina
284 General works
Vietnam
285 General

Documents and other collections
Other countries
Asia
Indochina
French Indochina
Vietnam -- Continued
286.A-Z Local, A-Z
Cambodia
287 General
288.A-Z Local, A-Z
Cochin China
289 General
290.A-Z Local, A-Z
Tongking
291 General
292.A-Z Local, A-Z
Thailand
293 General
294.A-Z Local, A-Z
Straits Settlements. Malay Peninsula
295 General
296.A-Z Local, A-Z
Indonesia
297 General
298.A-Z Local, A-Z
Philippine Islands
301 General
302.A-Z Local, A-Z
Japan
303 General
304.A-Z Local, A-Z
Korea
305 General
306.A-Z Local, A-Z
Iran
307 General
308.A-Z Local, A-Z
309 Former Soviet areas of Asia
309 General
310.A-Z Local, A-Z
Central Asia
311 General
312.A-Z Local, A-Z
Siberia
313 General
314.A-Z Local, A-Z
Turkey in Asia. Asia Minor

Documents and other collections
Other countries
Asia
Turkey -- Continued
315 General
316.A-Z Local, A-Z
322.A-Z Other, A-Z
e.g.
322.C8 Cyprus
322.P27 Pakistan
Indian Ocean islands
322.5 General works
322.6.A-Z By island or group of islands, A-Z
Africa
323 General works
Ethiopia
325 General
326.A-Z Local, A-Z
British Africa
327 General works
South Africa
328 General works
Cape of Good Hope
329 General
330.A-Z Local, A-Z
KwaZulu-Natal
331 General
332.A-Z Local, A-Z
Orange Free State
333 General
334.A-Z Local, A-Z
Transvaal
335 General
(336) Local
see S336.4+
Gauteng. Pretoria-Witwatersrand-Vereeniging
336.4 General
336.5.A-Z Local, A-Z
Mpumalanga. Eastern Transvaal
336.8 General
336.9.A-Z Local, A-Z
Limpopo. Northern Province. Northern Transvaal
337 General
337.2.A-Z Local, A-Z
North-West
337.5 General
337.6.A-Z Local, A-Z

Documents and other collections
  Other countries
    Africa
      British Africa -- Continued
338.A-Z   Other, A-Z
      Congo (Democratic Republic)
339   General
340.A-Z   Local, A-Z
      Egypt
341   General
342.A-Z   Local, A-Z
      French Africa
343   General works
        Algeria
345   General
346.A-Z   Local, A-Z
        Tunisia
346.5   General
346.6.A-Z   Local, A-Z
        West Africa
347   General
348.A-Z   Local, A-Z
        Madagascar
349   General
350.A-Z   Local, A-Z
354.A-Z   Other, A-Z
      German Africa
355   General works
        Burundi see S379.B94
        Tanzania
357   General
358.A-Z   Local, A-Z
        Rwanda
358.5   General
358.6.A-Z   Local, A-Z
        Cameroon
359   General
360.A-Z   Local, A-Z
        Southwest
361   General
362.A-Z   Local, A-Z
      Italian Africa
363   General
364.A-Z   Local, A-Z
      Liberia
365   General
366.A-Z   Local, A-Z

	Documents and other collections
	Other countries
	Africa -- Continued
	Morocco
367	General
368.A-Z	Local, A-Z
	Orange Free State see S333+
	Portuguese Africa
370	General works
	Mozambique
371	General
372.A-Z	Local, A-Z
	Angola
373	General
374.A-Z	Local, A-Z
375.A-Z	Other, A-Z
	e.g.
375.S2	Sao Tome and Principe
	South Africa see S328+
	Spanish Africa
377	General
378.A-Z	Local, A-Z
379.A-Z	Other, A-Z
	e.g.
379.B94	Burundi
	Australia
381	General works
382	Australian Capital Territory. Canberra
	New South Wales
383	General
384.A-Z	Local, A-Z
	Northern Territory
387	General
388.A-Z	Local, A-Z
	Queensland
389	General
390.A-Z	Local, A-Z
	Southern Australia
391	General
392.A-Z	Local, A-Z
	Tasmania
393	General
394.A-Z	Local, A-Z
	Victoria
395	General
396.A-Z	Local, A-Z
	Western Australia

Documents and other collections
Other countries
Australia
Western Australia -- Continued
397 General
397.5.A-Z Local, A-Z
New Zealand
397.7 General
397.8.A-Z Local, A-Z
Pacific islands
398 General
400.A-Z Individual, A-Z
400.G8 Guam
400.5 Developing countries
401 Agricultural economics
Including international societies and agencies, e.g. International Council for Scientific Agriculture
Cf. HD1429 International Institute of Agriculture
National, state, provincial, etc. see S21+
403 Agricultural missions, voyages, etc.
Class here works about missions, voyages, etc. involving more than one country
Collections
405 General
407 Collected writings of individual authors
Directories
408 General
By region or country
United States
409 General
409.5.A-.W By state, A-W
410.A-Z Other regions or countries, A-Z
411 Encyclopedias and dictionaries
Statistics
General agricultural statistics, including acreage, yield production, etc. see S21+; S419+
Agricultural statistics limited to economic aspects, including prices, consumption, trade see HD1421+
413 Tables
414 Calendars. Yearbooks. Almanacs
For popular farmers' almanacs (United States) see AY81.F3
Cf. SB450.965 Gardeners' almanacs
Biography
415 Collective
417.A-Z Individual, A-Z

History and conditions
Cf. HD113+ Economic history and conditions
419 General
Antiquity
Cf. GN799.A4 Origin and prehistory of agriculture
421 General works
423 Assyrians
425 Hebrews
427 Egyptians
429 Greeks
431 Romans
433 Middle ages
Cf. HD141+ Economic history
435 16th and 17th centuries
437 18th and 19th centuries
439 General agricultural conditions, world crop zones, etc.
By region or country
Including agricultural conditions and agricultural surveys
United States (and North America)
441 General works
By section
443 New England
444 Middle States
445 The South
Central States and the West see S441
448 The Southwest
449 Pacific Coast
451.A-.W By state, A-W
Canada
451.5.A1 General works
451.5.A2-Z Regions, provinces, etc.
451.7 Mexico
Europe
452 General works
Great Britain
453 Agricultural survey
455 General (and England alone)
457.A-Z Local, A-Z (England only)
Wales
458 General works
458.5.A-Z Local, A-Z
Scotland
459 General works
460.A-Z Local, A-Z
Northern Ireland
460.5 General works
460.6.A-Z Local, A-Z

History and conditions
By region or country
Europe -- Continued
Ireland (Republic or General)
461 General works
462.A-Z Local, A-Z (Republic only)
France
463 General works
464.A-Z Regions, provinces, etc, A-Z
Germany
Including West Germany
465 General works
466.A-Z Local, A-Z
e.g.
466.E37 East Germany
469.A-Z Other European countries and regions, A-Z
Subarrange each country by Table S3a
e.g.
469.A4 Alps (Table S3a)
469.S3 Scandinavia (Table S3a)
Asia
470.A1 General
470.A2-Z Regions, A-Z
471.A-Z By region or country, A-Z
Subarrange each country by Table S3a
471.3 Arab countries (General)
471.35 Islamic countries (General)
Indian Ocean islands
471.5 General works
471.6.A-Z By island or group of islands, A-Z
Africa
472.A1 General
472.A2-Z Regions, A-Z
473.A-Z By region or country, A-Z
Subarrange each country by Table S3a
Atlantic Ocean islands
473.5 General works
473.6.A-Z By island or group of islands, A-Z
Latin America
473.9 General works
Mexico see S451.7
South America
474 General
475.A-Z By region or country, A-Z
Subarrange each country by Table S3a
Central America
476.A1 General

History and conditions
By region or country
Central America -- Continued
476.A2-Z By region or country, A-Z
Subarrange each country by Table S3a
West Indies. Caribbean islands
477.A1 General
477.A2-Z By country, island, etc., A-Z
Subarrange each country, island, etc., by Table S3a
Australia
478.A1 General
478.A2-Z By state, A-Z
Subarrange each state by Table S3a
New Zealand
478.5.A1 General
478.5.A2-Z Local, A-Z
Pacific Ocean islands. Oceania
479 General
479.3.A-Z By island or group of islands, A-Z
480 Arctic regions
481 Tropics
482 Developing countries
Agricultural departments. Agricultural administration
484 General works
By region or country see S21+; S441+
Study and teaching. Research
484.4 General works
484.5.A-Z By region or country, A-Z
Agricultural legislation
see class K
General works
Classic authors (Greek and Roman)
Texts
see PA
491 Collections
492 Individual authors
493 Comprehensive works (Theory, progress, science)
Class here works for the library as distinguished from textbooks for the school and handbooks for everyday use
Breeding
Class here works on the general principles of breeding both plants and animals
For works limited to special plants, see the plant, e.g. SB189.5 Grain; SB191.W5 Wheat. For works limited to special animals, see the animal, e.g. SF201 Cattle
For works on general plant breeding see SB123+
For works on general animal breeding see SF105+

General works
Breeding -- Continued
494 General works
494.3 Germplasm resources
Cf. SB123.3+ Plants
Cf. SF105.3 Animals
494.33 Mutation breeding
Including space mutation breeding
494.35 Agricultural genome mapping (General)
494.5.A-Z Special aspects of agriculture as a whole, A-Z
494.5.A25 Aerial photography
494.5.A3 Aeronautics
Agricultural informatics see S494.5.D3
494.5.A39 Agricultural literature
494.5.A4 Agriculture as a profession. Vocational guidance
Cf. S559.5+ Employment surveys, etc.
Cf. SB50 Plant culture
Cf. SF80 Animal culture
494.5.A43 Agrobiodiversity
Including agrobiodiversity conservation
494.5.A45 Agroforestry. Agroforestry systems
Cf. S619.A37 Desertification control
Cf. S621.5.A38 Reclamation of land method
Cf. S627.A35 Soil conservation
Cf. SB172+ Multipurpose trees
494.5.A47 Agropastoral systems
Cf. SF140.P38 Pastoral systems
494.5.A65 Alternative agriculture. Appropriate technology
Artificial intelligence see S494.5.D3
494.5.A96 Authorship
Biological diversity in agriculture see S494.5.A43
Biology, Economic see S494.5.E25
494.5.B56 Biosystematics
494.5.B563 Biotechnology
Cf. S494.5.G44 Genetic engineering
Cf. SB106.B56 Crop biotechnology
Cf. SD387.B55 Forestry
Cf. SF140.B54 Animal biotechnology
Cf. SH136.B56 Aquaculture
494.5.C3 Cartography
494.5.C54 Classification
494.5.C6 Communication in agriculture
494.5.C64 Consultants
494.5.D3 Data processing. Agricultural informatics
Including artificial intelligence

General works
Special aspects of agriculture as a whole, A-Z -- Continued
494.5.D58 Diversification
For local (Documents and collections) see S21+
For local (History and conditions) see S441+
494.5.D6 Documentation
494.5.E25 Economic biology
Cf. SB107+ Economic botany
Cf. SF84+ Economic zoology
494.5.E4 Electronics
494.5.E5 Energy and agriculture
Including energy consumption
Cf. S494.5.S64 Solar energy
Cf. S675.4 Fuel consumption of agricultural machinery
Cf. SB288+ Energy crops
Cf. TJ163.5.A37 Energy conservation
494.5.E56 Entropy
494.5.E8 Estimating and reporting
Including surveying methods and statistical services
Experimentation see S539.5+
494.5.G44 Genetic engineering
Cf. SB123.57 Plant culture
494.5.G46 Geography
Class here general works on agricultural geography as a discipline
For works on world agricultural geography see S439
For works on local agricultural geography see S441+
Informatics, Agricultural see S494.5.D3
494.5.I47 Information services
Including agricultural information networks
494.5.I5 Innovations
Including technology transfer and innovation diffusion
494.5.I58 Inventions
Literature see S494.5.A39
494.5.M28 Materials handling
Cf. S571+ Farm produce handling
Mathematical models see S566.5
Operations research see S566.6+
494.5.P47 Permaculture
494.5.P485 Philosophy
494.5.P5 Plastics in agriculture
494.5.P73 Precision farming
494.5.P75 Productivity
For local (Documents and collections) see S21+
For local (History and conditions) see S441+
Cf. HD1401+ Economic aspects
494.5.P76 Psychology

General works
Special aspects of agriculture as a whole, A-Z -- Continued
Radioactive decontamination see S589.6
Radioactive tracers see S589.5
Recreational use of farms, ranches, etc. see GV198.945+
494.5.R34 Raised field agriculture
494.5.R4 Remote sensing
494.5.S64 Solar energy
Statistical services see S494.5.E8
Surveys see S494.5.E8
494.5.S86 Sustainable agriculture
For local (Documents and collections) see S21+
For local (History and conditions) see S441+
494.5.S95 Systems
Class here general works on agricultural and integrated agricultural systems
For works on world agricultural systems see S439
For works on local agricultural systems see S441+
494.5.U72 Urban agriculture
For local (Documents and collections) see S21+
For local (History and conditions) see S441+
Vocational guidance see S494.5.A4
494.5.W3 Water in agriculture
Cf. S618+ Irrigation water
Cf. TD927 Rural water supply
495 Textbooks
For British textbooks see S509+
For other foreign textbooks see S515+
For courses of study see S533+
Handbooks, etc.
496 General, international, etc.
For American (including Canadian) farmers
497 To 1815
499 1816-1865
501 1866-
501.2 1970-
Including "homesteading," i.e. self-sufficient living on a farm
For Southern farmers
503 To 1865
505 1866-
506.A-Z For other regions of the United States, A-Z
507.A-.W For states of the United States, A-W
For Canadian farmers
508.A1 General
508.A2-Z Provinces
For English farmers
509 To 1785

General works
Handbooks, etc.
For English farmers -- Continued
511 1786-1850
513 1851-1969
513.2 1970-
For others
515 To 1800
1801-
517.A2 General works
517.A3-Z By region or country, A-Z
518 Handbooks for women
519 Juvenile works
520 Pictorial works
Light literature. Popular works. Farm life, etc.
Class here works that are not scientific nor limited to one subject
Cf. BL325.A35 Comparative mythology
Cf. GR895 Folklore of agriculture
Cf. GT3470+ Country life (Manners and customs)
Cf. GT5810+ Customs relative to agriculture and hunting
Cf. HT421 Rural sociology
Cf. S496+ Handbooks, etc.
Cf. SB92+ Popular works on plant culture
Cf. SB103 Plant culture
Cf. SB455 Gardens and gardening
521 General works
By region or country
United States
521.5.A2 General works
521.5.A3-Z By region or state, A-Z
522.A-Z Other regions or countries, A-Z
523 Addresses, essays, lectures
Agricultural education
Cf. LC2780.2 Agricultural education of African Americans
Cf. S495 Textbooks
Cf. S678.5+ Agricultural engineering
530 Periodicals and societies
530.3 Congresses
Directories
530.5 General works
530.52.A-Z By region or country, A-Z
Biography see S415+
Schools. Study and teaching
531 General works
531.3 Teacher training
531.5 Audio-visual aids

Agricultural education
Schools. Study and teaching -- Continued
Laboratory manuals see S495
532 Agricultural work of missionaries
By region or country
United States
533 General works
533.F66 4-H Clubs
533.F8 Future Farmers of America
534.A-Z By region or state, A-Z
Including courses of study
535.A-Z Other regions or countries, A-Z
Individual colleges and institutions
536.5.A-Z International institutions. By name, A-Z
537.A-Z United States. By institution, A-Z
539.A-Z Other countries. By country, A-Z
Subarrange by institution. By name, A-Z
Research. Experimentation
Including experiment stations, laboratories, and research institutions
For publications of state-supported experiment stations see S21+
For descriptive works limited to individual state-supported experiment stations, etc. see S541+
Cf. S587.3+ Agricultural chemistry laboratories
539.5 Periodicals and societies
539.7 Congresses
Directories see S530.5+
540.A2 General works
540.A3-Z Special topics, A-Z
540.A58 Anthropological aspects
540.C57 Citizen participation
540.D38 Data processing
540.E25 Economic aspects (General)
540.E92 Evaluation
Farming systems research see S494.5.S95
540.F5 Field experiments
540.I56 International cooperation
540.L53 Library research
540.M34 Management
540.M38 Mathematical models
540.N82 Nuclear magnetic resonance spectroscopy
540.O53 On-farm research
540.S63 Sociological aspects
540.S7 Statistical methods
540.8.A-Z International institutions. By name, A-Z
By region or country

Agricultural education
Research. Experimentation
By region or country -- Continued
United States
Cf. S21.A2+ U.S. Department of Agriculture
541 General works
541.5.A-Z By region or state, A-Z
Under each state:
.x General works
.x2A-.x2Z Individual institutions. By name, A-Z
542.A-Z Other regions or countries, A-Z
Under each country:
.x General works
.x2A-.x2Z Individual institutions. By name, A-Z
542.3 Developing countries
Agricultural extension work
General and United States
544 General works
544.3.A-.W By state, A-W
544.5.A-Z Other regions or countries, A-Z
544.6 Developing countries
545 History, etc.
Class here general and nonofficial works only
For state documents see S31+
For foreign documents see S133+
Study and teaching. Research
545.5 General works
545.53.A-Z By region or country, A-Z
Historic farms
548 General works
By region or country
United States
548.4 General works
548.5.A-Z By region or state, A-Z
Subarrange by author
548.6.A-Z Other regions or countries, A-Z
Subarrange by author
Museums
549.A1 General works
549.A2-Z By region or country, A-Z
Under each country:
.x General works
.x2A-.x2Z Special. By name, A-Z
Exhibitions. Fairs
Cf. SF114+ Livestock exhibitions
550 Periodicals
550.5 General works

Agricultural education
Exhibitions. Fairs -- Continued
Organization. Methods of conducting fairs, etc.
551 General works
552 Prize competition. Regulations, etc.
552.5 Juvenile works
553.A-Z International. By place, A-Z
National, state, and local
By country
United States
554 General works
555.A-Z By region or state, A-Z
Subarrange each state by Table S3a
557.A-Z Other countries, A-Z
Subarrange each country by Table S3a
559.A-Z Exhibits of particular countries at various expositions. By country, A-Z
Employment surveys, manpower requirements, distribution and utilization of agriculturists and agricultural college graduates
Cf. HD1521+ Agricultural laborers
559.5 General works
By region or country
United States
559.6 General works
559.63.A-Z By region or state, A-Z
559.65.A-Z Other regions or countries, A-Z
Farm economics. Farm management
Class here works limited to technique, business methods, etc.
For public policy, etc. see HD1401+
560 Periodicals. Societies. Serials
560.2 Collected works (nonserial)
560.3 Congresses
560.45 Dictionaries. Encyclopedias
560.6 Information services
561 General works
561.3 Addresses, essays, lectures
By region or country
United States
General works see S561
561.6.A-Z By region or state, A-Z
562.A-Z Other regions or countries, A-Z
562.5 Study and teaching
563 Laying out farms, locating buildings, etc.
Insurance see HG9966+
Rents, taxes, valuation, etc. see HD28+; HJ9+
Sharing systems see HD1478.A3+; HD1491+

Farm economics. Farm management -- Continued

563.6 Personnel management

For local see S561.52+

Cf. HD1521+ Agricultural laborers

564 Labor productivity

564.5 Production standards

564.7 Record keeping

565 Safety measures (General)

Cf. S675.7 Farm machinery

565.7 Data processing

Accounting see HF5686.A36

Custom farmwork rates

565.85 General works

565.855.A-Z By region or country, A-Z

565.86 New agricultural enterprises

565.88 Agritourism. Recreational use of farms

Agricultural mathematics

Including farm management mathematics

565.97 Periodicals. Societies. Serials

566 General works

566.3 Problems, exercises, etc.

566.5 Mathematical models

566.55 Statistical methods

Cf. HD1421+ Economic aspects

Operations research. System analysis

566.6 General works

Programming

566.65 General works

566.7 Linear programming

566.8 Nonlinear programming

568 Dynamic programming

Custom farmwork rates see S565.85+

Postharvest technology. Marketing technology

Class here works limited to technique

For works limited to specific crops, see the crop, e.g. SB398.5 Grapes

For economic works on marketing and trade see HD28+

571 General works

571.5 Roadside marketing

Cooperative marketing see HD1483+

Methods and system of culture see S602.5+

Special methods for special areas see S604.3+

Farm buildings see S770+

	Agricultural chemistry. Agricultural chemicals
	For works limited to specific crops, see the crop, e.g. SB191.R5 Rice
	Cf. S592.5+ Soil chemistry
	Cf. S631+ Fertilizers
	Cf. SB128 Growth regulators
	Cf. SB950.9+ Pesticides
	Cf. SF253 Dairy chemistry
583	Periodicals. Societies. Serials
583.2	Congresses
584.A-Z	Documents. By country, A-Z
	For the United States Bureau of Chemistry see S585
584.4	Dictionaries. Encyclopedias
	Biography
584.5	Collective
584.52.A-Z	Individual, A-Z
	History and conditions
584.7	General works
584.75.A-Z	By region or country, A-Z
585	General works
585.4	Addresses, essays, lectures
585.8	Safety measures
	Cf. SB952.5 Pest control
	Methods of application
585.84	General works
585.87	Chemigation
	Study and teaching. Research
585.9	General works
585.93.A-Z	By region or country, A-Z
586	Tables
587	Analysis and experiments
587.25	Laboratory manuals
	Laboratories
587.3	General works
587.34.A-Z	By region or country, A-Z
	Under each country:
	.x — *General works*
	.x2A-.x2Z — *Individual laboratories, A-Z*
587.45	Natural products
587.5.A-Z	Special chemicals, A-Z
587.5.B65	Boron
587.5.C66	Copper
587.5.H4	Heavy metals
587.5.M54	Minerals
587.5.M64	Molybdenum
587.5.N5	Nitrogen
587.5.P56	Phosphorus

	Agricultural chemistry. Agricultural chemicals
	Special chemicals, A-Z -- Continued
587.5.P6	Potassium
587.5.S35	Saponins
587.5.S4	Selenium
587.5.S53	Silicon
587.5.S9	Sulfur
587.5.T7	Trace elements
587.5.Z55	Zinc
	Adjuvants
587.7	General works
587.73.A-Z	Special adjuvants, A-Z
587.73.S95	Surface active agents
587.73.V44	Vegetable oils
	Agricultural physics
588.4	Dictionaries. Encyclopedias
589	General works
	Study and teaching. Research
589.25	General works
589.27.A-Z	By region or country, A-Z
589.3	Optics in agriculture
589.5	Radioisotopes in agriculture
589.55	Nuclear accidents and agriculture
589.6	Radioactive decontamination
589.7	Agricultural ecology (General)
	For geographical treatment see S441+
	Agricultural conservation see S604.5+
	Agriculture and the environment
	Cf. S589.7 Agricultural ecology
	Cf. TD195.A34 Agricultural pollution
	Cf. TD930+ Agricultural wastes
589.75	General works
	By region or country
	United States
589.755	General works
589.757.A-Z	By region or state, A-Z
589.76.A-Z	Other regions or countries, A-Z
	Agricultural geology see QE37
	Plant growing media. Potting soils
	Cf. QK565.2 Cultural media for algae, etc.
589.8	General works
	Artificial media
589.85	General works
589.87.A-Z	Special media, A-Z
589.87.B37	Bark

Plant growing media. Potting soils
Artificial media
Special media, A-Z -- Continued
589.87.P43 Peat
Cf. S592.85 Peat soils
Cf. S661.2.P4 Soil amendment
Soils. Soil science
Cf. CC79.S6 Archaeology
Cf. QH84.8 Soil biology
Cf. QH541.5.S6 Soil ecology
Cf. QL110+ Soil fauna
Cf. QR111+ Soil micorogranisms
Cf. RA570+ Public health
Cf. S622+ Soil conservation and erosion
Cf. S631+ Fertilizers and manures
Cf. S661.7 Soil conditioners
Cf. SB973+ Soil disinfection
Cf. TA710+ Soil mechanics and engineering
Cf. TD878+ Soil pollution
Cf. TE208.5 Trafficability of soils
590 Periodicals. Societies. Serials
590.2 Congresses
Communication in soil science
590.4 General works
590.45 Soil science literature
Biography
590.6 Collective
590.63.A-Z Individual, A-Z
History
590.7 General works
590.73.A-Z By region or country, A-Z
591.A1-.A59 United States documents
591.A6-Z General works
591.3 Juvenile works
Study and teaching. Research
591.5 General works
591.55.A-Z By region or country, A-Z
591.7 Laboratory manuals
Museums
591.8 General works
591.84.A-Z International. By name, A-Z
591.85.A-Z By region or country, A-Z
Under each country:
.x *General works*
.x2A-.x2Z *Individual museums. By name, A-Z*
592 Encyclopedias and dictionaries
592.13 Data processing. Computer applications

Soils. Soil science -- Continued

592.135 Remote sensing

Cf. S592.145 Aerial photography in soil surveys

Soil surveys

For surveys of particular places see S599+

Cf. TE208+ Soil surveys in highway engineering

592.14 General works

592.143 Soil profiles

592.145 Aerial photography

592.147 Soil mapping

Soil classification

Cf. S592.6.A+ Special elements

Cf. S597.A+ Soils for special crops

592.16 General works

592.17.A-Z By order, great group, family, etc., A-Z

592.17.A37 Acrisols

592.17.A43 Alfisols

592.17.A57 Anthropogenic soils

592.17.A73 Arid soils. Desert soils

592.17.C45 Chernozem soils

Clay soils see S592.367

Desert soils see S592.17.A73

592.17.F45 Ferralsols

592.17.F55 Fluvisols

Forest soils see SD390+

592.17.F73 Fragipans

592.17.H57 Histosols

Humus see S592.8+

592.17.H93 Hydric soils. Hydromorphic soils

Loam soils see S592.357

592.17.M35 Mangrove soils

592.17.O95 Oxisols

Peat soils see S592.85

592.17.P63 Podzol

592.17.R43 Red soils

592.17.R45 Rendzinas

Sandy loam soils see S592.355

Sandy soils see S592.353

592.17.S64 Solonetz soils

592.17.S75 Steppe soils

592.17.T85 Tundra soils

592.17.U48 Ultisols

592.17.U73 Urban soils

592.17.V47 Vertisols

592.17.V65 Volcanic soils

Soils. Soil science -- Continued

592.185 Soil age

Including dating or age determination

For local see S599+

Cf. QE473 Paleopedology

592.2 Soil formation

Cf. QE473 Paleopedology

Soil physics

Cf. TA710.5 Testing for mechanical or engineering properties

592.3 General works

Soil texture

592.35 General works

592.353 Sandy soils

592.355 Sandy loam soils

592.357 Loam soils

592.358 Silt loam

592.367 Clay soils

Soil structure see S593.2

Soil aeration see S593.7

Soil optical properties

592.38 General works

592.4 Soil color

Soil temperature see S594.5

Soil chemistry

592.5 General works

592.53 Soil physical chemistry

592.55 Soil mineralogy

For local see S599+

Soil acidity. Acid soils

592.57 General works

592.575 Acid sulfate soils

592.6.A-Z Special soil chemical constituents, A-Z

592.6.A34 Agricultural chemicals

Cf. TD879.A35 Soil pollution

592.6.A4 Aluminum

592.6.A7 Arsenic

592.6.B28 Barite

592.6.B3 Barium

592.6.B6 Boron

592.6.C3 Calcium

592.6.C34 Carbohydrates

592.6.C35 Carbon

592.6.C36 Carbonates

592.6.C6 Cobalt

592.6.C67 Copper

592.6.E57 Enzymes

Soils. Soil science
Soil chemistry
Special soil chemical constituents, A-Z -- Continued
592.6.F58 Fluorine
592.6.G95 Gypsum
592.6.H43 Heavy metals
592.6.H47 Herbicides
592.6.I7 Iron
592.6.L4 Lead
592.6.M3 Magnesium
592.6.M35 Manganese
592.6.M64 Molybdenum
592.6.N5 Nitrogen
592.6.O73 Organic compounds
592.6.O9 Oxygen
592.6.P43 Pesticides
Cf. SB951.145.S65 Soil pesticides
Cf. TD879.P37 Soil pollution
592.6.P48 Phenolic acids
592.6.P5 Phosphorus
592.6.P58 Polycyclic aromatic hydrocarbons
592.6.P6 Potassium
592.6.S4 Selenium
592.6.S45 Serpentine
592.6.S85 Strontium
592.6.S9 Sulfur
Cf. S592.575 Acid sulfate soils
592.6.T7 Trace elements
592.6.Z55 Zinc
Soil biochemistry
For special organic chemical constituents see S592.6.A+
592.7 General works
Humus
592.8 General works
592.85 Peat soils
Cf. GB621+ Peat bogs
Cf. HD9559.P3+ Peat industry
Cf. S589.87.P43 Artificial plant growing medium
Cf. S661.2.P4 Soil amendment
Cf. TN837+ Peat production
593 Analysis and experiments
593.2 Soil structure
593.23 Soil compaction
Cf. TA749 Earthwork
Cf. TE210.4+ Highway engineering
593.25 Soil crusts and crusting
593.27 Subsoils

Soils. Soil science -- Continued

593.3 Soil colloids

Soil acidity see S592.57+

593.7 Soil aeration

593.75 Soil air

594 Soil moisture

Cf. S595.5 Irrigated soils

594.3 Soil respiration

594.5 Soil temperature

595 Alkali lands. Saline soil. Sodic soil

595.5 Irrigated soils

For local see S599+

596 Soils and the environment

For local see S599+

Cf. QH541.5.S6 Soil ecology

Cf. S592.17.A57 Anthropogenic soils

Cf. TD878+ Soil pollution

596.3 Soils and climate

For local see S599+

Soils and nutrition

596.5 General works

596.53 Soils and animal nutrition

Soils and crops. Soil-plant relationships. Soil productivity

For local see S599+

Cf. QK867+ Plant nutrition

Cf. QK900+ Plant ecology

596.7 General works

Forest soils see SD390+

596.75 Garden soils

597.A-Z Soils for special crops. By crop, A-Z

597.A65 Apple

597.B3 Babassu

597.C57 Citrus fruits

597.C6 Coffee

597.C65 Cotton

597.E53 Energy crops

597.F75 Fruit

597.G68 Grapes

597.G7 Grasses. Lawns

597.H48 Hevea

Lawns see S597.G7

597.L4 Legumes

597.M87 Mushrooms

597.O35 Oil palm

597.P55 Pine

597.P68 Potatoes

597.R5 Rice

Soils. Soil science
Soils and crops. Soil-plant relationships. Soil productivity
Soils for special crops. By crop, A-Z -- Continued

597.S56 Sisal
597.S65 Spruce
597.S84 Sugarcane
597.T35 Tangerine
597.T38 Tea
597.T4 Teak
597.T6 Tobacco
597.V4 Vegetables
598 Miscellaneous
Local
United States
Including North America
599.A1 General
Including regions
599.A3-.W States, A-W
Canada
599.1.A1 General
Including regions
599.1.A3-.Y Provinces, A-Y
599.2 Mexico
Central America
599.23.A1 General
Including regions
599.23.A3-Z Countries, A-Z
Subarrange each country by Table S3a
West Indies
599.25.A1 General
Including regions
599.25.A3-Z Countries, islands, or island groups, A-Z
Subarrange each country, island, or island group by Table S3a
Class works limited to a specific island within an island group with the group, treating the specific island as a locality within the group
South America
Including Latin America
599.3.A1 General
Including regions
599.3.A3-Z Countries, A-Z
Subarrange each country by Table S3a
Atlantic islands
599.35.A1 General
Including regions

Soils. Soil science
Local
Atlantic islands -- Continued
599.35.A3-Z Countries, islands, or island groups, A-Z
Subarrange each country, island, or island group by Table S3a
Class works limited to a specific island within an island group with the group, treating the specific island as a locality within the group
Europe
Cf. S599.45.A1+ Russia. Soviet Union. Russia (Federation)
599.4.A1 General
Including regions
599.4.A3-Z Countries, A-Z
Subarrange each country by Table S3a
Russia. Soviet Union. Russia (Federation)
Including Russia in Asia
For individual former Soviet republics other than Russia (in Europe) see S599.4.A1+
For individual former Soviet republics other than Russia (in Asia) see S599.6.A1+
599.45.A1 General of Russia (Federation) as a whole
599.45.A2-Z Locals of Russia (Federation), A-Z
Africa
599.5.A1 General
Including regions
599.5.A3-Z Countries, A-Z
Subarrange each country by Table S3a
Indian Ocean islands
599.55.A1 General
Including regions
599.55.A3-Z Countries, islands, or island groups, A-Z
Subarrange each country, island, or island group by Table S3a
Class works limited to a specific island within an island group with the group, treating the specific island as a locality within the group
Asia
Cf. S599.45.A1+ Russia in Asia
599.6.A1 General
Including regions
599.6.A3-Z Countries, A-Z
Subarrange each country by Table S3a
Australia
599.7.A1 General
Including regions

Soils. Soil science
Local
Australia -- Continued
599.7.A3-.W States, A-W
599.75 New Zealand
599.8.A-Z Other Pacific islands or island groups, A-Z
Subarrange each island or island group by Table S3a
Class works limited to a specific island within an island group with the group, treating the specific island as a locality within the group
599.9.A-Z Other regions, A-Z
e.g. Arctic regions, Antarctica, tropics
Agricultural meteorology. Crops and climate
For particular crops, see the crop in SB
Cf. S596.3 Soils and climate
Cf. SB454.3.W43 Weather information for gardeners
Cf. SD390.5+ Forest meteorology
600 Periodicals. Societies. Serials
600.2 Congresses
600.3 Directories
600.35 Dictionaries. Encyclopedias
Methodology
600.4 General works
600.43.A-Z Special methods, A-Z
600.43.D38 Data processing
600.43.M37 Mathematical models
600.43.S83 Statistical methods
Study and teaching. Research
600.45 General works
600.47 Laboratory manuals
600.5 General works
600.55 Juvenile works
600.57 Addresses, essays, lectures
By region or country
United States
600.6 General works
600.62.A-Z By region or state, A-Z
600.64.A-Z Other regions or countries, A-Z
600.7.A-Z Special topics, A-Z
Atmospheric greenhouse effect see S600.7.G73
600.7.B55 Blizzards
600.7.C54 Climatic changes
600.7.C93 Cyclones
Including hurricanes and typhoons
Drought tolerance see S600.7.D76
600.7.D76 Droughts. Drought tolerance
Cf. SB791 Plant pathology

Agricultural meteorology. Crops and climate
Special topics, A-Z -- Continued
600.7.E93 Evapotranspiration
600.7.F56 Flowering time
600.7.F76 Frost
600.7.G56 Global warming
600.7.G73 Greenhouse effect, Atmospheric
600.7.H37 Harvesting time
Hurricanes see S600.7.C93
600.7.P53 Planting time
600.7.R35 Rain and rainfall
600.7.R46 Remote sensing
Including the utilization of artificial satellites
600.7.S65 Solar radiation
600.7.S86 Storms
600.7.T45 Temperature
Typhoons see S600.7.C93
600.7.W43 Weather control
600.7.W45 Weather forecasting
600.7.W55 Wind
Agricultural ecology see S589.7
Crops and pollution see SB744.5+
Methods and systems of culture. Cropping systems
Cf. S494.5.A45 Agroforestry
602.5 General works
602.8 Fallowing
602.87 Shifting cultivation
602.88 Slash-mulch agricultural systems
603 Rotation of crops
603.5 Companion crops. Intercropping
Cf. SB283.5+ Catch crops
603.7 Double cropping. Multiple cropping
604 Tillage. Plowing
Cf. S683+ Implements
Special methods for special areas
Cf. S494.5.A45 Agroforestry
604.3 Alpine. Hill farming
Arid regions see S612+
604.33 Cold regions
Cf. SB109.7 Crops
604.37 Tropical
Cf. SB111.A2+ Tropical crops
604.4 Wetlands. Wetland agriculture
Including dambo farming
Cf. S621 Moors, marshes, and drainage

Agricultural conservation
Cf. S589.7 Agricultural ecology
Cf. TD195.A34 Agricultural pollution
Cf. TJ163.5.A37 Energy conservation
604.5 General works
By region or country
United States
604.6 General works
604.62.A-Z By region or state, A-Z
604.64.A-Z Other regions or countries, A-Z
Melioration: Improvement, reclamation, fertilization, irrigation, etc., of lands
Cf. TC801+ Reclamation and irrigation engineering
604.8 Periodicals. Societies. Serials
604.83 Congresses
604.84 Collected works (nonserial)
604.85 Dictionaries
605 General works
605.2.A-Z By region or country, A-Z
605.5 Organic farming. Organiculture
Cf. S654+ Organic fertilizers
Cf. SB453.5+ Organic gardening
Cf. SB974+ Organic plant protection
Special classes of lands and reclamation methods
606 Abandoned farm lands
607 Woodlands. Clearing
Cf. S679+ Clearing implements and explosives
608 Burning of lands
Deserts. Arid lands. Irrigation
Class here works on arid regions and irrigation agriculture
For works limited to specific crops, see the crop, e.g. SB189.45 Grain; SB191.R5 Rice
For works limited to dry farming see SB110
For farmers' manuals on irrigation agriculture see SB112
612 Periodicals. Societies. Serials
612.2 Congresses
612.3 Directories
612.4 Dictionaries. Encyclopedias
Study and teaching. Research
612.5 General works
612.55.A-Z By region or country, A-Z
612.8 History (General)
613 General works
614 Juvenile works
615 Addresses, essays, lectures
616.A-Z By region or country, A-Z

	Melioration: Improvement, reclamation, fertilization, irrigation, etc., of lands
	Special classes of lands and reclamation methods
	Deserts. Arid lands. Irrigation -- Continued
	Irrigation water
	For water requirements of specific crops, see the crop, e.g. SB189.45 Grain; SB191.R5 Rice
618	General works
	By region or country see S616.A+
618.4	Analysis. Measurement
	Quality
618.45	General works
618.47	Pollutants
	Composition
618.5	General works
618.6.A-Z	Special chemicals, A-Z
618.6.C35	Carbonate
619.A-Z	Other special topics, A-Z
619.A37	Agroforestry
	Chemigation see S585.87
619.C55	Climatic factors
619.D43	Deficit irrigation
619.E34	Efficiency, Irrigation
619.E53	Energy consumption
619.E57	Environmental aspects
619.F87	Furrow irrigation
	Landscape irrigation see SB475.82
	Microirrigation see S619.T74
619.N57	Nitrogen management
619.R44	Remote sensing
619.R85	Runoff irrigation
619.S24	Saline irrigation
619.S33	Scheduling of irrigation
	Cf. S619.D43 Deficit irrigation
	Sewage irrigation see TD670
	Soils see S595.5
619.S66	Sprinkler irrigation
619.S92	Subirrigation
619.S96	Supplemental irrigation
619.T36	Tank irrigation
619.T74	Trickle irrigation. Microirrigation
619.W37	Water duties
619.W38	Water harvesting
	Cf. S619.R85 Runoff irrigation
620	Saline environments
	Cf. S595 Alkali lands, saline soils
	Cf. SH138 Mariculture

Melioration: Improvement, reclamation, fertilization, irrigation, etc., of lands
Special classes of lands and reclamation methods -- Continued

621 Moors, marshes, etc. Drainage and ditching
Class here farmers' manuals only
For law and legislation, see class K
For works limited to economic aspects, public policy, etc. see HD1681+
For works limited to engineering see TC970+
Cf. S604.4 Wetland agriculture

621.5.A-Z Other, A-Z
621.5.A37 Agriculturally marginal lands
621.5.A38 Agroforestry for land reclamation
Cf. S619.A37 Desertification control
621.5.C47 Cerrados
621.5.C62 Coal-mined lands
Including coal mine waste
For works limited to surface mined lands see S621.5.S8
621.5.G73 Grasslands
Including prairies
621.5.H43 Heathlands
621.5.M48 Mined lands (General)
Mountains and hills see S604.3
621.5.O33 Oil-polluted lands
621.5.O34 Oil sands
621.5.P57 Pipelines
621.5.P59 Plants for land reclamation
(621.5.P73) Prairies
see S621.5.G73
621.5.Q35 Quarries
Revegetation see S627.R47
621.5.S3 Sand dunes
621.5.S65 Spoil banks
621.5.S8 Surface mined lands
621.5.V6 Volcanic land

Soil conservation and protection
Including soil degradation and erosion
Cf. SD390.4+ Forest soil erosion and conservation
Cf. TD878+ Soil pollution

622 Periodicals. Societies. Serials
622.2 Congresses
623 General works
623.3 Juvenile works
History and conditions
United States

Soil conservation and protection
History and conditions
United States -- Continued
624.A1 General works
624.A2-Z By region or state, A-Z
625.A-Z Other regions or countries, A-Z
625.7 Vocational guidance
Study and teaching. Research
626 General works
626.3.A-Z By region or country, A-Z
627.A-Z Special topics, A-Z
627.A3 Aerial photography
627.A35 Agroforestry
627.C57 Citizen participation
627.C58 Climatic factors
Including rain and rainfall
627.C65 Contour farming
Cover crops see SB284+
627.C76 Crop residue management
627.G68 Government policy
For local see S624+
627.H5 Hillside planting
627.I54 Incentives
627.M36 Mathematical models
627.P55 Plants for soil conservation
Including plant materials centers
627.P76 Projects
For individual local projects see S624+
627.R45 Remote sensing
627.R47 Revegetation
627.S66 Snow cover
627.S8 Streambank planting
For local see S624+
627.T4 Terracing
Fertilizers and improvement of the soil
For special fertilizers used on particular crops see S667.A+
Cf. HD9483+ Trade
Cf. S693.5 Equipment
Cf. SB742+ Deficiency diseases in plants
Cf. TP963+ Manufacture
631 Periodicals. Societies. Serials
631.3 Congresses
631.5 Dictionaries. Encyclopedias
633 General works
By region or country
United States
633.2 General works

Fertilizers and improvement of the soil
By region or country
United States -- Continued
633.3.A-Z Regions or states, A-Z
633.5.A-Z Other regions or countries, A-Z
635 Farm or home preparation, preservation, storage, etc.
637 Catalogs of manufacturers and dealers
Study and teaching. Research
638.5 General works
638.7.A-Z By region or country, A-Z
639 Analysis and experiments
For dealers' advertisements see S637
641 Inspection, legislation and administration
Including state serial documents
643 Lime and marl. Gypsum. Plaster of Paris
Including phosphogypsum
645 Potash. Potassium
647 Phosphates
649 Guano
Nitrogen and nitrates
Including ammonia, Chile saltpeter, urea, etc.
650.8 Periodicals. Societies. Serials
650.83 Congresses
651 General works
651.3 Nitrification inhibitors
Nitrogen-fixing plants see SB297+
652 Soil inoculation. Legume inoculation
For bacteriology of root nodules see QR113
652.3 Urease inhibitors
652.7 Silicon and silicates
Compound fertilizers see S631+
653.4 Trace elements (General)
653.5.A-Z Other special fertilizer chemical constituents, A-Z
653.5.B6 Boron
653.5.C6 Copper
653.5.M3 Magnesium
653.5.M35 Manganese
653.5.M6 Molybdenum
653.5.S84 Sulfur
653.5.Z56 Zinc
Organic fertilizers and manures
Including organic wastes as fertilizers
Cf. S649 Guano
Cf. S650.8+ Nitrogen and nitrates
654 General works
654.5 Biofertilizers
655 Farm manure

Fertilizers and improvement of the soil
Organic fertilizers and manures -- Continued
657 Sewage, sewage sludge, and night soil
659 Animal industry waste
Including blood, bone, fish-scrap, etc.
Vegetable fertilizers and amendments
Including compost and green manuring
Cf. SB195 Silage
Cf. SB284+ Cover crops and green manure crops
Cf. SB297+ Nitrogen-fixing plants
661 General works
661.2.A-Z Special, A-Z
661.2.M3 Marine algae
661.2.P4 Peat
Cf. S589.87.P43 Artificial plant growing medium
Cf. S592.85 Peat soils
661.2.S28 Sapropel
661.2.S85 Straw
661.2.W66 Wood chips
661.5 Mulching
661.7 Soil conditioners
Liquid fertilizers
662 General works
662.5 Folair feeding
663 Miscellaneous. Other fertilizers
667.A-Z Fertilizers for special crops. By crop, A-Z
For individual forest trees see SD397.A+
667.A2 Horticultural crops
667.A5 Alfalfa
667.A7 Apple
667.B3 Barley
667.B5 Beans
667.B57 Bermuda grass
667.C33 Cacao
667.C57 Coconut palms
667.C6 Coffee
667.C65 Conifers
667.C8 Corn. Maize
667.C85 Cotton
Field crops see S631+
667.F6 Forage crops
Forest fertilizers see SD408
667.F8 Fruit
667.G65 Grain
667.G68 Grapes
667.G7 Grasses
667.G74 Greenhouse plants

Fertilizers and improvement of the soil
Fertilizers for special crops. By crop, A-Z -- Continued

667.K5 Kikuyu grass
667.L4 Lettuce
Maize see S667.C8
667.M8 Mulberry
667.N6 Norway spruce
667.O45 Olive
667.O54 Onions
667.O7 Orange
667.P27 Papaya
Pasture fertilization see S667.G7
667.P38 Peanuts
667.P4 Pecan
667.P45 Peppers
667.P55 Pineapple
667.P8 Potatoes
667.R35 Range plants
667.R5 Rice
667.R68 Roses
667.S67 Sorghum
667.S75 Strawberries
667.S8 Sugar beets
667.S9 Sugarcane
667.S93 Sweet potatoes
667.T3 Tangerine
667.T6 Tobacco
667.T67 Tomatoes
667.T76 Tropical crops
667.V5 Vegetables
667.W5 Wheat

Soil conditioners see S661.7

Farm machinery and farm engineering

For works on particular types of machines for special crops see S715.A+

Cf. HD9486+ Agricultural machinery industry

Cf. TJ163.5.A37 Energy conservation in agriculture

Cf. TJ793 Internal combustion engines for agriculture machinery

Cf. TJ1480+ Manufacturing aspects of agricultural machinery

Cf. TL1+ Motor vehicles

671 Periodicals. Societies
671.3 Congresses
673 Directories
674 Encyclopedias and dictionaries
674.3 Agricultural engineering literature

Farm machinery and farm engineering -- Continued

Agricultural engineers, machinery operators, mechanics, etc.

674.4 General works

674.43.A-Z By region or country, A-Z

Biography

674.45 Collective

674.46.A-Z Individual, A-Z

674.5 History (General)

For history by region or country see S751+

675 General works

675.25 Juvenile works

675.3 Agricultural mechanics

675.4 Fuel consumption

675.5 Maintenance and repair. Farm shops

675.7 Safety measures

675.8 Costs

Tools and farm devices

Cf. SB454.8 Garden tools

676 General works

676.3 Catalogs

Local see S751+

676.5 Agricultural instruments, meters, etc.

677 General catalogs

Exhibits, etc.

678.A1 General works

678.A2-Z By region or country, A-Z

Under each country:

.x *General works*

.x2A-.x2Z *Special. By name, A-Z*

678.4 Vocational guidance

Study and teaching. Research

678.5 General works

678.53.A-Z By region or country, A-Z

678.56 Problems, exercises, examinations

678.57 Laboratory manuals

678.65 Robotics

678.7 Horticultural machinery

Cf. SB454.8 Garden equipment

Clearing implements

Including use of explosives in clearing land

679 General works

681 Catalogs

Soil working implements. Plows, etc.

683 General works

685 Catalogs

Seeding implements

687 General works

Farm machinery and farm engineering
Seeding implements -- Continued
689 Catalogs
Implements for caring for plants (Grafting, pruning, shelter, etc.)
691 General works
693 Catalogs
693.5 Fertilizer equipment
694 Spraying and dusting equipment
Harvesting implements and machinery
695 General works
696 Combines. Combine harvesters
697 Catalogs
Agricultural processing and processing machinery
Cf. SB129+ Crop handling
Cf. TP368+ Food industry and trade
Cf. TS1950+ Animal products
698 General works
698.5 Plant material cutting machinery
Threshing and related implements
699 General works
701 Catalogs
Storage
703 General works
705 Catalogs
Implements for direct preparation of crops for use
707 General works
709 Catalogs
Transportation and power transmission machinery
Cf. TL233+ Tractors (Manufacture)
711 General works
713 Catalogs
713.5 Wagons and carts
Cf. TS2001+ Manufacture
Waterlifting and transmission machinery see TJ899+
715.A-Z Implements and machinery for special crops. By crop, A-Z
Including planting, harvesting, and agricultural processing machinery for individual crops
715.B42 Beans
715.C33 Cabbage
715.C6 Corn
715.C64 Cotton
715.F67 Forage plants
715.G67 Grain
715.G7 Grapes
715.L48 Lettuce
715.M44 Melons

Farm machinery and farm engineering
Implements and machinery for special crops. By crop, A-Z -- Continued

715.M87	Mushrooms
715.O37	Oil palm
715.O4	Olives
715.P43	Peanuts
715.P48	Phragmites australis
715.P6	Potatoes
715.R5	Rice
715.S65	Sorghum
715.S89	Sugar beets
715.S9	Sugarcane
715.V4	Vegetables
715.W54	Wheat
	Implements for caring for farm animals see SF92
	Fences, gates see S790+
727	Miscellaneous
	e.g. Knots and splices
	By region or country
751	United States
760.A-Z	Other regions or countries, A-Z
760.5	Developing countries
	Agricultural structures. Farm buildings
	Cf. HD1393+ Valuation
	Cf. HD7289.A+ Rural housing
	Cf. NA8200+ Architecture
	Cf. S563 Farm layout
	Cf. SB195 Silos
	Cf. SB414.6+ Greenhouses
	Cf. SF91 Livestock housing
	Cf. SF494.5 Poultry housing
	Cf. TH4911+ Construction
770	Periodicals. Societies. Serials
772	Collected works (nonserial)
773	Congresses
774	Dictionaries and encyclopedias
	Directories
775	General works
775.3.A-Z	By region or country, A-Z
	Exhibitions
776	General works
776.4.A-Z	International. By place, A-Z
	Subarranged by year
776.6.A-Z	By region or country, A-Z
	Subarranged by author

Agricultural structures. Farm buildings -- Continued
778 History (General)
For local see S785+
780 General works
782 Juvenile works
783 Pictorial works
By region or country
United States
785 General works
786.A-Z By region or state, A-Z
787.A-Z Other regions or countries, A-Z
Fences. Gates
Cf. TH4965 Construction
790 General works
790.3 Electric fences
Conservation of natural resources
Including land conservation in general
Cf. HC1+ Economic aspects of natural resources
Cf. HD28+ Economic aspects of natural resources
Cf. S604.5+ Agricultural conservation
900 Periodicals and societies
912 Congresses
Documents
United States
914 Federal
916.A-Z Regions or states, A-Z
918.A-Z Other countries, A-Z
920 Directories
922 Encyclopedias and dictionaries
Exhibitions
924.A1 General works
924.A2-Z By region or country, A-Z
Under each country:
.x *General works*
.x2A-.x2Z *Special. By name, A-Z*
Biography
926.A2 Collective
926.A3-Z Individual, A-Z
History and conditions
928 General works
By region or country
United States
Cf. HC103.7 Natural resources (Economic aspects)
930 General works
932.A-Z Regions or states, A-Z
934.A-Z Other regions or countries, A-Z
936 Comprehensive works

Conservation of natural resources -- Continued
938 Textbooks
940 Juvenile literature
942 Essays and popular works
944 General special
944.5.A-Z Special topics, A-Z
944.5.A34 Aeronautics
944.5.C57 Citizen participation
944.5.C65 Communication
944.5.C67 Conservation plants
Including plant materials centers
Cf. S627.P55 Soil conservation
944.5.D36 Data processing
944.5.D42 Decision making
944.5.I57 International cooperation
944.5.L42 Leadership
944.5.N38 Natural resources conservation areas (General)
For local see S930+
944.5.P76 Projects
For local see S930+
944.5.P78 Protected areas (General)
For local see S930+
Cf. QH75+ Natural areas, wilderness areas, biosphere reserves, ecological reserves, landscape protection
Cf. QH90.75.A1+ Aquatic parks and reserves
Cf. QL81.5+ Wildlife refuges
Cf. SB481.A1+ National parks and reserves
Cf. SD426+ Forest reserves
Cf. SK357 Game reserves
944.5.P82 Public relations
944.5.S63 Social aspects
944.5.V64 Volunteer workers
945 Vocational guidance
Study and teaching. Research
946 General works
By region or country
United States
946.3 General works
946.32.A-Z By region or state, A-Z
946.34.A-Z Other regions or countries, A-Z
946.5 Audiovisual aids
Agricultural conservation see S604.5+
Land conservation
see S900+
Cf. S604.8+ Melioration of land
(950) Periodicals and societies
(952) General works

Conservation of natural resources
Land conservation -- Continued
(954.A-Z) By region or country, A-Z
Water conservation
Economic history see HD1690+
Engineering see TC401+; TD388+
Soil conservation see S622+
Forest conservation see SD411+
Conservation of grasslands
Formation and care of meadows see SB199
Soil conservation see S622+
Stock ranges see SF84.82+
Wildlife conservation see QL81.5+
Cf. QH75+ Protection of nature, scenery, natural monuments
(960) Periodicals and societies
(962) General works
(964.A-Z) By region or country, A-Z
Recreational resources conservation see GV191.642+
(970) General works
(972.A-Z) By region or country, A-Z
Marine resources conservation see GC1018
Mineral resources conservation see TN1+

Plant culture
For climatic aspects of particular crops, see the crop, e.g. SB191.M2 Corn
For soil aspects of particular crops see S597.A+
For fertilizers for particular crops see S667.A+
For machinery for particular crops see S715.A+
For diseases of particular crops see SB608.A+
Cf. HG9968 Crop insurance
Cf. QK1+ Botany
Cf. SD1+ Forestry

	Periodicals and societies
1	American
	For societies under state auspices see SB21
4	English
7	French
10	German
13	Other
	Congresses
16.A1-.A5	International congresses
16.A6-Z	By region or country, A-Z
	Documents
	United States
19	Federal
21	State, A-W
23	Great Britain
	For documents of colonies, etc. see SB29.A+
25	France
27	Germany
29.A-Z	Other, A-Z
39	Horticultural voyages, etc.
	Collections
41	General
43	Collected writings of individual authors
44	Directories
45	Encyclopedias and dictionaries
45.5	Nomenclature
	Communication in crop science
45.6	General works
45.65	Crop science in literature
46	Receipts and rule books. Calendars
50	Vocational guidance
	Study and teaching. Research
51	General works
51.8.A-Z	International institutions. By name, A-Z

Study and teaching. Research -- Continued

52.A-Z By region or country, A-Z

Under each country:

.x	*General works*
.x2A-.x2Z	*Local, A-Z*
.x3A-.x3Z	*Special schools or institutions. By name, A-Z*

School gardens and farms

Including children's gardens for school and home

For home gardens see SB457+

55 General

56.A-Z By place, A-Z

e.g. Report of Children's Farm School, New York

Exhibitions

57.A-Z International expositions. By place, A-Z

Subarranged by year

59.A-Z National and local. By place, A-Z

Subarranged by year

For exhibits of special plants, see the plants

Museums

For collections of special plants, e.g. gums, see the subject

60.A1 General works

60.A2-Z By region or country, A-Z

Under each country:

.x	*General works*
.x2A-.x2Z	*Special. By name, A-Z*

Biography

61 Collective

63.A-Z Individual, A-Z

e.g.

Appleseed, Johnny see SB63.C46

63.B9 Burbank, Luther

63.C46 Chapman, John

63.H5 Henderson, Peter

History and conditions

Cf. SB451+ Gardens and gardening

71 General

Antiquity

Cf. GN799.A4 Origin and prehistory of agriculture

73 General works

75 Greeks

77 Romans

79 Middle Ages

By region or country

United States

83 General works

History and conditions
By region or country
United States -- Continued
85.A-Z By region or state, A-Z
Subarrange each state by Table S3a
87.A-Z Other regions or countries, A-Z
Subarrange each country by Table S3a
General works
91 Comprehensive works
General and popular works for special regions
Cf. S521+ Popular works on agriculture in general
Cf. SB455 Popular works on gardens and gardening
United States
92 To 1800
93 1801-
94 American works in foreign languages
95 The South
Great Britain
97 To 1800
98 1801-
99.A-Z Other regions or countries, A-Z
102 Juvenile works
103 Essays and light literature
Cf. S521+ Light literature on agriculture in general
105 Addresses
106.A-Z Special aspects of crops and plant culture as a whole, A-Z
106.B56 Biotechnology
Including pollen biotechnology
For works limited to specific crops, see the crop, e.g. SB191.R5 Rice
Cf. TP248.27.P55 Plant biotechnology (General)
106.E25 Ecophysiology
Evolution see SB106.O74
106.G46 Genetics (General)
For works limited to special crops see the crop, e.g. SB191.R5 Rice
For works limited to general propagation see SB119+
106.I47 Improvement
For local (History and conditions) see SB83+
For local (Culture) see SB92+
106.M83 Mycorrhizas
Cf. QK604.2.M92 Mycology
106.O74 Origin and evolution
106.V43 Vegetation management

	Economic botany
	For economic botany of special plants, see the plant, e.g. Cereals SB189-SB191
	For medical botany see QK99.A1+
	Cf. QK101+ Phytogeography
	Cf. SD1+ Forestry
107	General and comprehensive works
107.5	Minor works
108.A-Z	By region or country, A-Z
	United States
108.U5	General works
108.U6A-.U6Z	By region or state, A-Z
109	Plant introduction
	For special areas see SB108.A+
	Methods for special areas
	Cf. S604.3+ Agriculture
109.7	Cold regions
110	Dry farming
	Tropical agriculture
111.A2	Periodicals. Societies. Serials
111.A3-Z	Monographs. By author
112	Irrigation farming
	Class here farmers' manuals on irrigation agriculture
	For works on arid regions and irrigation agriculture see S612+
112.5	Physiology
	Cf. SB130 Postharvest physiology
(113)	Nursery catalogs, etc.
	see SB118.485+
	Seeds. Seed technology
	Including seed growing and farms
	For special plants, see the plant, e.g. Wheat SB191.W5
	Cf. HD9019.S43+ Seed industry and trade
	Cf. QK660+ Botany
	Cf. SB732.8 Seed pathology
113.2	Periodicals. Societies
113.3	Congresses
113.4	Directories
	Study and teaching. Research
113.7	General works
113.75.A-Z	By region or country, A-Z
113.85	Laboratories
	Regulation, inspection, etc.
	Including certification, grading, and testing
114.A1	Societies
114.A3	General

Seeds. Seed technology
Regulation, inspection, etc. -- Continued
114.A4-Z By region or country
Subarrange each country by Table S3a
United States
114.U6 General works
114.U7A-.U7W By state, A-W
Seed projects
114.5 General works
114.53.A-Z By region or country, A-Z
115 Seed and plant catalogs
For works limited to specific plants, see the plant, e.g. SB362.3 Fruit; SB371 Peach
For works about special nurseries see SB118.48+
For works limited to nursery stock catalogs see SB118.485+
Cf. QK73.A+ Seed lists of botanical gardens
Seed growing. Seed farms
117 General works
117.2 History and conditions
By region or country
United States
117.3 General works
117.35.A-Z By region or state, A-Z
117.4.A-Z Other regions or countries, A-Z
118 Seed identification
118.25 Seed quality
Seed handling and postharvest technology
118.3 General works
118.32 Harvesting
118.34 Cleaning
118.36 Drying
118.38 Preservation. Protection
Including seed deterioration
118.4 Storage
118.43 Disinfection
118.44 Seed treatment
Including irradiation, stratification, etc.
118.45 Seed equipment and supplies
118.46 Synthetic seeds
Including somatic embryogenesis
Nurseries. Nursery industry
For works limited to a specific plant, see the plant, e.g. SB409 Orchids; SB411 Roses
For works on general plant propagation see SB119+
Cf. SB115 Seed and plant catalogs
118.48 Periodicals. Societies. Serials

Nurseries. Nursery industry -- Continued
Directories
Including nursery stock catalogs
118.485 General works
By region or country
United States
118.486 General works
118.487.A-Z By region or state, A-Z
118.488.A-Z Other regions or countries, A-Z
Biography see SB61+
118.5 General works
118.6 Economic aspects. Costs (General)
History and conditions
118.7 General works
By region or country
United States
118.73 General works
118.74.A-Z By region or state, A-Z
Subarrange each state by Table S3a
118.75.A-Z Other regions or countries, A-Z
Propagation
For works limited to special plants, see the plant, e.g. SB406.7+ Flowers; SB419 House plants
Cf. SB118.48+ Nurseries
119 General works
Special methods
121 Planting and transplanting. Sowing
Breeding, crossing, selection, etc.
123 General works
123.25.A-Z By region or country, A-Z
Germplasm resources
123.3 General works
123.34.A-Z By region or country, A-Z
123.45 Variety testing
123.5 Patents
Class here lists of patented plants
Including protected varieties
For legal works on plant patents, see class K
123.57 Genetic engineering. Transgenic plants
123.6 Cell and tissue culture
Cf. SB118.46 Somatic embryogenesis
123.65 Budding and grafting
123.7 Air layering
123.75 Plant cuttings. Mist propagation
124 Other special methods (not A-Z)

125 Training and pruning
For works limited to special plants, see the plant, e.g. SB359.45 Fruit
126 Artificial light gardening
Hydroponics. Soilless culture
Cf. S589.85+ Artificial plant growing media
126.5 General works
126.57.A-Z By region or country, A-Z
126.8 Flowering (General)
Cf. QK830 Botany
127 Forcing
Cf. SB414 Flowers
128 Growth regulators
Harvesting, curing, storage
For harvesting, curing, etc., of individual crops, see the crop, e.g. SB189.7+ Grain; SB442.5 Flowers and ornamental plants
129 General works
130 Postharvest physiology
Packing, shipment, and marketing see S571+
(133) Garden tools
see SB454.8
139 Miscellaneous
e.g. Electricity in horticulture
160 New crops (General)
For works limited to special crops, see the crop, e.g. SB169+ Tree crops
Tree crops
Including shrubs
Cf. S494.5.A45 Agroforestry
169 Periodicals. Societies. Serials
169.2 Congresses
170 General works
171.A-Z By region or country, A-Z
Multipurpose trees (General)
Cf. S494.5.A45 Agroforestry
172 General works
172.5.A-Z By region or country, A-Z
Food crops
Cf. S494.5.A45 Agroforestry
175 General works
176.A-S176.Z By region or country, A-Z
177.A-Z By plant, A-Z
Alkaloidal plants see SB265+
177.A52 Amaranths
Cf. SB191.A42 Grain
Cf. SB207.A52 Forage plants
Cf. SB351.A54 Vegetables

Food crops
By plant, A-Z -- Continued
Condiment plants see SB305+
177.E88 Euterpe edulis
Fruit see SB354+
Fungi, Edible see SB352.85+
177.G65 Goosefoots
Grain see SB188+
Herbs see SB351.H5
177.L45 Legumes
Cf. SB203+ Feed and forage legumes
Cf. SB297.4.L44 Nitrogen-fixing plants
Cf. SB317.L43 Legumes of multiple use
177.L85 Lupines
Cf. SB205.L9 Forage plants
Cf. SB317.L87 Economic plants
Cf. SB413.L86 Ornamental plants
Manna plants see SB317.M33
Marine algae see SH390+
Mushrooms see SB352.85+
Nuts see SB401+
Oilseed plants see SB298+
177.Q55 Quinoa
Root crops see SB209+
Spice plants see SB305+
Starch plants see SB309+
Sugar plants see SB215+
Tuber crops see SB209+
Vegetables see SB320+
Field crops
Cf. S21+ Crop reports, statistics
Cf. S494.5.E8 Estimating and reporting
Cf. S671+ Machinery
183 Periodicals. Societies. Serials
183.2 Congresses
Directories see SB44
Encyclopedias and dictionaries see SB45
Study and teaching. Research see SB51+
Field experiments see S540.F5
185 General works
Physiology
185.5 General works
185.6 Water requirements
185.7 Breeding
185.75 Varieties
185.78 Judging
Seed production see SB113.2+

Field crops -- Continued

185.8 Planting time. Harvesting time

186 Harvesting

186.2 Drying

186.3 Storage

186.5 Economic aspects of culture. Costs (General)

187.A-S187.Z By region or country, A-Z

Grain. Cereals

Cf. S671+ Machinery

188 Periodicals. Societies. Serials

188.2 Congresses

188.3 Directories

188.4 Dictionaries. Encyclopedias

Study and teaching. Research

188.5 General works

188.525.A-Z International institutions. By name, A-Z

188.53.A-Z By region or country, A-Z

188.55 Field experiments

188.6 Exhibitions

188.8 History (General)

189 General works

189.3 Straw

Cf. TS1109 Paper manufacture

Cf. TS1747.S7 Fiber industry

Physiology

189.4 General works

189.45 Water requirements. Irrigation

189.47 Varieties

Plant propagation

189.48 General works

189.5 Breeding

189.525 Germplasm resources

189.53 Genetic engineering

189.54 Cell and tissue culture

189.55 Seeds

189.57 Planting time. Harvesting time

189.6 Preharvest sprouting

Postharvest technology

189.7 General works

189.73 Harvesting

189.74 Threshing

189.75 Cleaning

189.77 Drying

189.8 Grading. Standards

190 Storage

190.3 Economic aspects of culture. Costs (General)

191.A-Z Individual cereals, A-Z

Field crops
Grain. Cereals
Individual cereals, A-Z -- Continued

191.A42 Amaranths
Cf. SB177.A52 Food crops
Cf. SB207.A52 Forage plants
Avena fatua see SB191.W53
191.B2 Barley
191.B9 Buckwheat
Corn see SB191.M2
Durra see SB191.S7
191.F66 Fonio
(191.I5) Indian rice
see SB191.W55
(191.K3) Kafir corn
see SB191.S7
Kaoliang see SB191.S7
191.M2 Maize. Corn
Cf. SB191.P64 Popcorn
Cf. SB351.C7 Sweet corn
191.M5 Millets
Milo see SB191.S7
191.O2 Oats
191.P4 Pearl millet
191.P64 Popcorn
191.R3 Ragi
191.R5 Rice
191.R53 Rice, Red
Cf. SB615.R43 Weed
191.R9 Rye
191.S7 Sorghum
Sweet corn see SB351.C7
191.T43 Teff
191.T7 Triticale
191.W5 Wheat
191.W53 Wild oat
191.W55 Wild rice
191.W57 Wild wheats
Including individual species
192.A-Z By region or country, A-Z
Forage crops. Feed crops
Including ranges of western United States
For care of cattle on ranges see SF84.82+
193 General works
193.3.A-Z By region or country, A-Z
193.5 Breeding
193.55 Seeds

Field crops
Forage crops. Feed crops -- Continued

195 Silage
For works limited to a special crop, see the crop, e.g.
SB191.M2 Corn
Cf. TH4935 Silos

Grasses
Cf. QK495.G74 Botany

197 General works
Local see SB202.A+
198 Hay and other dried forage plants
Cf. SB189.3 Straw
199 Formation and care of meadows. Pastures (General)
Cf. SB433+ Lawns
201.A-Z By plant, A-Z
201.A52 Andropogon furcatus
201.A53 Andropogon gayanus
201.B35 Bermuda grass
201.B47 Black grama grass
201.B5 Bluegrasses
Including individual species of bluegrass except Kentucky
Cf. SB201.K4 Kentucky bluegrass
201.B8 Bromegrasses
201.B9 Buffalo grass
201.B93 Buffelgrass
(201.C46) Cenchrus ciliaris
see SB201.B93
201.C73 Crested wheatgrass
201.D3 Danthonia
201.E46 Elymus sibiricus
201.E8 Esparto
201.F48 Fescue
201.F6 Foxtail
201.G8 Guinea grass
201.H3 Hardinggrass
201.I6 Indian rice
201.J5 Johnson grass
201.K4 Kentucky bluegrass
201.K54 Kikuyu grass
201.K57 Kioleria cristata
201.L6 Lolium
201.L65 Love grass
201.M4 Meadow fescue
201.M5 Mitchell grass
201.O6 Orchard grass
201.P3 Para grass
201.P35 Pennisetum purpureum

Field crops
Forage crops. Feed crops
Grasses
By plant, A-Z -- Continued
(201.P37) Perennial veldt grass
see SB201.V44
201.P42 Petrozavodsk orchard grass
201.P5 Phragmites australis
201.R3 Reed canary grass
201.R45 Rhodes grass
201.R52 Ricegrasses
Including individual species
201.R6 Roselle
201.R64 Rough fescue
201.R8 Ryegrasses
201.S8 Sudan grass
201.S95 Switchgrass
201.T34 Tall fescue
201.T5 Timothy grass
201.U75 Urochloa trichopus
201.V44 Veld grass
201.V46 Vetiver
201.W5 Wheatgrasses
Cf. SB201.C73 Crested wheatgrass
201.Z6 Zoysia japonica
202.A-Z By region or country, A-Z
Legumes
Cf. SB177.L45 Food legumes
Cf. SB297.4.L44 Nitrogen-fixing crops
Cf. SB317.L43 Legumes of multiple use
203 General works
203.3.A-Z By region or country, A-Z
205.A-Z Individual legumes, A-Z
205.A4 Alfalfa
205.B4 Berseem
Broad bean see SB205.F3
205.C37 Caucasus goat's rue
205.C64 Clover
205.C8 Cowpeas
Cf. SB351.C75 Vegetable
205.C85 Crotalaria
205.F3 Fava bean
Cf. SB351.F3 Food crop
Fenugreek see SB205.T7
205.K8 Kudzu
205.L4 Lespedeza
205.L7 Lotus

Field crops
Forage crops. Feed crops
Legumes
Individual legumes, A-Z -- Continued

205.L9 Lupines
Cf. SB177.L85 Food crops
Cf. SB317.L87 Economic plants
Cf. SB413.L86 Ornamental plants
205.M4 Medicago
205.P5 Pigeon pea
Cf. SB317.P54 Multiple use crop
205.S7 Soybean
205.S86 Stylosanthes
205.T35 Tamarugo
205.T67 Townsville stylo
205.T7 Trigonella. Fenugreek
Cf. SB317.F44 Multiple use crop
205.V58 Vetch
207.A-Z Other, A-Z
207.A52 Amaranths
Cf. SB177.A52 Food crops
Cf. SB191.A42 Grain
207.A77 Atriplex repanda
207.B54 Bilberry
207.B7 Brassica
207.C2 Cactus
207.C35 Ceanothus
207.C6 Comfrey
207.C86 Cup rosinweed
207.H35 Halophytes
Including salt-tolerant crops
207.K3 Kale
207.K6 Kochia
207.L52 Lichens
207.M35 Mangel-wurzel
207.P5 Phacelia
207.P64 Polygonum weyrichii
207.P8 Prickly pears
207.P93 Purshia tridentata
207.R36 Rape (Plant)
Cf. SB299.R2 Oilseed plant
207.S3 Salt-bush
Salt-tolerant crops see SB207.H35
207.S96 Sunflowers
Cf. SB299.S9 Oilseed plant
Cf. SB413.S88 Ornamental plants

	Field crops
	Forage crops. Feed crops -- Continued
(208.A-Z)	By region or country, A-Z see SB193.3.A+
	Root and tuber crops Cf. SB351.R65 Vegetables
209	General works
210.A-Z	By region or country, A-Z
211.A-Z	By plant, A-Z
211.A69	Araceae
	Artichoke, Jerusalem see SB211.J4
211.C3	Cassava
211.C5	Chicory
	Dasheen see SB211.T2
211.J4	Jerusalem artichoke
211.M23	Maca
	Mangel-wurzel see SB207.M35
211.M29	Manihot Cf. SB291.M32 Rubber plants
211.P3	Parsnip
211.P8	Potatoes
211.R8	Rutabaga
211.S9	Sweet potato
211.T2	Taro
211.T8	Turnip
211.Y3	Yam
	Sugar plants Cf. HD9100+ Sugar trade Cf. TP375+ Sugar manufacture
215	Periodicals. Societies. Serials
(216)	Directories (of cane growers and manufacturers of sugar) see TP375.5
217	General works
	Sugar beets
218	Periodicals. Societies. Serials
218.2	Congresses
	By region or country
219	United States
220.A-Z	Other regions or countries, A-Z
221	General works
	Sugar cane
226	Periodicals. Societies. Serials
226.2	Congresses
	By region or country
228	United States
229.A-Z	Other regions or countries, A-Z
231	General works

Field crops
Sugar plants -- Continued
235 Sorgo
239.A-Z Other sugar plants, A-Z
239.M3 Maple
239.P3 Palms
239.S75 Stevia rebaudiana
Textile and fiber plants
Cf. HD9850+ Textile trade
Cf. TS1300+ Textile industries
241 General works
242.A-Z By region or country, A-Z
Cotton
Cf. HD9070+ Cotton trade
245 Periodicals. Societies. Serials
245.2 Congresses
Documents (United States) see SB249
Documents (Other countries) see SB251.A+
249 General and United States
251.A-Z Other countries, A-Z
251.5 Sea Island cotton
(252) Ginning, baling, etc.
see TS1585
253 Flax
Cf. HD9155 Industry
Cf. SB299.F6 Oilseed plant
Cf. TS1700+ Manufacture
255 Hemp
Cf. HD9155 Hemp industry
Cf. SB295.C35 Cannabis
Cf. TS1733 Hemp manufactures
257 Jute
Cf. HD9156.J7+ Jute industry
259 Ramie
Cf. HD9156.R2+ Ramie industry
Cf. TS1544.R2 Textile industry
261.A-Z Other, A-Z
Cf. HD9156.A+ Fiber industries
Abaca see SB261.M3
261.A5 Ambary hemp. Kenaf
261.A6 Ananas erectifolius
Caroa see SB261.N4
(261.C5) Chamaerops humilis
see SB261.E87
261.E87 European fan palm
261.F56 Fique
261.F98 Furcraea

	Field crops
	Textile and fiber plants
	Other, A-Z -- Continued
261.H4	Henequen
261.K3	Kapok
	Kenaf see SB261.A5
(261.M25)	Maguey see SB317.A2
261.M27	Malva
261.M3	Manila hemp. Abaca
261.M6	Mitsumata
261.N4	Neoglaziovia variegata
261.P6	Phormium tenax
	Piteira see SB261.F98
261.P7	Posidonia australis
261.R6	Roselle
261.S4	Sisal
261.S63	Spanish moss
261.S86	Sunn hemp Cf. SB284.4.S96 Green manure crop
261.U7	Urena lobata
	Other field crops
	Alkaloidal plants Cf. SB293+ Medicinal plants
265	General works
	Cacao Cf. HD9200 Cocoa and chocolate industry
267	General works
268.A-Z	By region or country, A-Z
	Coffee Cf. HD9195+ Economic aspects
269	General works
270.A-Z	By region or country, A-Z
	Tea Cf. HD9195+ Economic aspects
271	General works
272.A-Z	By region or country, A-Z
	Tobacco Cf. HD9130+ Tobacco manufacture
273	General and United States
275	Analyses
276	Miscellaneous, including experiments
278.A-Z	By region or country, A-Z United States see SB273
279.A-Z	Other alkaloidal plants, A-Z
279.K64	Kola tree
279.M4	Mate

Field crops
Other field crops -- Continued
Aromatic plants see SB301+
Basketwork and matwork plants
Cf. SD397.O82 Osier culture
Cf. TS910 Basketmaking
281 General works
282.A-Z By region or country, A-Z
283.A-Z By plant, A-Z
283.J86 Juncus effusus
Catch crops
283.5 General works
283.55.A-Z By region or country, A-Z
Cover crops and green manure crops
284 General works
284.3.A-Z By region or country, A-Z
284.4.A-Z By plant, A-Z
284.4.L84 Lupinus perennis
284.4.S96 Sunn hemp
Cf. SB261.S86 Fiber plant
Dye plants
Cf. HD9999.C48+ Industry
Cf. QK98.7.A1+ Botany
Cf. TP890+ Technology
Cf. TT853+ Handicraft
285 General works
286.A-Z By region or country, A-Z
287.A-Z By plant, A-Z
287.A55 Anil
287.A58 Annatto tree
287.H46 Henna
287.I4 Indigofera
287.M3 Madder
Saffron see SB317.S2
287.W8 Woad
Energy crops
For individual energy crops, see the crop
Cf. SD536.5+ Fuelwood crops
288 General works
288.3.A-Z By region or country, A-Z
Green manure crops see SB284+
Gum and resin plants. Rubber plants
Cf. HD9161+ Rubber industry
Cf. TS1870+ Rubber manufacture
289 General works
Rubber plants (General)
290 General works

Field crops
Other field crops
Gum and resin plants. Rubber plants
Rubber plants (General) -- Continued

290.5.A-Z By region or country, A-Z
291.A-Z By plant, A-Z
291.A32 Acacia senegal
291.B3 Balata
Chicle see SB291.S3
291.E8 Eucommia ulmoides
291.G8 Guayule
291.G9 Gutta-percha
291.H4 Hevea
291.K6 Kok-saghyz
291.L35 Lannea coromandelica
291.M32 Manihot
Cf. SB211.M29 Root crops
Manilkara see SB291.S3
291.R48 Rhus
291.R49 Rhus verniciflua
Sapodilla see SB291.S3
291.S3 Sapotaceae. Manilkara. Sapodilla. Sapota. Chicle
For Manilkara kauki see SD397.M26
291.S6 Spindle tree
291.T3 Tau-saghz

Hydrocarbon-producing plants
Cf. SB289+ Gum and resin plants
Cf. SB298+ Oil-bearing and wax plants
291.5 General works
291.53.A-Z By region or country, A-Z

Insecticidal plants. Pesticidal plants
292.A2 General works
292.A4-Z By plant, A-Z
292.N44 Neem
Cf. SB952.N44 Neem insecticide
292.P8 Pyrethrum
Cf. SB952.P9 Insecticide
292.T4 Tephrosia vogelii

Medicinal plants (Culture only)
Cf. RS431.M37 Pharmacy
Cf. SB265+ Alkaloidal plants
293 General works
294.A-Z By region or country, A-Z
295.A-Z By plant, A-Z
295.A45 Aloe
295.A8 Asafoetida
295.A85 Atractylis ovata

Field crops
Other field crops
Medicinal plants (Culture only)
By plant, A-Z -- Continued

295.B4 Belladonna
295.B5 Betel nut
295.C25 Camellias
295.C3 Camphor
295.C32 Camptotheca acuminata
295.C35 Cannabis
Cf. SB255 Hemp
295.C4 Cascara
295.C45 Cephaelis ipecacuanha
295.C5 Cinchona
295.C6 Coca
295.C65 Coptis chinensis
295.C87 Curry leaf tree
295.D3 Datura innoxia
295.D5 Digitalis purpurea
295.E63 Ephedra
295.F74 Fritillaria
295.G35 Ganoderma
295.G37 Gastrodia elata
295.G5 Ginseng
(295.G55) Glycyrrhiza glabra
see SB295.L7
295.G6 Goldenseal
295.G7 Grapple plant
295.G8 Guarana
Hops see SB317.H64
295.H84 Horsemint
295.J2 Jacob's ladder
295.L7 Licorice
295.M34 Maca
Manna plants see SB317.M33
295.M5 Mentha
295.O65 Opium poppy
Cf. SB299.O65 Oilseed plant
295.P3 Pacific yew
295.P4 Peppermint
295.P6 Pinkeroot
295.P63 Piper betle
Poppy, Opium see SB295.O65
295.P84 Psilocybe
Including the various species
Pyrethrum see SB292.P8

Field crops
Other field crops
Medicinal plants (Culture only)
By plant, A-Z -- Continued

295.P87 Psyllium
Including individual psyllium-producing plants
295.Q38 Qat
295.R37 Rauvolfia serpentina
Saffron see SB317.S2
295.S37 Sassafras
295.S45 Senna
295.V34 Valeriana
295.V56 Violets

Nitrogen-fixing plants and trees
297 General works
297.3.A-Z By region or country, A-Z
297.4.A-Z By plant, A-Z
297.4.L44 Legumes
Cf. SB177.L45 Food legumes
Cf. SB203+ Feed and forage legumes
Cf. SB317.L43 Legumes of multiple use

Oil-bearing plants. Wax plants
298 General works
298.5.A-Z By region or country, A-Z
299.A-Z By plant, A-Z
299.A4 Aleurites
Cf. SB299.T8 Tung tree
299.B7 Brassica
Cf. SB317.B65 Economic plants
299.C23 Camellia oleifera
299.C25 Candelilla
299.C28 Carnauba palm
299.C3 Castor oil plant
299.C45 Chenopodium
299.C5 Chia
299.C6 Coconut palm
299.C7 Crambe abyssinica
299.E34 Eben tree
299.E78 Erythrina edulis
299.F6 Flax
Cf. HD9155 Industry
Cf. SB253 Fiber plant
299.J46 Jessenia bataua
299.J6 Jojoba
299.M2 Madi
299.M44 Melaleuca
299.O38 Oiticica tree

Field crops
Other field crops
Oil-bearing plants. Wax plants
By plant, A-Z -- Continued
Olive see SB367
299.O65 Opium poppy
Cf. SB295.O65 Medicinal plant
299.P3 Palms
Class here general works on oil palms and works on the African oil palm
For works on other palms, see the specific palm, e.g. SB299.C6 Coconut palm
299.P5 Phytelephas
Poppy, Opium see SB299.O65
299.R2 Rape (Plant)
Cf. SB207.R36 Forage plant
299.R5 Rhus succedanea
299.S2 Safflower
299.S4 Sesame
299.S9 Sunflowers
Cf. SB207.S96 Forage plant
Cf. SB413.S88 Ornamental plants
299.T3 Tallow tree
299.T8 Tung tree
299.U4 Ucuhuba
299.W3 Wax palms (General)
Wormseed see SB299.C45
Aromatic plants
Cf. SB454.3.F7 Fragrant gardens
Cf. TP983+ Perfume manufacture
301 General works
302.A-Z By region or country, A-Z
303.A-Z By plant, A-Z
303.B37 Basil
Cf. SB317.B25 Basils of multiple use
303.J37 Jasmine
303.L3 Lavenders
Cf. SB317.L37 Lavenders of multiple use
303.L4 Lemongrass
303.S34 Scented geraniums
303.S8 Sweet goldenrod
303.V4 Vetiver
Pesticidal plants see SB292.A2+
Spice and condiment plants
Cf. TX406+ Condiments, etc.
305 General works
306.A-Z By region or country, A-Z

Field crops
Other field crops
Spice and condiment plants -- Continued

307.A-Z By plant, A-Z
Black pepper see SB307.P5
307.C27 Capsicum annuum. Paprika
307.C3 Cardamoms
307.C5 Cinnamon
307.C6 Clove
307.C85 Cumin
307.G5 Ginger
307.H6 Horseradish
307.I4 Illicium verum
307.M87 Mustard
307.N8 Nutmeg
(307.P3) Paprika
see SB307.C27
307.P4 Peppers
Class here works on peppers grown for use as condiments and spices
For paprika see SB307.C27
For general works on peppers grown for use as vegetables see SB351.P4
307.P5 Piper nigrum. Black pepper
Saffron see SB317.S2
307.S34 Sage
307.T6 Tonka bean
307.V2 Vanilla
Starch plants
309 General works
311.A-Z By plant, A-Z
311.A7 Arrowroot
311.S3 Sago palm
Tannin plants
Cf. TS985 Tanning materials
313 General works
314.A-Z By region or country, A-Z
315.A-Z By plant, A-Z
315.A33 Acacia nilotica
315.G4 Geraniums
315.L4 Leather bergenia
315.R45 Rhus semialata
315.S9 Sumac
315.W3 Wattle
317.A-Z Other economic plants, A-Z
317.A16 Acanthophyllum
317.A2 Agave

Field crops
Other economic plants, A-Z -- Continued

317.A64 Aquatic plants
Cf. SB423+ Ornamental plants
Cf. SH388.7+ Algae culture
317.A68 Argania spinosa
317.A69 Arid regions plants
Including desert plants
Cf. SB427.5 Ornamental plants
317.A75 Astragalus
317.A85 Atriplex
317.A94 Azolla
317.B16 Babassu
317.B2 Bamboo
317.B23 Baobab
317.B25 Basil
Cf. SB303.B37 Aromatic plants
317.B65 Brassica
Cf. SB299.B7 Oilseed plants
317.B8 Broomcorn
317.C2 Cactus
317.C24 Calamus margaritae
317.C25 Calliandra calothyrsus
317.C255 Carob
317.C26 Caryota
317.C44 Chiranthodendron pentadactylon
317.C56 Coastal plants
317.C58 Cogon grass
317.C6 Comfrey
317.D82 Duckweeds
317.E58 Ensete
317.F33 Faidherbia albida
317.F44 Fenugreek
Cf. SB205.T7 Forage crop
317.F52 Ficus
317.F85 Fuller's teasel
317.G5 Giant reed
317.G57 Gliricidia sepium
317.G68 Gourds
Cf. SB413.G6 Ornamental gourds
317.G74 Grevillea robusta
317.G75 Guar
317.G77 Guazuma ulmifolia
Halophytes see SB317.S25
317.H45 Herbicide-resistant crops
317.H64 Hops
317.I4 Ilala palm

Field crops
Other economic plants, A-Z -- Continued

317.I58 Inulin-containing plants

317.K38 Kava

317.L37 Lavenders
Cf. SB303.L3 Aromatic plants

317.L4 Lead tree
Cf. SD397.L35 Forestry

317.L43 Legumes
Cf. SB177.L45 Food legumes
Cf. SB203+ Feed and forage legumes
Cf. SB297.4.L44 Nitrogen-fixing plants

317.L48 Leucaena

317.L87 Lupines
Cf. SB177.L85 Food crops
Cf. SB205.L9 Forage plants
Cf. SB413.L86 Ornamental plants

317.M28 Madhuca latifolia

317.M33 Manna plants

(317.M34) Margosa
see SB317.N43

Marine algae see SH390+

317.M38 Mauritia flexuosa

317.M47 Mesquite

317.M67 Moringa oleifera

317.M85 Mung bean

317.N43 Neem

317.N87 Nutgrass

317.N9 Nymphaea

Ocimum see SB317.B25

317.O68 Opuntia
Including prickly pears

Palm, Palmyra see SB317.P32

Palm, Peach see SB317.P43

317.P3 Palms (General)

317.P32 Palmyra palm

317.P35 Papaya
Cf. SB379.P2 Fruit

317.P36 Parkia biglobosa

317.P37 Paspalum hieronymii

317.P43 Peach palm

317.P54 Pigeon pea
Cf. SB205.P5 Forage crop

317.P76 Prosopis juliflora
Cf. SB615.P83 Weeds
Cf. SD397.P88 Forestry

Prickly pears see SB317.O68

Field crops
Other economic plants, A-Z -- Continued
317.R35 Raffia
317.R37 Rattan palms
317.R4 Reed
317.S2 Saffron
317.S25 Salt-tolerant crops. Halophytes
317.S27 Salvinia molesta
Seagrasses see SH393
Seaweed see SH390+
317.S46 Sesbania
Including Sesbania sesban
317.S7 Spanish broom
317.T48 Tequila agave
317.T52 Terminalia
317.T73 Trapa natans
317.T8 Turmeric
317.V44 Veld plants
317.W37 Water hyacinth
Cf. SB615.W3 Weed
317.W47 Wetland plants
317.Y82 Yucca
317.Z49 Zizania latifolia
Horticulture. Horticultural crops
Cf. SB115 Seed and plant catalogs (General)
Cf. SB446+ Horticultural service industry
Cf. SB450.9+ Gardening
317.5 Periodicals. Societies. Serials
317.52 Collected works (nonserial)
317.53 Congresses
Horticultural voyages see SB39
Directories
317.55 General
317.56.A-Z By region or country, A-Z
317.58 Dictionaries. Encyclopedias. Terminology
317.6 Vocational guidance
Study and teaching. Research
Cf. SB55+ School gardens
317.63 General works
317.65.A-Z By region or country, A-Z
317.68 Volunteer workers in horticulture. Master gardeners
Exhibitions
317.7 General works
317.73.A-Z International. By place, A-Z
National, state, and local. By country
United States
317.74 General works

Horticulture. Horticultural crops
Exhibitions
National, state, and local. By country
United States -- Continued
317.75.A-Z By region or state, A-Z
Subarrange each state by Table S3a
317.76.A-Z Other countries, A-Z
Subarrange each country by Table S3a
317.78 Judging. Standards
General works
317.8 Through 1800
317.9 1801-1950
318 1851-
Biography see SB61+
Horticultural literature
318.3 General works
318.34.A-Z By region or country, A-Z
318.36 Language. Authorship
History and conditions
318.5 General works
By region or country
United States
319 General works
319.2.A-Z By region or state, A-Z
319.3.A-Z Other regions or countries, A-Z
319.4 Economic aspects of culture. Costs (General)
Physiology
319.5 General works
319.53 Water requirements. Irrigation
Plant propagation
319.58 General works
319.6 Breeding
319.625 Cell and tissue culture
319.65 Seeds
Preparation for market
319.7 General works
319.73 Harvesting
319.75 Grading. Standards. Quality
319.76 Transportation
319.77 Storage
Pick-your-own farms
319.85 General works
By region or country
United States
319.86 General works
319.863.A-Z By region or state, A-Z
319.864.A-Z Other regions or countries, A-Z

Horticulture. Horticultural crops -- Continued
319.95 Sustainable horticulture
Vegetables
Cf. HD9220+ Vegetables industry
320 Periodicals. Societies. Serials
320.2 Congresses
320.25 Directories
320.27 Vegetable seed and plant catalogs
For works limited to specific vegetables, see the vegetable, e.g. SB349 Tomatoes
320.3 Dictionaries. Encyclopedias
Study and teaching. Research
320.4 General works
320.43.A-Z By region or country, A-Z
History
320.5 General works
By region or country
United States
320.6 General works
320.7.A-Z By region or state, A-Z
320.8.A-Z Other regions or countries, A-Z
320.9 General works
General cultural practices
321 General works
By region or country
United States
General works see SB321
321.5.A-Z By region or state, A-Z
322 Great Britain
323.A-Z Other regions or countries, A-Z
324 Juvenile works
324.3 Organic gardening
324.4 Container gardening
324.5 Indoor gardening
Cf. SB351.7+ Greenhouse culture
324.53 Sprouts
Vegetables and vegetable culture for special physiographic areas
324.55 General works
324.56 Tropical vegetables
Physiology
324.6 General works
324.64 Botanical chemistry. Composition
324.65 Water requirements. Irrigation
324.7 Breeding
324.73 Varieties
324.75 Seeds

	Vegetables -- Continued
324.85	Care and preparation of vegetables for market
	Including cold storage
	Cf. TX612.V4 Home storage of vegetables or types of vegetables
	Culture of individual vegetables or types of vegetables
325	Asparagus
327	Beans. Common bean
	Cf. SB203+ Feed and forage legumes
329	Beets
	Cf. SB207.M35 Mangel-wurzel
	Cf. SB218+ Sugar beets
331	Cabbage
	Including cabbage and cauliflower
333	Cauliflower
	Including broccoli and calabrese
335	Celery
	Including celeriac
337	Cucumber
339	Greens. Leafy vegetables
	Cf. SB351.S25 Salad greens
	Melons see SB379.M44
341	Onions
343	Peas
	Including pea shoots
	Cf. SB203+ Feed and forage legumes
	Potatoes see SB211.P8
345	Rhubarb
347	Squash. Pumpkin
349	Tomatoes
351.A-Z	Other, A-Z
351.A54	Amaranths
351.A95	Azuki
351.B35	Bambara groundnut
	Belgian endive see SB351.C5
	Bok choy see SB351.C53
	Broccoli see SB333
351.B7	Brussels sprouts
(351.C27)	Calabrese
	see SB333
351.C3	Carrots
351.C4	Chayote
351.C45	Chickpea
351.C5	Chicory. Belgian endive
351.C53	Chinese cabbage. Bok choy
351.C54	Chinese vegetables. Japanese vegetables
351.C58	Chive

Vegetables
Culture of individual vegetables or types of vegetables
Other, A-Z -- Continued

351.C67 Cole crops
Collards see SB351.K3
351.C69 Coriander
351.C7 Corn, Sweet
351.C75 Cowpea
Cf. SB205.C8 Forage plant
351.C8 Cucurbitaceae
Cf. SB337 Cucumber
Cf. SB347 Squash, pumpkins, etc.
Cf. SB379.M44 Melons
Cf. SB379.N28 Nara
351.D54 Dill
351.E5 Eggplant
351.E58 Endive. Escarole
Endive, Belgian see SB351.C5
Escarole see SB351.E58
351.F3 Fava bean
Cf. SB205.F3 Forage plant
351.F5 Fiddleheads
351.F74 French tarragon
351.G3 Garlic
351.H5 Herbs
Cf. GT5164 Manners and customs
Japanese vegetables see SB351.C54
351.K3 Kale. Collards
351.L36 Lamiaceae
351.L38 Lathyrus
351.L5 Leeks
351.L53 Lemon herbs
351.L55 Lentils
351.L6 Lettuce
351.L92 Lycium chinense
351.O5 Okra
351.O7 Orach
351.O74 Oregano
351.P25 Parsley
351.P3 Peanut
351.P4 Peppers
Class here general works on peppers and peppers grown for use as vegetables
For works on peppers grown for use as condiments and spices see SB307.P4
Pumpkin see SB347
351.R28 Radicchio

Vegetables
Culture of individual vegetables or types of vegetables
Other, A-Z -- Continued

351.R3 Radishes
351.R65 Root crops
Cf. SB209+ Field crops
351.R67 Rosemary
351.S25 Salad greens
351.S4 Sea kale
351.S7 Spinach
351.S76 Stem vegetables
351.S94 Swiss chard
Tarragon, French see SB351.F74
351.T48 Thymes
351.U3 Udo
351.U54 Umbelliferae (General)
For works on particular umbellifer plants, see the plant, e. g. see SB351.C3
351.V47 Vernonia
351.W3 Water-cress
Witloof see SB351.C5
Zucchini see SB347

Vegetable culture under glass, etc.
Cf. SB324.5 General indoor vegetable gardening
Cf. SB358 Fruit culture under glass
Cf. SB414.6+ General greenhouse culture

351.7 Periodicals. Societies. Serials
351.73 Congresses
Study and teaching. Research
351.8 General works
351.83.A-Z By region or country, A-Z
352 General works
History and conditions
352.3 General works
By region or country
United States
352.33 General works
352.34.A-Z By region or state, A-Z
352.35.A-Z Other regions or countries, A-Z
352.7 Equipment and supplies
Cf. SB414.6+ Greenhouses

Mushrooms. Edible fungi
Cf. QK617 Botany

352.85 Periodicals. Societies. Serials
352.87 Congresses
353 General works
353.3.A-Z By region or country, A-Z

Vegetables
Vegetable culture under glass, etc.
Mushrooms. Edible fungi -- Continued

353.5.A-Z By mushroom or fungus, A-Z
353.5.A35 Agaricus campestris
353.5.A95 Auricularia auricula-judae
Cultivated mushroom see SB352.85+
Ganoderma see SB295.G35
353.5.H47 Hericium erinaceus
(353.5.L46) Lentinus edodes
see SB353.5.S55
353.5.P55 Pleurotus
353.5.P67 Poria cocos
Psilocybe see SB295.P84
353.5.S55 Shiitake
353.5.T69 Tremella fuciforms
353.5.T74 Tricholoma matsutake
353.5.T78 Truffles
353.5.V64 Volvariella volvacea
353.5.W54 White matsutake

Fruit and fruit culture
Cf. HD9240+ Fruit trade

354 Periodicals. Societies. Serials
354.2 Collected works (nonserial)
354.3 Congresses
354.4 Dictionaries. Encyclopedias
Study and teaching. Research
354.47 General works
354.48.A-Z By region or country, A-Z
Museums
354.485 General works
354.486.A-Z By region or country, A-Z
Under each country:

.x	*General works*
.x2A-.x2Z	*Individual museums. By name, A-Z*

History and conditions
354.5 General works
354.6.A-Z By region or country, A-Z
354.8 General works
Cultural practices for special areas
355 General works
United States
General works see SB355
355.5.A-Z By region or state, A-Z
356 Great Britain
357 Other regions or countries
Not by region or country, A-Z

Fruit and fruit culture
Cultural practices for special areas
Other regions or countries, A-Z -- Continued
Tropics see SB359
357.2 Juvenile works
357.24 Organiculture
357.26 Container gardening
357.27 Indoor gardening
Cf. SB358 Greenhouse culture
Physiology
357.28 General works
357.283 Development
Including regulation
357.285 Water requirements. Irrigation
Breeding see SB359.35
357.33 Varieties
Cf. SB361 Illustration and description of choice fruits
357.5 Dwarf fruit trees
Fruit trade see HD9240+
358 Fruit culture under glass, etc.
Cf. SB357.27 General indoor fruit culture
359 Fruits and fruit culture for special physiographic areas
Including tropical fruit (General)
Plant propagation
359.3 General works
359.35 Breeding
359.4 Seeds
359.45 Vegetative propagation
Including grafting, budding, layering, rootstocks, etc.
(359.48) Plant and seed catalogs
see SB362.3
359.5 Pruning. Training
Care and preparation for market. Handling
Cf. HD9240+ Fruit industry
Cf. TP440+ Fruit processing and products
360 General works
360.3 Harvesting
360.4 Transportation
Cf. HE595.F7 Water
Cf. HE2321.F7 Rail
Cf. HE9788.4.F7 Air
360.5 Storage. Ripening
360.6 Grading. Standards. Quality
361 Illustration and description of choice fruits for culture
362 Fruit growers' directories

	Fruit and fruit culture -- Continued
362.3	Fruit seed and plant catalogs
	For works limited to specific fruit, see the fruit, e.g. SB371 Peach
	Culture of individual fruits or types of fruit
	Apple
363	General works
363.2.A-Z	By region or country, A-Z
	Varieties
363.3.A1	General
363.3.A2-Z	Special, A-Z
363.3.C6	Cox's Orange Pippin
363.3.J65	Jonagold
363.35	Harvesting
363.4	Storage. Ripening
363.5	Grading
363.6	Marketing. Packing, etc.
	Cf. HD9259.A5+ Economic history
364	Dates
365	Fig
367	Olive
	Citrus. Citrus fruits
369	General works
	By region or country
	United States
369.2.A1	General works
369.2.A2-Z	By region or state, A-Z
369.5.A-Z	Other regions or countries, A-Z
370.A-Z	Special, A-Z
370.C5	Citrus natsudaidai
370.C55	Citrus sudachi
370.G7	Grapefruit
370.L4	Lemon
370.L5	Lime
370.M34	Mandarin orange. Tangerine
370.O7	Oranges
370.P86	Pummelo
	Tangerine see SB370.M34
371	Peach
373	Pear
375	Pineapple
377	Plum
	Including prune
378	Stone fruit (General)
	Cf. SB401.A65 Almond
379.A-Z	Other fruits not grape nor berry, A-Z
379.A7	Apricot

Fruit and fruit culture
Culture of individual fruits or types of fruit
Other fruits not grape nor berry, A-Z -- Continued

379.A9 Avocado
379.B2 Banana
379.B8 Breadfruit
379.C34 Camu camu
379.C36 Cape gooseberry
379.C37 Carambola
379.C5 Cherry
(379.C57) Chinese hawthorn
see SB386.C73
379.D8 Durian
379.G8 Guava
Indian jujube see SB379.J8
379.J8 Jujube (Plant). Indian jujube
379.K58 Kiwifruit
379.L8 Litchi
379.L84 Longan
379.L85 Loquat
379.L87 Lucuma
379.M2 Mango
379.M25 Margosteen
379.M44 Melons. Muskmelon
379.M65 Mombin
Muskmelon see SB379.M44
379.N28 Nara
379.N3 Naranjilla
379.P2 Papaya
Cf. SB317.P35 General culture
379.P28 Passiflora mollissima
379.P3 Passion fruit
379.P4 Persimmon
379.P53 Pitahayas
379.P6 Pomegranate
379.P8 Prickly pears
Including Opuntia ficus-indica
Prune see SB377
379.Q7 Quince
379.R34 Rambutan
379.R57 Rose hips
379.R6 Roselle
379.S24 Salak
379.S35 Sclerocarya birrea
379.S74 Stenocereus
379.W38 Watermelon
379.W55 Wild loquat

Fruit and fruit culture -- Continued
Berries and small fruits

381 General works
383 Cranberry
385 Strawberry
386.A-Z Other, A-Z
386.B3 Barberry
386.B6 Blackberries
386.B7 Blueberries
386.B75 Bog blueberry
386.B8 Boysenberry
Cloudberry see SB386.R83
386.C73 Crataegus pinnatifida
386.C9 Currants
Including individual species
386.D48 Dewberry
386.G6 Gooseberries
386.H83 Huckleberries
386.L6 Loganberry
386.M39 Mayhaws
386.R24 Rabbiteye blueberry
386.R3 Raspberries
Including red raspberry
386.R83 Rubus chamaemorus. Cloudberry
386.S36 Saskatoon serviceberry
386.S4 Sea buckthorn
386.S6 Sorbus melanocarpa
386.V3 Vaccinium vitis-idaea

Grapes and grape culture. Viticulture
Including table grapes
Cf. HD9370+ Industry
Cf. TP544+ Wine and wine making

387 Periodicals. Societies. Serials
387.2 Congresses
387.4 Directories
387.5 Dictionaries. Encyclopedias
Study and teaching. Research
387.6 General works
387.63.A-Z By region or country, A-Z
387.65 Field experiments
387.67 Exhibitions
Biography
387.68 Collective
387.682.A-Z Individual, A-Z
History and conditions
387.7 General works
By region or country

Fruit and fruit culture
Grapes and grape culture. Viticulture
History and conditions
By region or country -- Continued
United States

387.75 General works
387.76.A-Z By region or state, A-Z
387.8.A-Z Other regions or countries, A-Z

General works
388.A1 Documents
388.A2-Z Other works

Cultural practices for special areas
389 United States and general American
390.A-Z Other American. By region or country, A-Z
European
391 General works
393 French, Belgian, Swiss
395 German, Austrian, Hungarian
396 Italian
396.2 Portuguese and Spanish
396.5 Russian
Including Asiatic Russian
397.A-Z Other European regions or countries, A-Z
398.A-Z Other regions or countries, A-Z

Physiology
398.2 General works
398.25 Water requirements. Irrigation
398.28 Varieties
398.3 Plant propagation
398.4 Organic viticulture
398.5 Care and preparation of grapes for market
399 Raisins
Including Levantine or Currant grapes, "Zante currants"

Nuts
401.A1-.A3 Periodicals. Societies. Serials
401.A4 General works
401.A45A-.A45Z By region or country, A-Z
401.A5-Z By plant, A-Z
401.A65 Almond
401.B7 Brazil nut
401.C3 Cashew
401.C4 Chestnut
401.C6 Coconut
401.F5 Filbert
Hazel see SB401.F5
401.M32 Macadamia nut
401.M326 Manketti

	Fruit and fruit culture
	Nuts
	By plant, A-Z -- Continued
	Peanut see SB351.P3
401.P4	Pecan
401.P46	Pinyon pines
401.P5	Pistachio
401.W3	Walnut
402	Other special
	Flowers and flower culture. Ornamental plants
403	Periodicals. Societies. Serials
403.Z5	History, etc., of garden clubs, etc.
403.16	Congresses
403.17	Collected works (nonserial)
403.2	Dictionaries and encyclopedias
403.45	Vocational guidance
403.5	Study and teaching. Research
	Florists' directories see SB442.87+
	History
404.5	General works
404.6.A-Z	By region or country, A-Z
	Biography
404.8.A1	Collective
404.8.A2-Z	Individual, A-Z
404.9	General works
	General cultural practices
405	General works
	By region or country
	United States
	General works see SB405
405.5.A-Z	By region or state, A-Z
406.A-Z	Other regions or countries, A-Z
406.5	Juvenile works
406.53	Organiculture
	Physiology
406.55	General works
406.57	Water requirements. Irrigation
	Ornamental plant and seed industry and marketing
	For works limited to a specific ornamental plant or flower, see the plant, e.g. Rose industry SB411.8+ Chrysanthemums SB413.C55
	Cf. SB419.3 House plant industry
	Cf. SB423.8+ Bedding plant industry
	Cf. SB442.8+ Cut flower industry and florists
406.6	General works
	By region or country
	United States

Flowers and flower culture. Ornamental plants
Ornamental plant and seed industry and marketing
By region or country
United States -- Continued
406.64 General works
406.65.A-Z By region or state, A-Z
406.66.A-Z Other regions or countries, A-Z
Ornamental plant and seed catalogs
Cf. SB445 Florists' catalogs
406.68 General works
406.685.A-Z By region or country, A-Z
Plant propagation
406.7 General works
406.8 Breeding
406.83 Sowing, planting, transplanting
406.87 Flowering
Identification
406.9 General works
406.93.A-Z By region or country, A-Z
Illustrations and descriptions of choice plants
407 General works
By region or country
United States see SB407
407.3 Other regions or countries, A-Z
Lists of ornamental plants
408 General works
By region or country
United States see SB408
408.3.A-Z Other regions or countries, A-Z
Culture of individual plants
Orchids
409.A1 Periodicals. Societies. Serials
409.A2 Congresses
409.A3-Z General works
409.3 Pictorial works
Exhibitions
409.35 General works
409.36.A-Z International. By place, A-Z
409.37.A-Z By region or country, A-Z
Biography
409.4 Collective
409.43.A-Z Individual, A-Z
409.48 History (General)
409.5.A-Z By region or country, A-Z
409.55 Economic aspects (General)
Plant propagation
Including in vitro propagation

Flowers and flower culture. Ornamental plants
Culture of individual plants
Orchids
Plant propagation -- Continued
409.58 General works
409.6 Breeding
409.7 Varieties
409.75 Miniature orchids
409.8.A-Z By group, type, or genus, A-Z
409.8.A53 Angraecum
409.8.B84 Bulbophyllum
409.8.C36 Catasetums
409.8.C38 Cattleyas
409.8.C95 Cymbidium
409.8.D45 Dendrobium
409.8.M38 Masdevallia
409.8.O53 Oncidium
409.8.P36 Paphiopedilum
409.8.P47 Phalaenopsis
409.8.S65 Slipper orchids
409.8.V36 Vanda
Roses
Cf. SB449.3.R67 Flower arrangement
410.9 Periodicals. Societies. Serials
410.93 Congresses
410.95 Dictionaries. Encyclopedias
411 General works
411.3 Pictorial works
Exhibitions. Showing
411.34 General works
411.35 Judging
411.36.A-Z International. By place, A-Z
411.37.A-Z By region or country, A-Z
Biography
411.4 Collective
411.42.A-Z Individual, A-Z
411.45 History (General)
411.5.A-Z By region or country, A-Z
Culture
General works see SB411
By region or country
United States see SB411
Other regions or countries see SB411.5.A+
411.54 Breeding
Varieties
411.6 General works
411.65.A-Z By group, type, or variety, A-Z

Flowers and flower culture. Ornamental plants
Culture of individual plants
Roses
Varieties
By group, type, or variety, A-Z -- Continued

411.65.C55 Climbing roses
411.65.D35 Damask roses
411.65.E53 English roses
411.65.G34 Gallica roses
411.65.H93 Hybrid tea roses
411.65.M55 Miniature roses
411.65.O55 Old roses
411.65.R84 Rugosa roses
411.65.S45 Shrub roses
411.7 Harvesting and postharvest technology
Rose industry
411.8 General works
411.83.A-Z By region or country, A-Z
413.A-Z Other plants, A-Z
413.A23 Acacia
(413.A25) Aconitum
see SB413.M64
413.A4 African violets
413.A43 Agapanthus
413.A45 Allium
413.A46 Aloe
413.A5 Amaryllis
413.A54 American elm
413.A58 Androsace
413.A6 Anemones
413.A64 Anthuriums
413.A647 Asparagus ferns
Including individual species
413.A7 Aster
413.A74 Astilbe
413.A8 Auricula
413.A9 Azaleas
413.B2 Bamboo
413.B4 Begonia
Bellflowers see SB413.C2
413.B57 Birthflowers
Bottle brushes see SB413.C175
413.B65 Bougainvillea
413.B66 Boxwood
413.B7 Bromeliads
413.B76 Brugmansia
413.B86 Butterfly bushes

	Flowers and flower culture. Ornamental plants
	Culture of individual plants
	Other plants, A-Z -- Continued
(413.C12)	Cactus see SB438+
413.C14	Calendula
413.C16	California poppy
413.C17	Calla lilies
413.C175	Callistemon
413.C18	Camellias
413.C2	Campanula
413.C25	Canna
413.C3	Carnation
413.C4	Ceanothus
413.C45	Chamaedorea
413.C5	Cherries, Flowering
413.C53	Christmas rose
	Christmas trees see SB428.3+
413.C55	Chrysanthemum
413.C6	Clematis
413.C63	Coleus
413.C634	Columbines
	Coniferae see SB428+
413.C64	Cornus
413.C644	Crabapples, Flowering
(413.C645)	Cranesbills see SB413.G35
413.C65	Crocuses
413.C86	Cyatheaceae
413.C88	Cycads
413.C9	Cyclamen
413.D112	Dactylanthus taylorii
413.D12	Daffodil. Jonquil. Narcissus
413.D13	Dahlia
413.D2	Daisies
413.D25	Daphnes
413.D3	Day lillies
413.D4	Delphinium
413.D68	Douglas fir
413.D72	Dracaena
	East Indian lotus see SB413.L82
413.E25	Easter lily
413.E27	Eastern hemlock
413.E35	Echinacea
413.E5	Elm
413.E68	Eremophila
413.E7	Ericaceae

Flowers and flower culture. Ornamental plants
Culture of individual plants
Other plants, A-Z -- Continued

413.E72 Ericas
413.E92 Eucalyptus
413.E95 Euphorbia
Ferns see SB429
Flowering cherries see SB413.C5
Flowering crabapples see SB413.C644
Flowering plums see SB413.P57
413.F6 Forsythia
413.F73 Freesias
413.F74 Fritillaria
413.F8 Fuchsia
413.G27 Gardenia
413.G3 Gentian
413.G35 Geraniums. Pelargoniums
Including hardy geraniums (cranesbills)
413.G36 Gerbera
413.G37 Gesneriaceae
413.G5 Gladiolus
413.G55 Gloxinias
413.G6 Gourds
Grasses, Ornamental (General) see SB431.7
413.G73 Grevillea
413.H38 Haworthia
(413.H4) Heath
see SB413.E72; SB413.H42
413.H42 Heather
413.H43 Hebe
413.H44 Heliconia
413.H443 Hellebores
Hemerocallis see SB413.D3
413.H52 Heuchera
413.H6 Hibiscus
413.H7 Hollies
413.H72 Honeysuckle
413.H73 Hosta
413.H9 Hyacinth
413.H93 Hydrangeas
413.I8 Iris
413.I84 Ivy
413.J32 Japanese black pine
413.J34 Japanese maple
Jonquil see SB413.D12
413.K3 Kalmia. Mountain laurel
413.L34 Lagerstroemia

Flowers and flower culture. Ornamental plants
Culture of individual plants
Other plants, A-Z -- Continued

	Larkspur see SB413.D4
413.L48	Lewisia
413.L65	Lilacs
413.L69	Lilies of the valley
413.L7	Lily
413.L73	Linden
413.L82	Lotus, East Indian
413.L86	Lupines Cf. SB177.L85 Food crops Cf. SB205.L9 Forage plants Cf. SB317.L87 Economic plants
413.L88	Lupinus texensis
	Lycopodium (General) see SB429
413.M34	Magnolias
413.M35	Maidenhair ferns
413.M36	Mammillaria (Cactus)
413.M365	Maple
413.M37	Marigolds
413.M42	Meconopsis
413.M64	Monkshoods
413.M65	Moonflower
413.M67	Morning glories
	Mosses (General) see SB433.55
	Mountain laurel see SB413.K3
413.M95	Myrica
	Narcissus see SB413.D12
413.N48	New Guinea impatiens
413.O34	Oak
413.O43	Oleander
413.P17	Palms
413.P2	Pansy
413.P3	Passiflora
	Pelargoniums see SB413.G35
413.P37	Penstemons
413.P4	Peonies Including tree peony
413.P43	Petunias
413.P47	Philodendrons
413.P5	Phlox
413.P54	Pine
413.P55	Pinks
413.P556	Platycerium
413.P557	Plectranthus
413.P56	Plumeria

Flowers and flower culture. Ornamental plants
Culture of individual plants
Other plants, A-Z -- Continued

413.P57 Plums, Flowering
413.P63 Poinsettias
Polyanthus see SB413.P7
413.P66 Poplar
413.P7 Primrose
413.P75 Proteaceae
413.R35 Ranunculaceae
413.R43 Red fescue
413.R44 Rhapis excelsa
413.R47 Rhododendrons
Including vireyas
Cf. SB413.A9 Azaleas
413.R7 Rock-rose
413.R8 Rohdea
413.R84 Rosaceae
413.S22 Salvia
413.S25 Sansevieria trifasciata
413.S26 Sarcocaulons
413.S28 Saxifraga
413.S43 Sedum
413.S63 Snapdragons
413.S64 Spireas
413.S86 Sulcorebutia
413.S88 Sunflowers
Cf. SB207.S96 Forage plants
Cf. SB299.S9 Oilseed plants
413.S9 Sweet pea
413.T5 Thuja
413.T52 Tillandsia
Tree peony see SB413.P4
413.T74 Trilliums
Tsuga canadensis see SB413.E27
413.T9 Tulip
413.V8 Violet
Vireyas see SB413.R47
413.W37 Waratahs
Water lilies (General) see SB423+
413.W44 Weigela
413.W54 Willows
413.W57 Wisteria
413.X36 Xanthorrhoea
413.Z54 Zinnia
414 Forcing

SB

Flowers and flower culture. Ornamental plants -- Continued
Greenhouses and greenhouse culture
Class here works on greenhouse culture of flowers and general greenhouse culture
Including conservatory plants and gardening
Cf. SB351.7+ Vegetables under glass
Cf. SB358 Fruit culture under glass
414.6 Periodicals. Societies. Serials
414.64 Congresses
414.7 Vocational guidance
Study and teaching. Research
414.73 General works
414.75.A-Z By region or country, A-Z
415 General works
History and conditions
415.4 General works
By region or country
United States
415.5 General works
415.55.A-Z By region or state, A-Z
415.6.A-Z Other regions or countries, A-Z
Illustrations and descriptions of notable greenhouses
415.8 General works
By region or country
United States
415.82 General works
415.83.A-Z By region or state, A-Z
Subarrange each state by Table S3a
415.84.A-Z Other regions or countries, A-Z
Subarrange each country by Table S3a
416 Greenhouse construction
Including design, environmental engineering, etc.
416.3 Window greenhouses and window greenhouse gardening
417 Glass gardens. Wardian cases
Cf. QH68 Vivariums. Terrariums
Container gardening
Cf. SB324.4 Vegetable gardening
Cf. SB433.5 Miniature gardens
418 General works
418.4 Equipment and supplies. Potting places
Including handicraft

Flowers and flower culture. Ornamental plants -- Continued
Indoor gardening and houseplants
Including window gardening
Cf. SB126 Artificial light gardening
Cf. SB324.5 Indoor vegetable gardening
Cf. SB416.3 Window greenhouse gardening
Cf. SB433.5 General miniature gardening
Cf. SB435.3 Indoor trees
419 General works
419.2 Juvenile works
419.23 Hydroponics
419.25 Interior landscaping
Including house plants in interior decoration
419.3 House plant industry and marketing
For marketing of particular houseplants see SB409+
419.5 Roof gardening. Balcony gardening
Including green roofs
Classes of plants
For works limited to specific genera, species, etc. see SB413.A+
421 Alpine plants. Rock-garden plants
Cf. SB459 Alpine and rock gardens
422 Annuals
Aquatic plants
Including waterlilies, water gardens, garden pools
Cf. SB317.A64 Economic plants
Cf. SF457.7 Aquarium plants
423 General works
423.3 Damp garden plants. Damp gardens
Arid regions plants see SB427.5
423.4 Autumn garden plants. Autumn gardening
Bedding plants. Beds
423.7 General works
423.75.A-Z By region or country, A-Z
Bedding plant industry and marketing
423.8 General works
423.83.A-Z By region or country, A-Z
Bonsai see SB433.5
424 Borders
Bulbs and tuberous plants
425 General works
Bulb industry
425.3 General works
425.34.A-Z By region or country, A-Z
Carnivorous plants see SB432.7
426 Chalk and limestone garden plants and gardens
427 Climbing plants. Vines

Flowers and flower culture. Ornamental plants
Classes of plants -- Continued
Damp garden plants see SB423.3
427.5 Desert plants. Desert gardening
Including arid regions plants
Cf. SB317.A69 Economic plants
427.8 Epiphytes. Air plants
Evergreen plants
Including conifers
428 General works
Christmas trees
428.3 General works
428.34.A-Z By region or country, A-Z
428.5 Everlasting flowers
429 Ferns and lycopodiums
431 Foliage plants
431.7 Grasses, Ornamental
Cf. SB433+ Lawns
432 Ground cover plants
432.5 Hanging plants
432.7 Insectivorous plants. Carnivorous plants
Lawns and turf
Cf. GV910 Bowling greens
Cf. GV975+ Golf greens
Cf. SB197+ Grasses as forage crops
Cf. SB431.7 Ornamental grasses
433 General works
By region or country
United States
433.15 General works
433.16.A-Z By region or state, A-Z
433.17.A-Z Other regions or countries, A-Z
433.2 Equipment and supplies
Including lawn mowers, leaf blowers, etc.
433.27 Lawn care industry
Turfgrasses industry
433.3 General works
433.34.A-Z By region or country, A-Z
Limestone garden plants see SB426
433.4 Low-allergen plants. Low-allergen gardens
433.5 Miniature plants. Miniature gardens
Including bonsai, hòn non bộ,penjing, and saikei
Cf. SB417 Glass gardens
Cf. SB419+ Miniature indoor gardens
433.55 Mosses. Moss gardening
433.6 Night-flowering plants. Night gardens
433.8 Peat garden plants

Flowers and flower culture. Ornamental plants
Classes of plants -- Continued
434 Perennials
434.3 Prairie plants. Prairie gardening
434.5 Rain forest plants. Rain forest gardens
434.7 Shade-tolerant plants. Gardening in the shade
Shrubs and ornamental trees. Arboriculture
Cf. SB428.3+ Christmas trees
Cf. SB433.5 Bonsai
435 General works
435.2 Equipment and supplies
435.3 Indoor trees (General)
By region or country
United States
435.5 General works
435.52.A-Z By region or state, A-Z
Subarrange each state by Table S3a
435.6.A-Z Other regions or countries, A-Z
Subarrange each country by Table S3a
435.65 Plant introduction
For local see SB435.5+
Plant propagation
435.7 General works
435.73 Breeding
435.76 Pruning
435.8 Tree repairing. Tree surgery
Cf. SD406 Forestry
435.85 Tree climbing
Cf. SD387.T74 Forestry
436 Street trees. Trees in cities (General). Urban forestry
For local see SB435.5+
437 Hedges, screens, and windbreaks
Cf. SD409.5 Forestry
(437.5) By individual type of shrub or tree
see SB413.A+
Valuation. Appraisal
437.6 General works
437.65.A-Z By region or country, A-Z
437.7 Tree hazard evaluation
Succulent plants. Cactus
438 General works
Industry and marketing
438.3 General works
438.34.A-Z By region or country, A-Z
Trees see SB435+
438.8 Variegated plants
Vines see SB427

Flowers and flower culture. Ornamental plants
Classes of plants -- Continued
Wild plants. Wild flowers. Native plants
Including landscaping with native plants, natural landscaping, and natural gardens
439 General works
By region or country
United States
General works see SB439
439.24.A-Z By region or state, A-Z
439.26.A-Z Other regions or countries, A-Z
439.28 Seeds
Including seedheads
Wild flower industry. Native plant industry
Including wild plant trade
439.3 General works
439.35.A-Z By region or country, A-Z
439.5 Winter garden plants. Winter gardening
439.6 Woodland garden plants. Woodland gardening
439.8 Xerophytes. Drought-enduring plants. Dry gardens
Cf. SB427.5 Desert plants
Cf. SB438+ Succulent plants
Flower shows. Exhibitions
For exhibits of special flowers, see the flower, e.g. SB411 Roses
Cf. SB449.15 Flower arrangement shows
441 General works
441.4 Judging
441.5 Floral parades
For local see SB441.7+
441.6.A-Z International. By place, A-Z
Subarrange by year
National, state, and local
By region or country
United States
441.7 General works
441.73.A-Z By region or state, A-Z
Subarrange each state by Table S3a
441.75.A-Z Other regions or countries, A-Z
Subarrange each country by Table S3a
442.5 Care and preparation of cut flowers, foliage, and potted ornamental plants for market
Including cold storage
For particular flowers or ornamental plants see SB409+
Cf. SB419.3 House plant industry

Flowers and flower culture. Ornamental plants -- Continued
Marketing. Cut flower industry. Florists
For marketing of particular flowers or ornamental plants see SB409+
Cf. SB449+ Floristry

442.8 Periodicals. Societies. Serials
442.85 Congresses
Directories
442.87 General works
442.873.A-Z By region or country, A-Z
443 General works
By region or country
United States
443.3 General works
443.35.A-Z By region or state, A-Z
443.4.A-Z Other regions or countries, A-Z
445 Florists' designs, catalogs, etc.
Cf. SB449+ Flower arrangement and decoration
445.5 Dried flower industry
Horticultural service industry
Cf. SB317.5+ Horticulture
446 Periodicals. Serials
446.2 Congresses
446.25 Directories
446.38 Vocational guidance
446.4 Study and teaching. Research
446.44 Problems, exercises, examinations
446.5 General works
By region or country
United States
446.55 General works
446.57.A-Z By region or state, A-Z
446.6.A-Z Other regions or countries, A-Z
447 Preservation and reproduction of flowers, fruits, etc.
447.5 Bonkei. Tray landscapes
Flower arrangement. Floral decorations. Floristry
Including cut flowers used in flower arrangements
Cf. SB442.8+ Florists
449 General works
449.12 History
Biography
449.13 Collective
449.132.A-Z Individual, A-Z
449.15 Flower arrangement shows
Cf. GR780+ Language of flowers
Cf. SB441+ Flower shows
449.2 Equipment (Containers, accessories, etc.)

Flowers and flower culture. Ornamental plants
Flower arrangement. Floral decorations -- Continued

449.3.A-Z Special materials, A-Z
449.3.A7 Artificial materials
449.3.C3 Candles
449.3.D7 Dried materials
Including preserved flower pictures
Cf. SB447 Flower preservation
449.3.D8 Driftwood
449.3.F6 Foliage
449.3.F7 Fruits and vegetables
449.3.G46 Gesneriaceae
449.3.H47 Herbs
449.3.P65 Potted plants
449.3.P7 Pressed flowers
Including pressed flower pictures
449.3.R67 Roses
449.3.S44 Silk flowers
Cf. TT890.7 Handicraft
449.3.T76 Tropical flowers
449.3.W5 Wild flowers
Special applications and types
449.48 General works
449.5.A-Z By application or type, A-Z
449.5.B65 Bouquets. Posies
Cf. SB449.5.B7 Bridal bouquets
449.5.B7 Bridal bouquets
449.5.C3 Christmas decorations
449.5.C4 Church decoration
449.5.C6 Corsages
449.5.F84 Funeral decorations
449.5.J4 Jewish festivals
449.5.L4 Leis
449.5.M56 Miniature flower arrangement
449.5.P3 Parties
Posies see SB449.5.B65
449.5.T86 Tussie mussies
449.5.W4 Weddings
449.5.W74 Wreaths
Cf. TT899.75 Handicraft
Japanese flower arrangement
450 General works
450.2 History
Teachers and masters
450.28 Collective
450.3.A-Z Individual, A-Z
450.5.A-Z Special schools, A-Z

Flowers and flower culture. Ornamental plants
Flower arrangement. Floral decorations
Japanese flower arrangement
Special schools, A-Z -- Continued

450.5.E67 Enshū school
450.5.I4 Ikenobō school
450.5.K67 Ko school
450.5.K68 Koryū Sokenryū
450.5.K69 Kōshū school
450.5.M56 Mishō school
450.5.O4 Ohara school
450.5.O68 Omuro school
450.5.R54 Rikyū Koryū
450.5.R89 Ryūsei school
450.5.S4 Senkei school
450.5.S58 Sōbi school
450.5.S6 Sōgetsu school
450.6 Utensils
450.65 Special applications
450.67 American flower arrangement
450.7 Chinese flower arrangement
450.73 French flower arrangement
450.78 Indonesian flower arrangement
450.8 Korean flower arrangement
450.87 Thai flower arrangement

Gardens and gardening
Cf. RM735.7.G37 Therapeutic use
Cf. SB317.5+ Horticulture
Cf. SB317.68 Master gardeners
Cf. SB320+ Vegetable gardening
Cf. SB354+ Fruit culture
Cf. SB403+ Flower gardening

450.9 Periodicals. Societies. Serials
450.92 Collected works (nonserial)
450.93 Congresses
Directories
450.94 General works
450.943.A-Z By region or country, A-Z
Guidebooks to gardens see SB465+
450.95 Dictionaries. Encyclopedias
450.96 Handbooks, charts, etc.
450.965 Almanacs. Calendars. Yearbooks
Exhibitions see SB317.7+
450.97 General works
Early works through 1800 see SB317.8
Gardening literature see SB318.3+
450.98 Pictorial works

SB

Gardens and gardening -- Continued
History and conditions
Class here works on the history of practical gardening and gardens
For works on the history of notable gardens and garden design see SB465+
451 General works
By region or country
United States
451.3 General works
451.34.A-Z By region or state, A-Z
451.36.A-Z Other regions or countries, A-Z
Culture methods
453 General works
By region or country
United States
General works see SB453
453.2.A-Z By region or state, A-Z
453.3.A-Z Other regions or countries, A-Z
Organic gardening
Cf. S605.5 Organic farming
Cf. S654+ Organic fertilizers
Cf. SB324.3 Vegetable gardening
Cf. SB974+ Organic plant protection
453.5 General works
453.6 Companion planting
454 General special
454.3.A-Z Special topics, A-Z
454.3.A76 Arts and crafts gardens
454.3.B52 Bible plants
Botany for gardeners see QK50
Butterfly gardening see QL544.6
454.3.C62 Collectibles
454.3.C64 Color in gardening
454.3.C67 Cottage gardening and gardens
454.3.E35 Edible forest gardens
454.3.E53 Environmental aspects
454.3.E95 Experiments
454.3.E95 Experiments
454.3.F45 Feng shui gardens
454.3.F7 Fragrant gardens
Cf. SB301+ Aromatic plants
Gardening to attract wildlife see QL59
454.3.G84 Guerrilla gardens
Cf. SB457.3 Community gardens. Allotment gardens
454.3.M43 Mediterranean climate
454.3.P45 Philosophy

Gardens and gardening
Special topics, A-Z -- Continued
454.3.P57 Planting time
Plants, Small see SB454.3.S53
454.3.R37 Rare garden plants
454.3.R43 Recycling
454.3.S25 Sanctuary gardens
454.3.S52 Sheltered gardens
454.3.S53 Small plants (General)
Including natural dwarf and miniature plants
Cf. SB419+ Miniature indoor gardens
Cf. SB433.5 Miniature ornamental plants and gardens
454.3.S63 Social aspects. Gardens and society
454.3.T43 Tea gardens
454.3.W43 Weather
454.6 Garden centers (Retail trade)
454.8 Equipment and supplies. Garden tools
For equipment used in commercial vegetable growing see S715.V4
Cf. HD9486.5+ Gardening equipment industry
455 Light literature. Popular works
455.3 Addresses, essays, lectures
Gardens for special classes and groups of persons
Children's gardens
Including juvenile works on gardening
Cf. SB55+ School gardens and farms
457 General works
457.2 Plants for play environments
457.3 Community gardens. Allotment gardens
Cf. SB454.3.G84 Guerrilla gardens
457.35 Monastery gardens
457.4.A-Z Other, A-Z
457.4.A34 Aged. Older people
Cf. SB475.9.A35 Landscape architecture
457.4.H36 Handicapped. People with disabilities
457.4.H64 Homeless persons
Older people see SB457.4.A34
People with disabilities see SB457.4.H36
457.4.T44 Teenagers
Special styles and types of gardens
For works limited to individual plants see SB409+
For works limited to special classes of plants see SB421+
457.5 General works
457.52 Vernacular gardens
Cultural and ethnic garden styles and types
Cf. SB466.A+ Gardens in particular places

Gardens and gardening
Special styles and types of gardens
Cultural and ethnic garden styles and types -- Continued

457.527 African American gardens
457.53 American gardens
457.534 Australian gardens
457.536 Baroque gardens
457.54 British gardens
457.547 Byzantine gardens
457.55 Chinese gardens
457.58 Dutch gardens
457.585 Edwardian gardens
457.6 English gardens
457.63 European gardens
457.65 French gardens
457.68 Georgian gardens
457.8 Islamic gardens
457.85 Italian gardens
458 Japanese gardens
458.2 Korean gardens
458.3 Latin gardens
458.35 Medieval gardens
458.4 Mogul gardens
458.46 Oriental gardens
458.5 Persian gardens
Cf. SB457.8 Islamic gardens
458.54 Renaissance gardens
458.55 Roman gardens
458.6 Turkish gardens
458.7 Victorian gardens

Special materials and physiographic areas
Alpine gardens see SB459
Chalk gardens see SB426
Damp gardens see SB423.3
Desert gardening see SB427.5
Dry gardens see SB439.8
458.94 High altitude gardening
458.95 Hillside gardening
Limestone gardens see SB426
Peat gardens see SB433.8
459 Rock gardens. Alpine gardens
Including wall gardens
Cf. SB421 Rock and alpine garden plants
Cf. SB475.5 Stone (Landscape gardening)
459.6 Sandy soil gardening
460 Seaside gardening
Wall gardens see SB459

	Gardens and gardening
	Special styles and types of gardens
	Special materials and physiographic areas -- Continued
	Water gardens see SB423+
	Special techniques
461	Formal gardens
	Cf. SB457.527 Cultural and ethnic styles
	Cf. SB465+ Notable gardens
463	Topiary work
463.5	Vertical gardening
	Including arbors and trellises
	Illustrations, descriptions, and history of notable gardens
	For works on gardens and antiquities, see D-F
	For works on special cultural and ethnic garden styles and types see SB457.527+
465	General works
466.A-Z	By region or country, A-Z
	Under each country (except where otherwise provided):
	.x General works
	.x2A-.x2Z Local, A-Z
	.x3A-.x3Z Special gardens, A-Z
	e.g.
	Germany
466.G3	General works
466.G35A-.G35Z	Local, A-Z
466.G4A-.G4Z	Special gardens, A-Z
	Japan
	Cf. SB458 Japanese gardens (as a type)
466.J3	General works
466.J32A-.J32Z	Local, A-Z
466.J33A-.J33Z	Special gardens, A-Z
	United States
466.U6	General works
466.U65A-.U65Z	Local, A-Z
466.U7A-.U7Z	Special gardens, A-Z
	Garden archaeology
466.7	General works
466.75.A-Z	By region or country, A-Z
467	Conservation and restoration of historic gardens
	For special places see SB466.A+
467.8	Management of large gardens
	Including maintenance
	For special places see SB466.A+
	Landscape gardening. Landscape architecture
469	Periodicals. Societies. Serials
469.2	Collected works (nonserial)
469.23	Congresses

Landscape gardening. Landscape architecture -- Continued
469.25 Dictionaries and encyclopedias
Directories
469.3 General works
By region or country
United States
469.33 General works
469.34.A-Z By region or state, A-Z
469.35.A-Z Other regions or countries, A-Z
Landscape architecture as a profession. Landscape architects
469.37 General works
469.375 Women in landscape architecture. Women landscape architects
469.38 Employment surveys, manpower requirements, distribution and utilization of landscape architects (General)
By region or country
United States
469.384 General works
469.385.A-Z By region or state, A-Z
469.386.A-Z Other regions or countries, A-Z
Communication in landscape gardening and landscape architecture
469.39 General works
469.393 Information services
469.395 Computer network resources
Including the Internet
Study and teaching. Research
469.4 General works
469.43.A-Z By region or country, A-Z
469.5.A-Z Special schools, A-Z
469.6 Problems, exercises, examinations
Exhibitions
469.75 General works
469.77.A-Z International. By place, A-Z
Subarrange by year
469.78.A-Z By region or country, A-Z
Subarrange by author
Biography
469.9 Collective
470.A-Z Individual, A-Z
Including collections of their designs
History and conditions
Cf. SB451+ History of gardens in general
Cf. SB465+ History of notable gardens
470.5 General works
By region or country

Landscape gardening. Landscape architecture
History and conditions
By region or country -- Continued
United States
470.53 General works
470.54.A-Z By region or state, A-Z
470.55.A-Z Other regions or countries, A-Z
470.7 Symbolism of gardens
General works
471 To 1875
472 1876-
Practical works on landscaping. Handbooks, manuals, etc.
For works limited to home grounds and small estates see SB473
472.3 General works
472.32.A-Z By region or country, A-Z
472.4 Addresses, essays, lectures
472.45 Landscape design (General). Garden design (General)
Cf. SB473 Home grounds
472.47 Drawings
Landscaping industry
Including economics and management
Cf. SB446+ Horticultural service industry
472.5 General works
By region or country
United States
472.53 General works
472.535.A-Z By region or state, A-Z
472.54.A-Z Other regions or countries, A-Z
472.55 Landscape contracting
472.56 Specifications
472.565 Estimates and cost
Equipment and supplies (Farm machinery) see S678.7
Equipment and supplies (Garden tools) see SB454.8
472.7 Urban landscape architecture. Urban vegetation management
For local see SB470.53+; SB472.32.A+
Cf. NA9052 Urban beautification
472.8 Historic preservation and restoration
Cf. SB467 Historic gardens
Cemeteries see RA626+
Driveways see TE279.3
Fences, gates see TH4965
Garden structures see TH4961+
Garden toolsheds see TH4962
Garden walks see TH4970
Gazebos see TH4963

Landscape gardening. Landscape architecture
473 Home grounds. Small estates
Industrial sites see TS190.5
473.2 Patio gardening. Courtyard gardening
Cf. NA8375 Patio architecture
Cf. TH4970 Patio construction
Lawns see SB433+
473.4 Lighting
473.5 Ornaments and furniture
Cf. NA8450 Ornamental buildings for parks and gardens
475 Mazes. Labyrinths
Paths see TE280+
Roads see TE177+
475.5 Stone
Cf. SB459 Rock gardens
Trees and shrubs see SB435+
Topiary work see SB463
Water in landscape architecture
Cf. NA9400+ Fountain architecture
Cf. SB423+ Water gardens
Cf. TH4977 Fountain construction
475.8 General works
475.82 Landscape irrigation
475.83 Water conservation. Xeriscaping
475.9.A-Z Other special topics, A-Z
475.9.A35 Aged. Older people
Cf. SB457.4.A34 Gardening
475.9.C55 Climatic factors
475.9.D37 Data processing
475.9.D47 Desert landscape architecture
475.9.E35 Edible landscaping
475.9.E53 Energy conservation
475.9.F57 Firescaping
475.9.F67 Forest landscape design
Cf. SD387.L35 Landscape management in forestry
475.9.H54 Hillside landscape architecture
Native plant landscaping see SB439+
Older people see SB475.9.A35
475.9.S72 Standards
475.9.S95 Surveying
475.9.W48 Wetland landscape design
476 Miscellaneous
e.g. Forestry esthetics
(476.4) Drawings
see SB472.47
Specifications see SB472.56
Estimates and costs see SB472.565

Parks and public reservations
Including works on theory, management, history, etc.
Cf. QH75+ Nature reserves, wilderness areas
Cf. QH91.75.A1+ Marine parks and reserves
Cf. QH101+ Natural history of particular parks
Cf. RA604 Environmental health
Cf. SD426+ Forest reserves
Cf. TD931 Sanitary engineering

481.A1 Periodicals. Societies. Serials
481.A2 Congresses
481.A4-Z General works
481.3 Juvenile works
Biography
481.5 Collective
481.6.A-Z Individual, A-Z
By region or country
United States
Including general works on the theory, management, and history of parks and monuments at the national, state, and local level
For collective description of national, state, and local parks and public reservations, see E
For works on individual national, state, or local parks and monuments, including theory, management, etc., see E-F
Documents
482.A1-.A29 Serials
482.A3 Monographs. By date of publication
482.A4 General works
482.A5-Z By region or state, A-Z
Under each state:
.x *General works*
.x2A-.x2Z *Cities, A-Z*
(483) Cities
see SB482.A5+
Other regions or countries
Class here works on the theory, management, and history of collective and individual parks and reservations
484.A-Z By region or country, A-Z
e.g.
484.C2 Canada
For collective description of Canadian national, provincial, and local parks and public reservations see F1011
For works on individual Canadian national, provincial, or local parks and monuments, including theory, management, etc. see F1035.8+

Parks and public reservations
By region or country -- Continued
485.A-Z By city, A-Z
Class here works on the theory and management of collected and individual city parks
For descriptive works on collected and individual city parks, see D and F
486.A-Z Special topics, A-Z
486.D46 Design. Designs and plans
486.F34 Facilities
Cf. NA6930 Building architecture
Cf. TH4711 Building construction
486.F54 Finance
486.F56 Fire management
486.H35 Handicapped. People with disabilities
486.I57 Interpretive programs
486.M33 Maintenance
486.M35 Management
People with disabilities see SB486.H35
486.P76 Protection
486.P82 Public opinion
486.P83 Public use
486.S53 Search and rescue operations
486.S65 Social aspects
486.V35 Vandalism
486.V62 Vocational guidance
486.V64 Volunteer workers
Pests and diseases
599 Periodicals. Societies. Serials
599.2 Congresses
600 Dictionaries
600.5 Directories
601 General works
603 Minor
Urban pests
Cf. SB938 Insect pests
603.3 General works
603.33.A-Z By region or country, A-Z
603.5 Garden pests and diseases
Cf. SB608.O7 Ornamental plants
Cf. SB761+ Ornamental trees and shrubs
Cf. SB974+ Organic plant protection
605.A-Z By region or country, A-Z
Study and teaching. Research see SB950.57+
608.A-Z By individual or type of plant or tree, A-Z
For particular insects see SB945.A+
608.A2 Abies grandis

Pests and diseases
By individual or type of plant or tree, A-Z -- Continued

608.A25	Acacia
608.A27	Acer pseudoplatanus
608.A37	African violets
608.A42	Agathis alba
608.A5	Alfalfa
608.A515	Almond
608.A517	Amaranths
608.A518	American chestnut
608.A52	Anthuriums
608.A6	Apple
608.A7	Arabidopsis thaliana
608.A77	Ash
608.A79	Aspen
608.A8	Asparagus
608.A84	Avocado
608.A9	Azaleas
608.B14	Bamboo
608.B16	Banana
608.B2	Barley
608.B3	Bean
608.B4	Beets
608.B45	Berries
608.B5	Birch
608.B63	Blueberry
608.B65	Bluegrass
608.B67	Boxwood
608.B68	Brassica
608.B7	Brazil nut
608.B78	Brussels sprouts
608.B85	Bulbs
608.B88	Butternut
608.C14	Cabbage
608.C17	Cacao
608.C18	Cactus
608.C2	Calla lily
608.C24	Callitropsis nootkatensis
608.C25	Camphor tree
608.C27	Canavalia
608.C28	Cannabis. Hemp
608.C29	Cardamoms
608.C3	Carnation
608.C32	Carrots
608.C33	Cassava
608.C34	Casuarina cunninghamiana
608.C35	Cauliflower

Pests and diseases
By individual or type of plant or tree, A-Z -- Continued

608.C38 Cedar
608.C39 Celery
608.C43 Cherry
608.C45 Chestnut
608.C455 Chickpea
608.C46 Chrysanthemum
608.C48 Cinchona
608.C5 Citrus. Citrus fruits
Citrus fruits see SB608.C5
608.C55 Clover
608.C58 Coconut palm
608.C6 Coffee
608.C67 Cole crops
608.C7 Conifers
608.C76 Cork tree
Corn see SB608.M2
608.C8 Cotton
608.C85 Cowpea
608.C87 Cranberry
608.C875 Crataegus
Creeping bentgrass see SB608.T87
608.C877 Crucifers
608.C88 Cucumber
608.C885 Cucurbits
608.C888 Currant
608.C89 Cyclamen
608.D3 Dahlia
608.D35 Date palm
608.D44 Dendrobium
608.D6 Douglas fir
608.E2 Eggplant
608.E5 Elm
608.E55 Entandrophragma
608.E82 Eucalyptus
608.E83 Eucalyptus camaldulensis
608.E87 European beech
608.F24 Fava bean
608.F3 Ferns
Field crops see SB599+
608.F35 Fig
608.F37 Filbert
608.F4 Fir
608.F5 Flax
Flowers see SB608.O7
608.F59 Foliage plants

Pests and diseases
By individual or type of plant or tree, A-Z -- Continued

608.F62 Food crops
608.F63 Forage plants
Including pasture plants
608.F7 Foxtail
608.F8 Fruit
608.G38 Gentianella scopulorum
608.G4 Gerbera
608.G5 Ginseng
608.G55 Gladiolus
608.G6 Grain
608.G7 Grape
608.G8 Grasses
Cf. SB608.T87 Turfgrasses
608.G82 Greenhouse plants
Cf. SB936 Economic entomology
608.G9 Guarana
608.G93 Guayule
608.H3 Hardwoods
608.H4 Hemlock
Hemp see SB608.C28
608.H45 Herbs
608.H47 Heritiera fomes
608.H5 Hevea
608.H56 Hippophae rhamnoides
608.H7 Honeysuckle
608.H8 Hops
608.H82 Horseradish
608.H83 Horticultural crops
608.H84 House plants
608.I63 Incense cedar
608.I7 Iris
608.J3 Japanese cherry
608.J34 Jarrah
608.J4 Jerusalem artichoke
608.J77 Jute
(608.K3) Kafir corn
see SB608.S6
608.K57 Kiwifruit
608.L27 Landscape plants
608.L3 Larch
608.L4 Legumes
608.L5 Lemon
608.L52 Lespedeza
608.L523 Lettuce
608.L53 Lily

Pests and diseases
By individual or type of plant or tree, A-Z -- Continued

608.L55 Lima bean
608.L58 Liriodendron tulipifera
608.L6 Lodgepole pine
608.L85 Lupines
608.M2 Maize. Corn
608.M27 Mangium
608.M3 Mango
608.M32 Mangrove plants
608.M34 Maple
608.M38 Medicinal plants
608.M4 Melons
608.M45 Mesquite
608.M5 Millets
608.M8 Mulberry
608.M9 Mushrooms
Including individual species and genera
608.M94 Myrtle beech
608.N67 Norway spruce
608.N673 Nothofagus
608.N674 Nothofagus fusca
608.N676 Nursery stock
608.N68 Nuts
608.O115 Oak
608.O2 Oats
608.O25 Ohia lehua
608.O27 Oil palm
608.O3 Oilseed plants
608.O4 Olive
608.O5 Onions
608.O6 Orange
608.O65 Orchid
608.O7 Ornamental plants (General)
Including flowers
Ornamental woody plants see SB761+
608.P15 Pacific madrone
608.P22 Palms
608.P23 Papaya
Pasture plants see SB608.F63
608.P24 Paulownia kawakamii
608.P25 Pea
608.P3 Peach
608.P37 Peanut
608.P4 Pear
608.P42 Pearl millet
608.P45 Pecan

Pests and diseases
By individual or type of plant or tree, A-Z -- Continued

608.P5	Pepper
608.P56	Phragmites australis
608.P63	Pigeon pea
608.P65	Pine
608.P72	Pineapple
608.P73	Pistachio
608.P76	Plane tree
608.P77	Plum
608.P774	Polish larch
608.P7745	Ponderosa pine
608.P775	Poplar
608.P78	Poppy
608.P79	Populus tremuloides
608.P8	Potatoes
608.P85	Proteaceae
608.R2	Rape
608.R25	Raspberry
608.R33	Red spruce
608.R37	Restionaceae
608.R43	Rhododendrons
608.R5	Rice
608.R7	Root crops
608.R8	Rose
608.R85	Rubus
608.R9	Rye
608.S33	Sandalwood
608.S42	Sea buckthorn
	Shade trees see SB761+
	Shrubs see SB761+
608.S44	Scots pine
608.S46	Siberian larch
608.S5	Silk tree
608.S54	Silver fir
608.S57	Snapdragon
608.S59	Solanaceae
608.S6	Sorghum
608.S7	Soybean
608.S8	Spruce
608.S83	Stone fruit
608.S85	Strawberry
608.S88	Sugar beet
608.S89	Sugar maple
608.S9	Sugarcane
608.S92	Sunflower
608.S945	Sweet clover

SB

Pests and diseases
By individual or type of plant or tree, A-Z -- Continued

608.S95 Sweet pea
608.S98 Sweet potato
608.T26 Taro
608.T28 Taxus
608.T3 Tea
608.T33 Teak
608.T4 Teosinte
608.T6 Timothy
608.T7 Tobacco
608.T75 Tomato
Trees see SB761+
608.T8 Tropical crops
Cf. SB724 Plant diseases in the tropics
608.T85 Tulip
608.T87 Turfgrasses
Including individual species
608.T9 Turnip
608.U42 Umbelliferae
608.V4 Vegetables (General)
608.V44 Veld grass
608.W3 Walnut
608.W32 Walnut, English
608.W33 Watermelon
608.W47 Western larch
608.W5 Wheat
608.W6 White ash
608.W64 White spruce
608.W65 Willow

Weeds, parasitic plants, etc.
For works on weed control of special plants see SB608.A+
For forest weeds and their control see SB761+
Cf. SB951.4+ Herbicides (General)

610 Periodicals. Societies. Serials
610.2 Congresses
611 General works
Study and teaching. Research
611.3 General works
611.34.A-Z By region or country, A-Z
611.4 Economic aspects (General)
Biological control (General)
611.5 General works
611.6 Microbiological methods. Microbial herbicides
By region or country, A-Z
United States

	Pests and diseases
	Weeds, parasitic plants, etc.
	By region or country, A-Z
	United States -- Continued
612.A2	General works
612.A3-Z	By region or state, A-Z
613.A-Z	Other regions or countries, A-Z
613.5	Invasive plants
	For local see SB612.A2+
	Aquatic weeds
614	General works
614.3.A-Z	By region or country, A-Z
614.7	Phreatophytes
615.A-Z	Individual weeds, etc., A-Z
615.A27	Absinth wormwood
615.A52	Ambrosia artemisiifolia
615.A65	Apera spica-venti
615.A78	Artemisia frigida
	Asiatic witchweed see SB615.W58
	Avena fatua see SB615.W54
	Bindweed, Field see SB615.F54
615.B72	Bracken fern
615.B74	Broom snakeweed
615.C4	Canada thistle
615.C42	Celastrus orbiculatus
615.C43	Chinese clematis
615.C45	Chromolaena odorata
615.C47	Cladophora
615.C5	Climbing hempweed
	Climbing spindle berry see SB615.C42
615.C63	Cogon grass
615.C65	Common dandelion
615.D29	Dalmatian toadflax
615.D6	Docks
615.D85	Dwarf mistletoes
615.E23	Echium plantagineum
615.E54	English ivy
615.E87	Eurasian watermilfoil
615.F54	Field bindweed
615.F68	Fountain grass
(615.F75)	Fringed sagebrush see SB615.A78
615.G2	Garlic
615.G23	Garlic mustard
615.G52	Giant hogweed
615.G67	Gorse
615.H4	Heather

SB

Pests and diseases
Weeds, parasitic plants, etc.
Individual weeds, etc., A-Z -- Continued

615.H45	Hemp sesbania
	Hempweed, Climbing see SB615.C5
615.H54	Hieracium lepidulum
615.H66	Honey mesquite
615.H93	Hydrilla
615.H95	Hydrocotyle ranuculoides
615.H97	Hymenachne amplexicaulis
615.H98	Hypericum perforatum
615.I39	Imperata
(615.I4)	Imperata cylindrica see SB615.C63
615.J34	Japanese knotweed
615.K55	Knapweeds
615.K83	Kudzu
615.L24	Lagorosiphon major
615.L35	Lantana camara
615.L42	Lead tree
615.L43	Leafy spurge
615.L56	Linaria vulgaris
615.M3	Marsh horsetail
615.M38	Medusahead wildrye
615.M39	Melaleuca quinquenervia
615.M4	Mesquite
615.M43	Miconia calvescens
615.M45	Mikania micrantha
615.M46	Mimosa pigra
615.M5	Mistletoes Cf. SB615.D85 Dwarf mistletoes
615.M65	Morella faya
(615.M94)	Myrica faya see SB615.M65
	Oriental bittersweet see SB615.C42
615.P25	Pampas grasses Including individual species
615.P28	Parthenium hysterophorus
615.P3	Paspalum distichum
(615.P38)	Paterson's curse see SB615.E23
615.P45	Phyla canescens
615.P54	Plectonema boryanum
615.P66	Populus tremuloides
615.P8	Prickly pears

Pests and diseases
Weeds, parasitic plants, etc.
Individual weeds, etc., A-Z -- Continued

615.P83 Prosopis juliflora
Cf. SB317.P76 Multipurpose plant
Cf. SD397.P88 Forestry
615.P86 Purple loosestrife
615.Q3 Quack grass
615.R3 Ragweeds
615.R4 Red alder
615.R43 Red rice
Cf. SB191.R53 Crop
615.R44 Reed canary grass
615.S2 Sagebrush
Including individual species
615.S35 Senna obtusifolia
615.S4 Serrated tussock
615.S58 Small-leaf spiderwort
615.S62 Sow thistles
615.S63 Spartina
(615.S74) Striga
see SB615.W58
615.S84 Sulphur cinquefoil
615.T25 Tamarisks
615.T4 Thistles
615.T96 Typha
615.V44 Veld grass
615.W3 Water hyacinth
Cf. SB317.W37 Economic plant
615.W54 Wild oat
615.W56 Willows
615.W58 Witchweeds
Including Asiatic witchweed

Poisonous plants
Cf. QK100.A1+ Botany
617 General
By region or country
United States
617.4 General works
617.45.A-Z By region or state, A-Z
617.5.A-Z Other regions or countries, A-Z
618.A-Z Individual plants, A-Z
618.D4 Death camas
618.M5 Milkweed
618.M6 Mountain laurel
618.P6 Poison ivy
618.S7 Sneezeweed

Pests and diseases -- Continued
Plant pathology
621-723 By region or country (Table S1)
Add number in table to SB600
724 Tropics
Cf. SB608.T8 Diseases of tropical crops
Periodicals and societies see SB599
Directories see SB600.5
727 Congresses
728 Dictionaries. Encyclopedias
Including nomenclature
Biography
729.5 Collective
729.6.A-Z Individual, A-Z
731 General works
732 Minor miscellaneous
732.4 Vocational guidance
Study and teaching. Research
732.5 General works
732.54.A-Z By region or country, A-Z
732.56 Laboratory manuals
732.58 Economic aspects (General)
732.6 Biological control of phytopathogenic microorganisms (General)
732.65 Molecular aspects
732.7 Plant-pathogen relationships
732.73 Diseased plant anatomy and physiology
732.75 Phytotoxins. Allelopathy and allelopathic agents (General)
732.8 Seed pathology. Seed-borne plant diseases (General)
Including seed-borne phytopathogens
Cf. SB118.43 Disinfection
732.87 Soilborne plant diseases
Including root diseases
Cf. SB741.R75 Root rots
733 Fungus diseases
Cf. SB951.3 Fungicides
734 Bacterial diseases
736 Virus diseases
737 Mycoplasma diseases
738 Phytoplasma diseases
741.A-Z Individual and groups of diseases or pathogens, A-Z
For works limited to a specific plant see SB608.A+
741.A48 Alternaria
741.A55 Anthracnose
741.A7 Armillaria root rot
Including Armillaria mellea
741.B33 Bacterial wilt diseases

Pests and diseases
Plant pathology
Individual and groups of diseases or pathogens, A-Z -- Continued
Cf. SB741.R35 Ralstonia solanacearum

741.B6 Black rot
741.B73 Botryodiplodia theobromae
Botryotinia see SB741.B74
741.B74 Botrytis. Botryotinia
741.C42 Charcoal rot
741.C45 Chlorosis
741.C6 Clubroot
741.C73 Colletotrichum
741.C9 Crown gall
741.D3 Damping-off
741.D68 Downy mildew
741.E7 Ergot
741.F6 Fire blight
741.F9 Fusarium
741.G35 Ganoderma
741.H38 Heterobasidion annosum
741.L45 Leaf spots
741.M65 Mildew
Cf. SB741.D68 Downy mildew
Cf. SB741.P72 Powdery mildews
741.M75 Mosaic diseases
741.P58 Phytophthora
741.P59 Phytophthora cinnamomi
741.P715 Potyviruses
741.P72 Powdery mildews
741.P76 Pseudomonas syringae
741.P95 Pythium
741.R35 Ralstonia solanacearum
741.R38 Red band needle blight
741.R75 Root rots
741.R8 Rusts
741.S38 Scleroderris canker
741.S6 Smuts
741.V45 Verticillium. Verticillium wilts
741.W44 Wilt diseases
741.X35 Xanthomonas
741.5 Tumors
Cf. SB767 Galls
Nutrition disorders. Deficiency diseases
Cf. QK746+ Chemical agents affecting plants
742 General works

Pests and diseases
Plant pathology
Nutrition disorders. Deficiency diseases -- Continued

743.A-Z Special. By compound, element, or group of elements, A-Z
Cutter compounds by principal element
743.B6 Boron
743.I75 Iron
743.M25 Magnesium
743.M3 Manganese
743.P68 Potassium
743.T7 Trace elements
743.Z55 Zinc

Pesticide effects
744 General works
744.25 Herbicides
Cf. QK753.H45 Plant physiology

Pollution effects. Crops and pollution
Cf. QK750+ Plant physiology
744.5 General works
By type of pollution
745 Air pollution, smoke, fumes, etc.
Cf. QK751 Plant physiology
745.4 Acid deposition. Acid precipitation
746 Radioactive substances
Cf. QK753.R33 Plant physiology
Cf. S589.6 Decontamination
747.A-Z Other pollutants, A-Z
747.F58 Fluorides
747.O95 Ozone, Atmospheric
747.S84 Sulfur dioxide

750 Disease and pest resistance
Cf. SB933.2 Insect resistance

Diseases and pests of trees and shrubs
Including forest health, forest insects, weeds, etc.
For individual trees or types of trees see SB608.A+
For wounds and mutilation, tree surgery, etc. see SD406
Cf. QK840 Reparative processes in plants
761 General works
By region or country
United States
762 General works
763.A-Z By region or state, A-Z
764.A-Z Other regions or countries, A-Z

Pests and diseases
Plant pathology
Diseases and pests of trees and shrubs -- Continued
765 Tree and forest declines
For particular trees see SB608.A+
For local see SB762+
767 Galls and gall insects
For special insects see QL1+
770 Tree cavities. Tree hollows. Tree holes
For local see SB762+
Individual trees see SB608.A+
781 Damage from frosts, freezing, hail, and ice
Cf. QK756 Plant physiology
785 Effect of floods
Cf. QK870+ Plant physiology
791 Effect of drought
Cf. QK754.7.D75 Plant physiology
Cf. S600.7.D76 Agricultural meteorology
793 Effect of wind
Cf. QK754.7.W55 Plant physiology
795.A-Z Other, A-Z
795.F6 Forking
Economic zoology see SF84+
Economic entomology
For insects injurious to humans see RA639.5
For works on general insect pests of specific plants see SB608.A+
For individual insects (including those associated with a specific plant) see SB945.A+
For works limited to beneficial insects see SF517+
For insects injurious to animals see SF810.A3+
Cf. QL461+ Zoology
Cf. SB761+ Forest insects
Cf. SB767 Galls and gall insects
Cf. SB951.5+ Insecticides
818 Periodicals. Societies. Serials
818.2 Congresses
818.5 Dictionaries. Encyclopedias. Terminology
821-923 Documents. By country (Table S1)
Add number in table to SB800
931 General works
931.3 Juvenile works
(932) Biological control of insects
see SB933.3
933 Minor works. Pamphlets
Study and teaching. Research
933.14 General works

SB

Pests and diseases
Economic entomology
Study and teaching. Research -- Continued
933.16.A-Z By region or country, A-Z
933.2 Insect resistance. Insect resistant plants
Biological control
933.25 Periodicals. Societies. Serials
933.27 Congresses
933.3 General works
933.32.A-Z By region or country, A-Z
933.33 Entomophagous arthropods and insects
933.334 Nematodes
Microbiological methods. Microbial insecticides
Cf. SB942 Insect diseases
933.34 General works
933.37 Viral insecticides
933.5 Semiochemicals
Including sex attractants
933.6 Sterilization
933.7 Temperature
By region or country
United States
934 General works
934.5.A-Z By region or state, A-Z
935.A-Z Other regions or countries, A-Z
Forest insects see SB761+
936 Greenhouse pests
Cf. SB608.G82 Diseases and pests
937 Storage pests
Cf. TP373.3 Food processing
938 Urban pests
939 Scale insects
Cf. QL523.C7 Corimelaenidae (Zoology)
940 Mites
Including Acariformes
Cf. QL458+ Acari (Zoology)
Cf. RA641.M5 Public health
Cf. SB951.6 Miticides
Cf. SF810.M5 Veterinary medicine
942 Diseases of insects, mites, etc.
Cf. SB933.34+ Microbiological control of insects
945.A-Z Individual and groups of insects, mites, etc., A-Z
Including transmission of plant diseases by individual insects, etc., and control and insecticide resistance of individual insects, etc.
Acariformes see SB940
945.A22 Acarus siro

Pests and diseases
Economic entomology
Individual and groups of insects, mites, etc., A-Z -- Continued

945.A224 Adelges
945.A226 African armyworm
945.A23 Agromyzidae
945.A26 Alfalfa midge
945.A3 Alfalfa weevil
945.A33 Ambermarked birch leafminer
945.A34 Amrasca devastans
945.A4 Ants
945.A5 Aphids
(945.A52) Aphis fabae
see SB945.B38
945.A527 Apple clearwing moth
945.A74 Argentine ant
945.A8 Armyworms
945.A83 Asian longhorned beetle
945.A86 Atta
945.B24 Balsam woolly adelgid
945.B28 Banana root borer
945.B3 Bark beetles
945.B38 Bean aphid
945.B422 Beet armyworm
945.B424 Beetles
945.B427 Bemisia
945.B44 Black cutworm
Boll weevil see SB945.C8
945.B83 Borers
945.B89 Brown planthopper
945.B9 Browntail moth
945.C24 Cabbage maggot
945.C26 Cacao pod borer
945.C337 Capnodis tenebrionis
945.C44 Cercopidae
945.C47 Chilo
945.C49 Chilotraea polychrysa
945.C5 Chinch bug
945.C523 Choristoneura murinana
945.C525 Chortoicetes terminifera
(945.C53) Chrysophtharta bimaculata
see SB945.T27
945.C55 Cicada, Periodical
945.C67 Coccidae
945.C68 Cockchafers
945.C7 Codling moth

Pests and diseases
Economic entomology
Individual and groups of insects, mites, etc., A-Z -- Continued

945.C723 Collembola
Colorado potato beetle see SB945.P68
Contarinia medicaginis see SB945.A26
945.C8 Cotton-boll weevil
945.C865 Cranberry girdler
945.C888 Ctenarytaina eucalypti
945.C92 Cutworms
945.C95 Cyclamen mite
945.D38 Dendroctonus micans
945.D44 Desert locust
945.D48 Diabrotica
945.D5 Diamondback moth
945.D53 Diaspididae
945.D75 Douglas fir beetle
945.D76 Douglas fir tussock moth
945.D87 Dysdercus
945.E48 Emerald ash borer
945.E52 Empoasca fabae
945.E65 Epilachna
945.E73 European chafer
945.E75 European corn borer
945.E78 European pine shoot moth
945.E845 Eurygaster integriceps
945.F535 Fire ants
945.F64 Florida wax scale
945.F7 Forest tent caterpillar
(945.F74) Formica rufa
see SB945.W67
945.F8 Fruit fly
945.G53 Granary weevil
945.G65 Grasshoppers
945.G75 Green peach aphid
945.G9 Gypsy moth
945.H27 Heliothis
945.H274 Heliothis armigera
945.H28 Heliothis zea
945.H29 Hemispherical scale
945.H294 Hemlock woolly adelgid
945.H9 Hyphantrai cunea
Imported fire ant see SB945.F535
945.I68 Ips typographus
945.J27 Janetiella oenophila
945.J3 Japanese beetle

Pests and diseases
Economic entomology
Individual and groups of insects, mites, etc., A-Z -- Continued

945.K45 Khapra beetle
945.L27 Large timberworm
Leaf cutting ants see SB945.A86
945.L5 Leafhoppers
945.L55 Leafminers
945.L6 Leopard moth
945.L63 Lepidoptera
945.L65 Leucaena psyllid
945.L68 Liriomyza trifolii
Locust, Seventeen-year see SB945.C55
945.L7 Locusts
945.L8 Lucerne flea
945.M32 Macrotermes gilvus
945.M5 Mediterranean flour moth
945.M54 Mediterranean fruit fly
945.M56 Melon-flies
Mites see SB940
945.M7 Mole crickets
945.M74 Monochamus urussovi
Moths see SB945.L63
945.M78 Mountain pine beetle
945.M96 Mythimna separata
945.N4 Neodiprion sertifer
945.N46 Neotermes
945.N53 Nezara viridula
945.N57 Nipaecoccus viridis
945.N8 Nun moth
945.O37 Oligonychus ununguis
945.O4 Olive fly
945.O57 Oporinia autumnata
945.O63 Oriental fruit fly
945.O65 Oriental fruit moth
945.O77 Oryctes rhinoceros
945.P2 Pales weevil
945.P35 Pea aphis
945.P36 Peach twig-borer
945.P47 Pentatomidae. Stinkbugs
945.P48 Pepper weevil
Periodical cicada see SB945.C55
945.P58 Phyllophaga
945.P59 Phylloxera
945.P618 Pine bud moth
945.P619 Pine gall midge

Pests and diseases
Economic entomology
Individual and groups of insects, mites, etc., A-Z -- Continued

(945.P6235) Pine-shoot moth
see SB945.E78
Plant lice see SB945.A5
945.P644 Planthoppers
945.P66 Poplar and willow borer
945.P68 Potato beetle
945.P7 Potato tuberworm
945.P73 Prays oleae
945.P78 Psylla
945.P95 Pyralidae
945.R44 Red locust
945.R45 Red spider
945.R457 Rhagoletis cerasi
945.R458 Rhammatocerus schistocercoides
945.R48 Ribbed pine-borer
945.R49 Rice gall midge
945.R495 Rice hispa
945.R57 Rice weevil
945.R7 Rocky Mountain locust
945.S2 San Jose scale
945.S25 Satin moth
945.S3 Sawflies
Scale insects see SB939
945.S35 Scarabaeidae
Seventeen-year locust see SB945.C55
945.S46 Shoot flies
945.S5 Sitona
945.S57 Sorghum shoot fly
945.S635 Southern pine beetle
945.S64 Southwestern corn borer
945.S645 Sphaeraspis salisburiensis
945.S647 Spiders
945.S673 Spirea aphid
945.S68 Spodoptera littoralis
945.S69 Spruce bark beetles
945.S697 Spruce bud moth
945.S7 Spruce budworm
Spruce budworm, Western see SB945.W539
945.S74 Stem borers
Stinkbugs see SB945.P47
945.S83 Sugarcane borer
945.S86 Sweetpotato whitefly
945.T25 Tanymecus dilaticollis

Pests and diseases
Economic entomology
Individual and groups of insects, mites, etc., A-Z -- Continued

945.T27 Tasmanian eucalyptus leaf beetle
945.T36 Tent caterpillars
945.T45 Termites
Cf. TA423.7 Deterioration and preservation of wood
Timberworm, Large see SB945.L27
945.T6 Thrips
945.T76 Tomato pinworm
945.T78 Tortricidae
945.T87 Turnip aphid
945.T9 Tyroglyphidae
945.W3 Wasps
945.W53 Western corn rootworm
945.W539 Western spruce budworm
945.W56 Wheat bulb fly
945.W563 Wheat curl mite
945.W57 White-fringed beetles
945.W62 White pine weevil
945.W65 Wireworms
945.W67 Wood ant
945.W68 Wood borers
945.W7 Woolly apple aphid
945.X94 Xyleborus destruens
945.Z43 Zeiraphera rufimitrana

Pest control and treatment of diseases. Plant protection
Including integrated pest management
For control of pests and diseases of specific plants see SB608.A+
For treatment of special diseases see SB621+
For control of specific pests in general see SB818+
Cf. HD9718.5.P47+ Pest control industry
Cf. TH9041 Pest control in buildings

950.A1 Periodicals. Societies. Serials. Yearbooks
950.A2 Congresses
950.A3-Z General works, treatises, and textbooks
Directories
950.15 General works
950.152.A-Z By region or country, A-Z
By region or country
United States
950.2.A1 General works
950.2.A2-Z By region or state, A-Z
950.3.A-Z Other regions or countries, A-Z
Study and teaching. Research

Pests and diseases
Pest control and treatment of diseases. Plant protection
Study and teaching. Research -- Continued

950.57 Periodicals. Societies. Serials
950.6 Congresses
950.7 General works
950.725.A-Z International institutions. By name, A-Z
950.73.A-Z By region or country, A-Z

Under each country:

.x	*General works*
.x2A-.x2Z	*Local, A-Z*
.x3A-.x3Z	*Special schools or institutions. By name, A-Z*

950.76.A-Z Special topics, A-Z
950.76.E44 Electrophoresis
(950.8-.83) Urban pests
see SB603.3+

Pesticides
Cf. HD9660.P3+ Pesticides industry
Cf. QH545.P4 Ecology
Cf. QP82.2.P4 Physiological effect
Cf. QP801.P38 Animal biochemistry
Cf. RA1270.P4 Toxicology
Cf. S592.6.P43 Behavior and movement in soils
Cf. S694 Equipment
Cf. TD196.P38 Pollution
Cf. TD427.P35 Water pollution
Cf. TD887.P45 Air pollution
Cf. TP248.P47 Chemical technology
Cf. TX571.P4 Food adulteration

950.9 Periodicals. Societies. Serials
950.92 Collected works (nonserial)
950.93 Congresses
950.95 Dictionaries. Encyclopedias
951 General works
951.13 Juvenile works
951.14 Addresses, essays, lectures
By region or country see SB950.2+
Special pesticides
951.145.A-Z Special types of pesticides, A-Z
951.145.B54 Biodegradable pesticides
951.145.B68 Botanical pesticides
951.145.C65 Controlled release pesticides
951.145.L54 Light-activated pesticides
Microbial pesticides see SB976.M55
951.145.N37 Natural pesticides
951.145.S65 Soil pesticides

Pests and diseases
Pest control and treatment of diseases. Plant protection
Pesticides
Special pesticides
Special types of pesticides, A-Z -- Continued
951.145.S97 Systemic pesticides
Special classes of pesticides (by target)
Acaricides see SB951.6
951.15 Algicides
951.3 Fungicides
Herbicides
Cf. QK753.H45 Plant physiology
Cf. SB611.6 Microbial herbicides
951.4 General works
951.45 Herbicide safeners
Insecticides
Cf. SB933.34+ Microbial insecticides
Cf. SB933.37 Viral insecticides
951.5 General works
951.54 Botanical insecticides
951.6 Miticides. Acaricides
951.65 Molluscicides
951.7 Nematocides
Piscicides see SH157.7
951.8 Rodenticides
952.A-Z Individual pesticides, A-Z
952.A54 Aminopropiophenones
952.A7 Arsenic compounds
952.A82 Atrazine
952.B43 Benzoylphenyl ureas
952.B5 Bipyridinium compounds
952.B6 Bordeaux mixture
952.B65 Boverin
952.B68 Brodifacoum
952.B7 Bromides
952.B75 Bromomethane
952.C3 Carbamates
952.C4 Chlordan
952.C44 Chlorine compounds (General)
952.C45 Chloromethylpropene
952.C49 Chlorpyrifos
952.C6 Copper compounds
952.C62 Copper naphthenate
952.D2 DDT
952.D33 Deet
952.D43 Diatomaceous earth
952.D5 Dichlorophenoxyacetic acid

Pests and diseases
Pest control and treatment of diseases. Plant protection
Pesticides
Special pesticides
Individual pesticides, A-Z -- Continued

	Dipterex see SB952.T7
952.F45	Fenitrothion
952.F55	Fluorine compounds
952.G58	Glyphosate
952.G74	Green Muscle (Trademark)
(952.H4)	Hexachlorocyclohexane see SB952.L56
952.I46	Imidazolinones
952.I6	Iodine compounds
952.L56	Lindane
952.M15	MCPA
952.M38	Mercury compounds (General)
952.N44	Neem insecticide
952.N54	Nicotinoids
952.O4	Oil
952.P3	Parathion
952.P37	Pentachlorophenol
(952.P4)	Petroleum
952.P45	Phenoxyalkanoic acids
952.P5	Phosphorus compounds
952.P67	Porphyrins
952.P68	Potassium cyanide
952.P88	Pyrethroids
952.P9	Pyrethrum Cf. SB292.P8 Plant culture
952.Q5	Quinoline
952.S6	Sodium fluoroacetate
952.S63	Sodium pentachlorophenate
952.S94	Sulfur compounds (General)
952.T45	Terbutryn
952.T7	Trichlorfon
952.T72	Trichlorophenoxyacetic acid
952.T74	Triclopyr
952.5	Safety measures
	Methods of application
952.8	General works
	Applicators (Persons)
952.85	General works
	By region or country
	United States
952.86	General works
952.863.A-Z	By region or state, A-Z

Pests and diseases
Pest control and treatment of diseases. Plant protection
Pesticides
Methods of application
Applicators (Persons)
By region or country -- Continued
952.87.A-Z Other regions or countries, A-Z
953 Spraying. Dusting
For works limited to a specific agent see SB952.A+
Cf. S694 Equipment
955 Fumigation of plants and plant products
For works limited to a specific agent see SB952.A+
Cf. SB973.3 Soil fumigation
957 Resistance to pesticides
For resistance to pesticides by specific insects, etc. see SB945.A+
For resistance to pesticides by specific animals see SB993.5+
959 Miscellaneous
Study and teaching. Research
959.6 General works
959.7.A-Z By region or country, A-Z
960 Analysis and experiments
960.5.A-Z Special topics, A-Z
960.5.R33 Radioactive tracers
961 Tables, formulae, etc.
964 Evaluation
965 Certification
Economic aspects
969.6 General works
969.8.A-Z By region or country, A-Z
Policy
970 General works
970.4.A-Z By region or country, A-Z
Soil disinfection
Cf. SB951.145.S65 Soil pesticides
973 General works
973.3 Fumigation
973.5 Heat treatment
Organic plant protection
For organic plant protection of specific plants see SB608.A+
For organic control of specific weeds, parasitic plants, etc. see SB610+
For organic control of specific animals see SB992+
974 General works

Pests and diseases
Pest control and treatment of diseases. Plant protection
Organic plant protection -- Continued
Biological control
For biological control of special pests see SB611.5+
975 General works
975.5.A-Z By region or country, A-Z
976.A-Z Special biological pest control agents, A-Z
976.A78 Arthropoda
976.F85 Fungi
976.I56 Insects
Microbial pesticides see SB976.M55
976.M55 Microorganisms. Microbial pesticides
976.M58 Mites
976.N46 Nematoda
Cf. SB933.334 Insect control
978 Sterilization of pests
For sterilization of specific insects, etc. see SB933.6
For sterilization of specific animals see SB992+
Inspection. Quarantine
Including plant quaratine facilities
979.5 Periodicals. Societies. Serials
979.6 Collected works (nonserial)
979.7 Congresses
980 General works
By region or country
United States
981 General works
983.A-Z By region or state, A-Z
985.A-Z Other regions or countries, A-Z
Pest introduction. Nonindigenous pests
For individual and groups of pests see SB610+
Cf. SB613.5 Invasive plants
Cf. SH174.5+ Aquatic pests (Fish culture)
990 General works
990.5.A-Z By region or country, A-Z
Economic zoology applied to crops. Agricultural zoology
Including animals injurious and beneficial to plants
Cf. QL1+ Zoology
Cf. SB818+ Economic entomology
Cf. SF84+ General economic zoology
992 Periodicals. Societies. Serials
992.2 Collected works (nonserial)
992.3 Congresses
992.4 Dictionaries. Encyclopedias
993 General works

Economic zoology applied to crops. Agricultural zoology -- Continued
993.23 Juvenile works
993.25 Pictorial works
993.27 Addresses, essays, lectures
By region or country
United States
993.3 General works
993.32.A-Z By region or state, A-Z
993.34.A-Z Other regions or countries, A-Z
Vertebrates
993.4 General works
By region or country
United States
993.43 General works
993.44.A-Z By region or state, A-Z
993.45.A-Z Other regions or countries, A-Z
Mammals
993.5 General works
By region or country
United States
993.6 General works
993.65.A-Z By region or state, A-Z
993.7.A-Z Other regions or countries, A-Z
994.A-Z Special mammals, A-Z
994.A64 Aplodontia
Coyote see SF810.7.C88
994.C82 Coypu
994.D4 Deer
Dogs see SF810.7.D65
Ermine see SF810.7.E74
994.G58 Goats
994.K35 Kangaroos
994.M5 Mice
994.M7 Moles (Animals)
994.M73 Moose
994.M85 Muskrats
994.P72 Predators
Cf. SF810.5+ Predator control
994.R15 Rabbits
994.R2 Rats
Cf. RA641.R2 Public health
994.R6 Rodents
Cf. SB951.8 Rodenticides
994.S55 Skunks
994.S67 Squirrels
994.T74 Trichosurus vulpecula

Economic zoology applied to crops. Agricultural zoology
Vertebrates
Mammals
Special mammals, A-Z -- Continued
Wolves see SF810.7.W65
Birds
995 General works
995.25 Scarecrows and other crop protection devices
By region or country
United States
995.3 General works
995.34.A-Z By region or state, A-Z
995.36.A-Z Other regions or countries, A-Z
996.A-Z Special birds, A-Z
996.C3 Cattle egret
996.C6 Crow
996.D5 Dickcissel
996.M3 Magpie
996.M5 Meadowlark
996.P8 Purple martin
996.Q44 Quelea
996.S7 Sparrow
996.S75 Starling
996.S8 Swallow
996.T5 Thrush
996.W7 Woodpecker
996.Y4 Yellow-bellied sapsucker
998.A-Z Other, A-Z
998.B82 Bufo marinus
998.B85 Burrowing nematode
998.D49 Ditylenchus
998.D5 Ditylenchus dipsaci
998.E4 Earthworms
Cf. SF597.E3 Earthworm culture
998.G37 Gastropoda
998.G53 Giant African snail
998.G64 Golden nematode
998.H35 Helicidae
998.H46 Heterodera
Heterodera rostochiensis see SB998.G64
998.I57 Insect nematodes
998.L64 Longidoridae
998.M45 Meloidogyne. Root-knot nematodes
998.M64 Mollusks
998.N4 Nematodes
Cf. SB951.7 Nematocides
998.P54 Pinewood nematode

Economic zoology applied to crops. Agricultural zoology
Other, A-Z -- Continued
998.R4 Rattlesnakes
Root-knot nematodes see SB998.M45
998.S59 Slugs (Mollusks)
998.S68 Soybean cyst nematode
998.T75 Trichodoridae
1110 Miscellaneous pamphlets
Not to be cataloged

Forestry
Cf. QK474.8+ Trees
Cf. S494.5.A45 Agroforestry
1 Periodicals. Societies. Serials
Documents
Class here serial documents
For special documents of a monographic character see SD131+
United States
11 Federal documents
12.A-.W States, A-W
Other regions or countries
Canada
13 General
14.A-Z Local, A-Z
Mexico
15 General
16.A-Z Local, A-Z
Central America
17 General
18.A-Z Local, A-Z
West Indies
19.A15 General
19.A6-Z Individual islands
e.g.
19.C8 Cuba
21 South America
Argentina
23 General
24.A-Z Local, A-Z
Bolivia
25 General
26.A-Z Local, A-Z
Brazil
27 General
28.A-Z Local, A-Z
Chile
29 General
30.A-Z Local, A-Z
Colombia
31 General
32.A-Z Local, A-Z
Ecuador
33 General
34.A-Z Local, A-Z
35 Guianas
French Guiana

Documents
Other regions or countries
South America
Guianas
French Guiana -- Continued
36.3 General
36.4.A-Z Local, A-Z
Guyana. British Guiana
36.5 General
36.6.A-Z Local, A-Z
Suriname. Dutch Guiana
36.7 General
36.8.A-Z Local, A-Z
Paraguay
37 General
38.A-Z Local, A-Z
Peru
39 General
40.A-Z Local, A-Z
Uruguay
41 General
42.A-Z Local, A-Z
Venezuela
43 General
44.A-Z Local, A-Z
Europe
Great Britain. England
45 General
46.A-Z Local, A-Z
Wales
47 General
48.A-Z Local, A-Z
Scotland
49 General
50.A-Z Local, A-Z
Northern Ireland
50.5 General
50.6.A-Z Local, A-Z
Ireland
51 General
52.A-Z Local, A-Z
Austria
53 General
54.A-Z Local, A-Z
Belgium
55 General
56.A-Z Local, A-Z

	Documents
	Other regions or countries
	Europe -- Continued
	Denmark
57	General
58.A-Z	Local, A-Z
	France
59	General
60.A-Z	Local, A-Z
	Germany
61	General
62.A-Z	Local, A-Z
	Greece
63	General
64.A-Z	Local, A-Z
	Netherlands
65	General
66.A-Z	Local, A-Z
	Italy
67	General
68.A-Z	Local, A-Z
	Norway
69	General
70.A-Z	Local, A-Z
	Portugal
71	General
72.A-Z	Local, A-Z
	Soviet Union
73	General
74.A-Z	Local, A-Z
	Spain
75	General
76.A-Z	Local, A-Z
	Sweden
77	General
78.A-Z	Local, A-Z
	Switzerland
79	General
80.A-Z	Local, A-Z
	Turkey
81	General
82.A-Z	Local, A-Z
83.A-Z	Other divisions of Europe, A-Z
	Asia
	China
85	General
86.A-Z	Local, A-Z

Documents
Other regions or countries
Asia -- Continued
86.5 Taiwan
India
87 General
88.A-Z Local, A-Z
Japan
89 General
90.A-Z Local, A-Z
Iran
91 General
92.A-Z Local, A-Z
Philippines
93 General
94.A-Z Local, A-Z
Siberia
95 General
96.A-Z Local, A-Z
97.A-Z Other divisions of Asia, A-Z
e.g.
97.C4 Sri Lanka
Indian Ocean islands
98 General works
98.3.A-SB98.3.Z By island or group of islands, A-Z
Africa
Egypt
99 General
100.A-Z Local, A-Z
103.A-Z British Africa, A-Z
105.A-Z Other divisions of Africa, A-Z
Australia
110 General
111.A-Z Local, A-Z
New Zealand
112 General
113.A-Z Local, A-Z
115.A-Z Pacific islands, A-Z
117 Almanacs
118 Congresses
119 Voyages, etc.
Collections
121 Works of several authors
123 Collected writings of individual authors
126 Dictionaries and encyclopedias
Directories
126.5 General works

Directories -- Continued
By region or country
United States
126.6 General works
126.65.A-Z By region or state, A-Z
126.7.A-Z Other regions or countries, A-Z
Biography
127 Collected
129.A-Z Individual, A-Z
History of forestry. Forest conditions
131 General works
By region or country
America
139 General works
North America
140 General works
United States
143 General works
144.A-.W By region or state, A-W
e.g.
144.A112 East
144.A115 Lake States
144.A117 Middle West
144.A12 New England
144.A128 Northwestern States
144.A13 Pacific Northwest
144.A14 Rocky Mountains
144.A15 South
144.A17 Tennessee Valley
144.A18 West
145-245 Other countries (Table S2)
Add number in the table to SD144
246 Northern Hemisphere
247 Tropics
247.5 Developing countries
Communication in forestry
248.5 General works
248.7 Information services
248.8 Computer network resources
Including the Internet
Forestry education. Study and teaching
250 Periodicals. Societies. Serials
250.3 Collected works (nonserial)
250.4 Congresses
Directories
250.5 General works
250.53.A-Z By region or country, A-Z

Forestry education. Study and teaching -- Continued
251 General works
251.25 Outlines, syllabi, etc.
251.3 Addresses, essays, lecture
251.5 Audiovisual aids
By region or country
United States
252 General works
254.A-Z By region or state, A-Z
Under each state:
.x General works
.x2A-.x2Z Local, A-Z
.x3A-.x3Z Special schools or universities. By name, A-Z
Other regions or countries
America
North America
255-256 Canada (Table S4)
257-258 Mexico (Table S4)
259-260 Central America (Table S4)
261-262 West Indies (Table S4)
South America
Including Latin America in general
263 General works
265-266 Argentina (Table S4)
267-268 Bolivia (Table S4)
269-270 Brazil (Table S4)
271-272 Chile (Table S4)
273-274 Colombia (Table S4)
275-276 Ecuador (Table S4)
Guianas
277 General works
French Guiana
278.3 General works
278.4.A-Z Local, A-Z
278.45.A-Z Special schools or universities. By name, A-Z
Guyana. British Guiana
278.5 General works
278.6.A-Z Local, A-Z
278.65.A-Z Special schools or universities. By name, A-Z
Suriname. Dutch Guiana
278.7 General works
278.8.A-Z Local, A-Z
278.85.A-Z Special schools or universities. By name, A-Z
279-280 Paraguay (Table S4)
281-282 Peru (Table S4)
283-284 Uruguay (Table S4)

Forestry education. Study and teaching
By region or country
Other regions or countries
America
South America -- Continued
285-286 Venezuela (Table S4)
Atlantic Islands
286.5 General works
286.6.A-Z By island or group of islands, A-Z
Subarrange each by Table S5
Europe
287 General works
289-290 Great Britain. England (Table S4)
291-292 Wales (Table S4)
293-294 Scotland (Table S4)
Northern Ireland
294.5 General works
294.6.A-Z Local, A-Z
294.65.A-Z Special schools or universities. By name, A-Z
295-296 Ireland (Table S4)
297-298 Austria (Table S4)
299-300 Belgium (Table S4)
301-302 Denmark (Table S4)
303-304 France (Table S4)
305-306 Germany (Table S4)
307-308 Greece (Table S4)
309-310 Holland (Table S4)
311-312 Italy (Table S4)
313-314 Norway (Table S4)
315-316 Portugal (Table S4)
317-318 Russia. Soviet Union. Russia (Federation) (Table S4)
Cf. SD341+ Russia in Asia. Siberia
319-320 Spain (Table S4)
321-322 Sweden (Table S4)
323-324 Switzerland (Table S4)
325-326 Turkey (Table S4)
327.A-Z Other regions or countries, A-Z
Subarrange each by Table S5
Asia
329 General works
331-332 China (Table S4)
333-334 India (Table S4)
335-336 Japan (Table S4)
337-338 Iran (Table S4)
339-340 Philippines (Table S4)
341-342 Russia in Asia. Siberia (Table S4)
Central Asia

Forestry education. Study and teaching
By region or country
Other regions or countries
Asia
Central Asia -- Continued
342.5 General works
342.6.A-Z Local, A-Z
342.65.A-Z Special schools or universities. By name, A-Z
343-344 Turkey in Asia (Table S4)
345.A-Z Other regions or countries, A-Z
Subarrange each by Table S5
e.g.
345.T3-.T33 Taiwan (Table S5)
Africa
347 General works
349-350 Egypt (Table S4)
352.A-Z Other regions or countries, A-Z
Subarrange each by Table S5
Indian Ocean islands
352.5 General works
352.6.A-Z By island or group of islands, A-Z
Subarrange each by Table S5
353-354 Australia (Table S4)
354.2 New Zealand
Pacific Area
354.8 General works
Pacific islands. Oceania
354.9 General works
355.A-Z By island or group of islands, A-Z
Subarrange each by Table S5
355.5 Developing countries
Forestry extension
355.7 General works
355.73.A-Z By region or country, A-Z
Research. Experimentation
Including experiment stations and research institutions
356 Periodicals. Societies. Serials
356.2 Collected works (nonserial)
356.3 Congresses
Directories see SD250.5+
356.4 General works
356.43 Addresses, essays, lectures
356.48.A-Z International institutions. By name, A-Z
By region or country
United States
356.5 General works

Forestry education. Study and teaching
Research. Experimentation
By region or country
United States -- Continued

356.52.A-Z By region or state, A-Z

Under each state:

.x	*General works*
.x2A-.x2Z	*Individual institutions. By name, A-Z*

356.54.A-Z Other regions or countries, A-Z

Under each country:

.x	*General works*
.x2A-.x2Z	*Individual institutions. By name, A-Z*

356.6.A-Z Special topics, A-Z
356.6.E94 Experiments
356.6.M35 Management
356.6.P75 Provenance trials

For particular trees see SD397.A+

Laboratories
356.7 General works
356.72.A-Z By region or country, A-Z

Under each country:

.x	*General works*
.x2A-.x2Z	*Individual laboratories. By name, A-Z*

Museums
357.A1 General works
357.A2-Z By region or country, A-Z

Under each country:

.x	*General works*
.x2A-.x2Z	*Individual museums. By name, A-Z*

Exhibitions, etc.
358.A1 General works
358.A2-Z By region or country, A-Z

Under each country:

.x	*General works*
.x2A-.x2Z	*Individual exhibitions. By name, A-Z*

Experimental forests and areas
358.5 General works
By region or country
United States
358.7 General works
358.8.A-Z By region or state, A-Z

Class individual experimental forests, except federal forests, with the state

For individual federal experimental forests see SD359.A+

359.A-Z Individual federal experimental forests, A-Z

Forestry education. Study and teaching
Experimental forests and areas
By region or country -- Continued
360.A-Z Other regions or countries, A-Z
361 Miscellaneous
Arbor day. Forest week
363 General works
By region or country
United States see SD363
363.3.A-Z Other regions or countries, A-Z
373 General works
375 Popular works
376 Juvenile works
381 Addresses, essays, lectures
381.5 Data processing
Description of remarkable trees, individual and collective
For historic trees, see class D
For folklore of trees see GR785
Cf. QK474.8+ Botany
383 General works
383.3.A-Z By region or country, A-Z
385 Popular description of forest trees
387.A-Z Special aspects of forestry, A-Z
387.A25 Aerial photography
387.A3 Aeronautics
Cf. SD421.43+ Aeronautics in forest fire control
387.A66 Appropriate technology
387.B48 Biomass
For local see SD139+
For particular trees see SD397.A+
387.B53 Biometrics
387.B55 Biotechnology
Boreal forestry see SD387.T34
387.C37 Carbon sequestration
387.C47 Citizen participation
387.C58 Clearcutting
387.C63 Coarse woody debris
387.C66 Consultants
387.C67 Continuous cover forestry
387.C68 Coppice forests
387.C69 Cover crops
Data processing see SD381.5
387.D43 Decision making
387.D6 Documentation. Literature
387.E33 Efficiency, Forestry
387.E58 Environmental aspects of forestry
Cf. TD428.F67 Water pollution

Special aspects of forestry, A-Z -- Continued

387.E78 Ethical aspects. Professional ethics

387.E85 Exotic forests and forestry
For local see SD139+
For particular trees see SD397.A+

387.F36 Fast growing trees
For local see SD139+
For particular trees see SD397.A+

387.F52 Fire management
Including prescribed burning for forest management
Cf. SD420.5+ Forest fires

(387.F55) Floodplain forestry
see SD410.5

387.F58 Forecasting

387.F59 Forest canopies

387.F594 Forest litter
For local see SD139+

387.F6 Forestry as a profession

387.G73 Grazing

(387.I54) Information services
see SD248.7

387.I57 Innovations

387.L3 Labor productivity

387.L33 Landowners

387.L35 Landscape management
Cf. SB475.9.F67 Forest landscape design

Literature see SD387.D6

387.M3 Mapping

387.M33 Mathematics
Including mathematical models
Cf. SD387.S73 Statistical methods

387.M8 Multiple use
Cf. SD427.M8 Forest reserves (U.S.)

387.O43 Old growth forests
Including old growth forest conservation
For local see SD139+

387.P5 Plastics

387.P69 Private forests
For local see SD139+

Professional ethics see SD387.E78

387.P74 Projects
For works limited to specific government projects see SD561+

387.P8 Public health

Recreational use see GV191.67.F6

387.R4 Remote sensing

Special aspects of forestry, A-Z -- Continued
387.S3 Safety measures
Cf. SD421.4 Forest fires
387.S52 Short rotation forestry
387.S53 Site quality and classification
For local see SD139+
For particular trees see SD397.A+
387.S545 Snags
387.S55 Social aspects
387.S69 Standards
For local, see SD139+
387.S73 Statistical methods
387.S75 Statistical services
387.S86 Surveys
Class here works on surveying methods
For works on the results of surveying see SD11+
387.S87 Sustainable forestry
For local see SD139+
For particular trees see SD397.A+
387.S94 Symbolic aspects
387.T34 Taigas. Boreal forestry
For local see SD139+
387.T5 Time study
387.T74 Tree climbing
Cf. SB435.85 Arboriculture
387.V6 Volunteer workers
387.W57 Women in forestry
387.W6 Woodlots
388 Forestry machinery and engineering
Including logging machinery
388.5 Tools and implements
Including instruments, meters, etc.
389 Forest roads
Cf. TE229.5 Engineering
Forest soils
390 General works
390.3.A-Z By region or country, A-Z
Soil erosion and conservation
390.4 General works
390.43.A-Z By region or country, A-Z
Forest meteorology. Forest microclimatology
Cf. SD421.37 Fire weather
Cf. SD425 Forests and floods
390.5 General works
390.6.A-Z By region or country, A-Z
390.7.A-Z Special topics, A-Z
Atmospheric greenhouse effect see SD390.7.G73

Forest meteorology. Forest microclimatology
Special topics, A-Z -- Continued
Atmospheric ozone see SD390.7.O95
390.7.C55 Climatic changes
390.7.G73 Greenhouse effect, Atmospheric
390.7.O95 Ozone, Atmospheric
390.7.R34 Rain and rainfall
390.7.S56 Snow
390.7.S65 Solar radiation
390.7.S85 Storms
390.7.T44 Temperature
390.7.W56 Wind
Sylviculture
391 General and popular works
392 Sylvicultural systems
393 Economic aspects. Finance. Cost of growing timber
Including forestry investment
For local see SD139+
For particular trees see SD397.A+
Cf. SD430+ Forest exploitation and utilization
Natural history of forest trees
395 General works
396 Growth
396.5 Thinning
397.A-Z Description, value, and culture of individual species or groups, A-Z
Cf. QK495.A1+ Botany
397.A18 Abies alba
397.A185 Abies concolor
397.A186 Abies densa
397.A2 Acacia
397.A22 Acacia decurrens
397.A25 Acacia mearnsii
397.A253 Acacia melanoxylon
397.A26 Acacia nilotica
397.A28 African blackwood
397.A32 Agathis
397.A33 Agathis alba
397.A38 Albizia
397.A382 Albizia amara
(397.A385) Albizia falcataria
see SD397.F34
397.A4 Alder
397.A44 Alnus glutinosa
397.A48 American chestnut
397.A483 American holly
397.A485 American linden

Sylviculture
Natural history of forest trees
Description, value, and culture of individual species or groups, A-Z -- Continued

397.A488 American sycamore
397.A5 Amur cork tree
397.A53 Andira inermis
397.A54 Annamocarya sinensis
397.A56 Araucaria
397.A58 Arizona cypress
397.A6 Ash
397.A7 Aspen
397.A76 Atlantic white cedar
397.A82 Aucomea klaineana
397.B17 Bael
397.B19 Baldcypress
397.B2 Balsam fir
397.B23 Balsam poplar
Bamboo see SB317.B2
397.B4 Beech
Beech, European see SD397.E83
(397.B45) Betula pendula
see SD397.E845
397.B5 Birch
397.B514 Black cherry
397.B516 Black locust
397.B52 Black poplar
Cf. SD397.H93 Hybrid black poplar
397.B53 Black spruce
Black walnut see SD397.W2
397.B54 Black willow
397.B56 Borneo ironwood
397.B58 Bornmueller fir
397.B6 Boxwood
397.B67 Brazilian firetree
397.B7 Brazilian pine
397.B88 Butternut
397.C3 Caesalpinia
397.C33 California black oak
397.C333 Calliandra calothyrsus
397.C335 Calocedrus formosana
397.C337 Candlenut tree
397.C339 Caragana arborescens
397.C34 Cassia
397.C344 Casuarina
397.C35 Catalpa
397.C37 Cathaya argyrophylla

Sylviculture
Natural history of forest trees
Description, value, and culture of individual species or groups, A-Z -- Continued

397.C38 Caucasian fir
397.C4 Cedar
397.C434 Cedar of Lebanon
397.C442 Chamaecyparis
397.C445 Chamaecyparis formosensis
397.C446 Chamaecyparis nootkatensis
397.C447 Chamaecyparis obtusa
397.C45 Chamaecyparis thyoides
397.C47 Chaparral
397.C5 Chestnut
397.C52 China fir
397.C524 Chinese white poplar
397.C53 Chorisia speciosa
397.C56 Cilician fir
397.C57 Cinchona
Coast redwood see SD397.R3
397.C6 Cocobolo
397.C66 Colorado spruce
397.C7 Conifers
397.C77 Cordia goeldiana
397.C79 Cork oak. Cork tree
Cork tree see SD397.C79
397.C8 Cottonwood
397.C86 Cryptomeria japonica
397.C87 Cunninghamia konoshii
397.C872 Cupressaceae
397.C9 Cypress
397.D24 Dactylocladus stenostachys
397.D3 Dahurian larch
397.D33 Dalbergia latifolia
397.D34 Dalbergia sissoo
397.D37 Dawn redwood
397.D48 Diospyros
397.D5 Dipterocarpaceae
397.D65 Dogwood
397.D7 Douglas fir
397.D72 Downy birch
397.D76 Drimys winteri
397.D87 Durmast oak
Eastern black walnut see SD397.W2
397.E27 Eastern hemlock
397.E29 Eastern redcedar
397.E42 Elm

Sylviculture
Natural history of forest trees
Description, value, and culture of individual species or groups, A-Z -- Continued

397.E46 Emory oak
397.E5 Engelmann spruce
397.E54 English oak
397.E58 Enterolobium cyclocarpum
397.E8 Eucalyptus
397.E814 Eucalyptus camaldulensis
(397.E815) Eucalyptus diversicolor
see SD397.K27
397.E818 Eucalyptus globulus
397.E82 Eucalyptus grandis
(397.E823) Eucalyptus marginata
see SD397.J36
397.E824 Eucalyptus regnans
397.E825 Eucalyptus saligna
397.E827 European ash
397.E828 European aspen
397.E83 European beech
397.E834 European hornbeam
397.E836 European larch
397.E84 European Turkey oak
397.E845 European white birch
397.E85 Evergreens
397.F34 Falcataria moluccana
397.F5 Fir
397.G52 Giant sequoia
397.G55 Gliricidia maculata
397.G56 Gmelina arborea
397.G58 Gonystylus bancanus
397.G6 Gossweilerodendron balsamiferum
397.G7 Grass tree
397.G72 Greek fir
397.G73 Greek juniper
Guaiacum see SD397.L5
397.G97 Gyrinops ledermannii
397.H24 Hackberry
397.H3 Hardwoods
Hemlock, Western see SD397.W45
Hemlocks see SD397.T78
397.H54 Hevea
397.H57 Hiba arborvitae
397.H6 Hickory
397.H67 Honduras mahogany
397.H93 Hybrid black poplar

Sylviculture
Natural history of forest trees
Description, value, and culture of individual species or groups, A-Z -- Continued

	Ilomba see SD397.P9
397.I53	Incense cedar
	Ipil see SD397.L4
397.J34	Japanese larch
397.J36	Jarrah
397.J8	Juniperus
397.K27	Karri
397.K3	Kauri
397.K43	Khaya anthotheca
397.K53	Knema attenuata
397.L25	Lafoensia glyptocarpa
397.L3	Larches
397.L35	Lead tree Cf. SB317.L4 Multipurpose plant
397.L4	Leucaena glauca
397.L46	Libocedrus
397.L47	Libocedrus bidwillii
397.L48	Licania rigida
397.L5	Lignum vitaes. Guaiacum
397.L6	Lindens
397.L63	Liriodendron tulipifera
397.L64	Live oak
397.L65	Locust
397.M16	Maesopsis eminii
397.M18	Magnolias
397.M2	Mahogany
397.M23	Mangium
397.M24	Manglietia glauca
397.M25	Mangrove
397.M26	Manilkara kauki
397.M3	Maple
	Maple, Sugar see SD397.S775
397.M4	Mesquite
	Metasequoia glyptostroboides see SD397.D37
397.M64	Montanoa
397.M65	Mopane
397.M66	Mora
397.M84	Mulanje cedar
397.N6	Norway spruce
397.N64	Nothofagus
397.N65	Nothofagus procera
397.N66	Nothofagus pumilio
397.O12	Oak

Sylviculture
Natural history of forest trees
Description, value, and culture of individual species or groups, A-Z -- Continued

397.O36 Ocotea rodiaei
397.O74 Oriental spruce
397.O8 Osage orange
397.O82 Osier
397.P28 Paper birch
397.P29 Parkia nitida
397.P3 Paulownia
397.P318 Paulownia kawakamii
397.P319 Paulownia tomentosa
397.P4 Pecan
397.P47 Persimmon
397.P53 Picea jezoensis
397.P54 Picea schrenkiana
Pine
397.P55 General
397.P562 Aleppo pine
397.P564 Austrian pine
Including Corsican pine
397.P565 Balkan pine
397.P568 Pinus brutia
397.P57 Pinus canariensis
397.P572 Pinus caribaea
397.P5723 Chir pine
397.P573 Cluster pine
Corsican pine see SD397.P564
397.P574 Pinus eldarica
397.P5745 Pinus griffithii
Italian stone pine see SD397.P61124
397.P575 Jack pine
397.P576 Pinus kesiya
397.P578 Pinus koraiensis
397.P58 Loblolly pine
397.P585 Lodgepole pine
397.P59 Longleaf pine
397.P597 Pinus merkusii
397.P598 Montezuma pine
Pinus nigra see SD397.P564
397.P61115 Pinus oocarpa
397.P6112 Pinus patula
397.P61124 Pinus pinea. Italian stone pine
397.P6114 Pinyon pines
397.P6115 Ponderosa pine
397.P6117 Pinus radiata

Sylviculture
Natural history of forest trees
Description, value, and culture of individual species or groups, A-Z
Pine -- Continued

397.P612 Red pine
397.P614 Scots pine
397.P615 Scrub pine
397.P617 Shortleaf pine
397.P619 Pinus sibirica
397.P623 Slash pine
397.P63 Sugar pine
397.P64 Swiss pine
397.P644 Pinus taiwanensis
397.P647 Western white pine
397.P65 White pine
397.P75 Yellow pines
397.P77 Piptadenia communis
397.P8 Plane tree
397.P835 Podocarpus
397.P838 Podocarpus imbricata
397.P85 Poplar
397.P853 Populus alba
397.P855 Populus tremuloides
397.P87 Port Orford cedar
397.P88 Prosopis juliflora
Cf. SB317.P76 Multipurpose plant
Cf. SB615.P83 Weed
397.P9 Pycnanthus angolensis
397.P97 Pyrenean oak
397.Q3 Quebracho
397.Q35 Quercus frainetto
397.R15 Ramin
397.R16 Rasamala
397.R18 Red alder
(397.R2) Red gum
see SD397.S78
397.R25 Red oak
397.R3 Redwoods
Including coast redwood
Cf. SD397.D37
Cf. SD397.G52
397.R49 Rhizophora
397.R5 Rhizophoraceae
397.R54 Rhododendrons
397.R62 Robinia
397.S16 Sacred fir

Sylviculture
Natural history of forest trees
Description, value, and culture of individual species or groups, A-Z -- Continued

397.S2	Saksaul
397.S22	Salix alba
397.S23	Salix tetrasperma
397.S24	Sandalwood
397.S26	Santalum spicatum
	Sequoia sempervirens see SD397.R3
397.S48	Shorea
397.S5	Shorea robusta
397.S513	Siberian fir
397.S515	Siberian larch
	Silver fir see SD397.A18
397.S52	Simal
397.S56	Sitka spruce
397.S6	Sorbus
397.S77	Spruce
397.S775	Sugar maple
397.S78	Sweetgum
397.S8	Sycamore
397.S98	Syzygium cordatum
397.T34	Taiwania cryptomerioides
397.T35	Tamarack
397.T4	Teak
397.T45	Terminalia ivorensis
397.T47	Terminalia superba
397.T5	Thuja
397.T53	Thuja occidentalis
397.T66	Totara
397.T78	Tsuga
	Tsuga canadensis see SD397.E27
	Tulip tree see SD397.L63
397.T87	Tupelo
397.V27	Valley oak
397.V3	Valonia oak
397.V57	Virola surinamensis
397.W2	Black walnut
397.W45	Western hemlock
397.W454	Western larch
397.W46	Western redcedar
397.W47	White spruce
397.W48	Whitebark pine
397.W5	Willow
397.Y44	Yellow birch
397.Y442	Yellow buckeye

Sylviculture
Natural history of forest trees
Description, value, and culture of individual species or groups, A-Z -- Continued

397.Y46 Yew
397.Z35 Zambezi teak

Forest nurseries
Cf. SD401+ Sylviculture methods

397.7 Periodicals. Societies. Serials
397.73 Collected works (nonserial)
397.75 Congresses
398 General works

By region or country
United States

398.4 General works
398.42.A-Z By region or state, A-Z
398.43.A-Z Other regions or countries, A-Z
399 Tree introduction
For special areas see SD131+
For special trees see SD397.A+
Cf. SB109 Plant introduction
Cf. SB435.65 Ornamental trees
Cf. SD387.E85 Exotic forests and forestry

399.5 Tree breeding and selection. Forest genetics
399.7 Forest genetic resources conservation

Methods

401 General works

Seeds

401.5 General works

Seed growing. Seed orchards

401.6 General works
401.64.A-Z By region or country, A-Z
401.7 Inspection, certification, grading, and testing

Handling and postharvest technology

401.8 General works
402 Harvesting and collecting
402.3 Cleaning
402.35 Drying
402.4 Preservation. Protection
402.45 Storage

Propagation

403 General works

Clonal forestry

403.4 General works
403.5 Cell and tissue culture

Seedlings

404 General works

Sylviculture
Methods
Propagation
Seedlings -- Continued
404.25 Bareroot seedlings
404.3 Container seedlings
405 Transplanting
405.4 Protection of seedlings
406 Tree repairing
Cf. SB435.8 Ornamental trees
407 Pruning
408 Use of fertilizers
Including sewage sludge disposal
For individual forest trees see SD397.A+
Irrigation
408.15 General works
408.154.A-Z By region or country, A-Z
408.2 Drainage
Afforestation and reforestation
Cf. SD387.E85 Exotic forests and forestry
Cf. SD410.3+ Methods for special areas
409 General works
409.5 Windbreaks, shelterbelts, etc.
Cf. SB437 Horticulture
Methods for special areas
410.3 Arid regions
Including desertification control
Cold regions
410.38 General works
410.4 Frozen ground
410.5 Floodplains
410.7 Peatlands
410.9 Wetlands
Conservation and protection
Cf. SB599+ Plant pests and diseases
Cf. SD387.O43 Old growth forest conservation
Cf. SD399.7 Forest genetic resources conservation
411 General works
Biography
411.5 Collective
411.52.A-Z Individual, A-Z
By region or country
United States
412 General works
413.A-Z By region or state, A-Z
414.A-Z Other regions or countries, A-Z

Conservation and protection -- Continued
Forest influences
Cf. GF54.5 Human ecology
Cf. QH541.5.F6 Forest ecology
Cf. SD390.5+ Forests and climate
Cf. SD425 Forests and floods
416 General works
416.3.A-Z By region or country, A-Z
Deforestation
Including control
Cf. SD411+ Forest conservation
Cf. SD537.5+ Logging
418 General works
418.3.A-Z By region or country, A-Z
Damage by elements
419 General works
Forest fires and wildfires
Cf. QH545.F5 Fire ecology
Cf. SD387.F52 Fire management
420.5 Periodicals. Societies. Serials
420.55 Collected works (nonserial)
420.6 Congresses
420.67 Dictionaries. Encyclopedias. Terminology
Study and teaching. Research
420.7 General works
420.73.A-Z By region or country, A-Z
421 General works
421.23 Juvenile works
421.233 Addresses, essays, lectures
Biography
421.24 Collective
421.25.A-Z Individual, A-Z
By region or country
United States
421.3 General works
421.32.A-Z By region or state, A-Z
421.34.A-Z Other regions or countries, A-Z
Forecasting
421.36 General works
421.37 Fire weather
Cf. SD390.5+ Forest meteorology
421.375 Detection
421.38 Equipment and supplies
Including chemical retardants
For aeronautical equipment see SD421.43+
421.4 Safety measures
Aeronautics

Conservation and protection
Damage by elements
Forest fires and wildfires
Aeronautics -- Continued
421.43 General works
421.435 Smokejumping
421.45.A-Z Other special topics, A-Z
421.45.D37 Data processing
421.45.E25 Economic aspects
421.45.I58 Investigation
421.45.M37 Mathematical models
421.45.V64 Volunteer workers
Ground cover fires
421.47 General works
421.5 Grassland fires
424 Earth movements. Landslides
Forest soil erosion see SD390.4+
Storms see SD390.7.S85
425 Floods, forests and water supply
Cf. GB842 Forest hydrology
Cf. GB843 Karst hydrology
Cf. GB1201+ Floods
Forest reserves
United States
General
Documents
426.A1-.A3 Collections
426.A5 Separate. By date
Including rules, etc.
426.A6-Z General works
427.A-Z Special subjects, A-Z
427.C5 Claims
427.C53 Clearcutting
427.E35 Economic aspects
427.G8 Grazing
427.H7 Homesteads
427.L3 Land exchange
427.M8 Multiple use
Recreational use see GV191.67.F6
427.R35 Ranger stations
427.T5 Timber
427.T7 Trespass
427.W3 Water resources
428.A2A-.A2Z By region or state, A-Z
Class individual reserves, except national forests, with the state
For national forests see SD428.A3+

Conservation and protection
Forest reserves
United States -- Continued
428.A3-Z Individual national forests, A-Z
Other countries see SD567+
Exploitation and utilization
Cf. SD388 Forestry machinery and engineering
Cf. TS800+ Technology
430 Periodicals. Societies. Serials
431 General works
431.5 Working plans
432 Companies for exploitation. Cooperatives
433 Testing, technology, laboratories, including timbers (from producers' standpoint)
Cf. SD356.7+ Forestry laboratories
Cf. TA420 Strength of materials
Timber trees
434 General
For special trees see SD397.A+
By region or country
United States
435 General works
436.A-Z By region or state, A-Z
Other regions or countries
America
North America
437-438 Canada (Table S3)
439-440 Mexico (Table S3)
441-442 Central America (Table S3)
443-444 West Indies (Table S3)
South America
Including Latin America in general
445 General works
447-448 Argentina (Table S3)
449-450 Bolivia (Table S3)
451-452 Brazil (Table S3)
453-454 Chile (Table S3)
455-456 Colombia (Table S3)
457-458 Ecuador (Table S3)
Guianas
459 General works
460.3-.4 French Guiana (Table S3)
460.5-.6 Guyana. British Guiana (Table S3)
460.7-.8 Suriname. Dutch Guiana (Table S3)
461-462 Paraguay (Table S3)
463-464 Peru (Table S3)
465-466 Uruguay (Table S3)

Exploitation and utilization
Timber trees
By region or country
Other regions or countries
America
South America -- Continued

467-468 Venezuela (Table S3)
Atlantic islands
468.5 General works
468.6.A-Z By island or group of islands, A-Z
Europe
469 General works
471-472 Great Britain. England (Table S3)
473-474 Wales (Table S3)
475-476 Scotland (Table S3)
476.5-.6 Northern Ireland (Table S3)
477-478 Ireland (Table S3)
479-480 Austria (Table S3)
481-482 Belgium (Table S3)
483-484 Denmark (Table S3)
485-486 France (Table S3)
487-488 Germany (Table S3)
489-490 Greece (Table S3)
491-492 Holland (Table S3)
493-494 Italy (Table S3)
495-496 Norway (Table S3)
497-498 Portugal (Table S3)
499-500 Russia. Soviet Union. Russia (Federation) (Table S3)
Cf. SD523+ Russia in Asia. Siberia
501-502 Spain (Table S3)
503-504 Sweden (Table S3)
505-506 Switzerland (Table S3)
507-508 Turkey (Table S3)
509.A-Z Other regions or countries, A-Z
Asia
511 General works
513-514 China (Table S3)
515-516 India (Table S3)
517-518 Japan (Table S3)
519-520 Iran (Table S3)
521-522 Philippines (Table S3)
523-524 Russia in Asia. Siberia (Table S3)
524.5-.6 Central Asia (Table S3)
525-526 Turkey in Asia (Table S3)
527.A-Z Other regions or countries, A-Z
e.g.
527.T3 Taiwan

Exploitation and utilization
Timber trees
By region or country
Other regions or countries -- Continued
Africa
528 General works
531.A-Z By region or country, A-Z
Australia
533 General works
534.A-Z By state or territory, A-Z
534.2 New Zealand and adjacent islands
534.5.A-Z Atlantic islands, A-Z
535.A-Z Pacific islands, A-Z
535.3 Tropics
535.7 Wood quality and variation
For particular trees see SD397.A+
536 Sections of woods and descriptive text
Lumber inspection see TS825
Pulpwood crops
For particular trees see SD397.A+
536.3 General works
536.35.A-Z By region or country, A-Z
Fuelwood crops. Fuelwood
Including gathering and cutting
For particular trees see SD397.A+
Cf. HD9769.F84+ Industry
Cf. SB288+ Energy crops
Cf. TP324 Fuel
536.5 General works
536.6.A-Z By region or country, A-Z
Logging
Cf. SD387.C58 Clearcutting
Cf. SD388 Forestry machinery
Cf. TJ1350+ Hoisting and conveying machinery
Biography
537.5 Collective
537.52.A-Z Individual, A-Z
538 General works
By region or country
United States
538.2.A1 General works
538.2.A2-Z By region or state, A-Z
538.3.A-Z Other regions or countries, A-Z
Log brands
538.8 General works
538.83.A-Z By region or country, A-Z

Exploitation and utilization -- Continued
Transportation
Cf. TF678 Logging railways
539 General works
Aerial methods. Aeronautics
539.5 General works
539.53 Balloon
539.57 Skyline
Trucking
539.8 General works
539.83.A-Z By region or country, A-Z
By water. Log driving. Booms. Rafting
540 General works
540.3.A-Z By region or country, A-Z
541 Utilization
Non-timber forest resources. By-products
Cf. TP996.W6 Wood waste
543 General works
543.3.A-Z By region or country, A-Z
543.4 Bark
543.5 Mast (Nuts)
Slash
544 General works
544.3 Slashburning
547 Turpentine orcharding
Valuation, measurement, etc.
551 General
553 Accretion and yield
Measurement. Scaling
555 General works
557 Tables, etc.
Cf. HF5716.L8 Tables of cost, quantity, weight, etc., of lumber
(559) Assessment and taxation
see HJ4167 etc.
Administration. Policy
For serial documents see SD11+
561 General works
By country
Class here only monographs
For serials see SD11+
United States
565 General and Federal
566.A-.W States, A-W
567-667 Other countries (Table S2)
Add number in the table to SD566
669 Tropics

Administration. Policy
By country -- Continued
669.5 Developing countries

Animal culture
Cf. HD9410+ Animal industry (Economic aspects)
Cf. HG9968.6 Livestock insurance
Cf. HV4701+ Humane and inhumane treatment of animals
Cf. QL1+ Zoology
Cf. SF84+ Economic zoology
Cf. SF409 Small animals
Cf. SF411+ Pets
Cf. TS1950+ Animal products
Periodicals. Societies. Serials
Cf. SF191, SF221, etc.
For associations under state auspices see SF17
1.A1 History, organization, etc.
1.A2-Z General
5 Congresses
Documents
Class here serial documents
For documents of a monographic character see SF41+
United States
11 Federal
13.A-.W States, A-W
15.A-Z Other countries, A-Z
17 Associations under state auspices
(19) Yearbooks
see SF1.A1+
21 Dictionaries. Encyclopedias
21.5 Names
Communication in animal culture
22 General works
22.5 Animal culture literature
Directories
23 General
By region or country
United States
25 General works
26.A-Z By region or state, A-Z
27.A-Z Other regions or countries, A-Z
Biography
31 Collective
33.A-Z Individual, A-Z
History and conditions
Cf. GN799.A4 Origin and prehistory of domestic animals
41 General works
By region or country
51 United States (including separate states and sections)
53 Great Britain
55.A-Z Other regions or countries, A-Z

Relation of animal culture to plant culture see S602.5+
61 Comprehensive works. Textbooks
Including general care of livestock
Handbooks, manuals, etc. Practical works
American (United States)
63 Through 1840
65 1841-1975
65.2 1976-
67.A-Z By region or state, A-Z
English
69 To 1785
71 1786-1975
71.2 1976-
Other regions or countries
74 Through 1800
75 1801-1975
1976-
75.2 General works
75.3.A-Z By region or country, A-Z
75.5 Juvenile works
76 Pictorial works
76.5 Light literature
76.6 Addresses, essays, lectures
77 Miscellaneous
(78) Draft animals
see SF180
80 Vocational guidance
Study and teaching. Research
81 General works
81.5 Audiovisual aids
82.5.A-Z International institutions. By name, A-Z
83.A-Z By region or country, A-Z
Under each country:

.x	*General works*
.x2A-.x2Z	*Local, A-Z*
.x3A-.x3Z	*Individual institutions. By name, A-Z*

Exhibitions see SF114+
Economic zoology
Cf. QL1+ Zoology
Cf. QL99 Medical zoology
Cf. RA639+ Animals as carriers of disease
Cf. SB992+ Animals injurious and beneficial to plants
Cf. SF810.5+ Predator control
84 Periodicals. Societies. Serials
84.23 Collected works (nonserial)
84.25 Congresses
84.27 Dictionaries. Encyclopedias

Economic zoology -- Continued

84.3 General works

84.33 Juvenile works

84.35 Pictorial works

84.37 Addresses, essays, lectures

By region or country

United States

84.4 General works

84.43.A-Z By region or state, A-Z

84.45.A-Z Other regions or countries, A-Z

Wildlife resources. Wildlife utilization

Cf. QL81.5+ Wildlife conservation

Cf. SK351+ Wildlife management

Cf. SK590+ Wild animal trade

84.6 General works

84.64.A-Z By region or country, A-Z

Rangelands. Range management. Grazing

For forage plants on ranges see SB193+

For grazing in forests see SD427.G8

84.82 Periodicals. Societies. Serials

84.84 Congresses

Study and teaching. Research

Including experimental ranges

84.86 General works

84.865.A-Z By region or country, A-Z

85 General works

By region or country

United States

85.3 General works

85.35.A-Z By region or state, A-Z

85.4.A-Z Other regions or countries, A-Z

85.43 Developing countries

85.6.A-Z Special topics, A-Z

85.6.B56 Biodiversity

85.6.D43 Decision making

Including decision support systems

85.6.E82 Evaluation

85.6.F57 Fire management. Prescribed burning

85.6.M36 Mapping

85.6.P56 Photography

Prescribed burning see SF85.6.F57

85.6.R45 Remote sensing

Reseeding see SF85.6.R49

85.6.R49 Revegetation. Reseeding

85.6.W38 Water supply

Weed control see SB610+

87 Acclimatization
Cf. SF140.C57 Climatic factors
88 Handling
89 Transportation
91 Housing and environmental control
For housing of particular animals, see the animal
Cf. NA8230 Architecture
Cf. TH4930 Construction
92 Equipment and supplies
Including catalogs
Behavior see SF756.7
Feeds and feeding. Animal nutrition
For feeding of particular animals, see the animal
Cf. SF854+ Deficiency diseases
94.5 Periodicals. Societies. Serials
94.55 Collected works (nonserial)
94.6 Congresses
94.65 Dictionaries. Encyclopedias
95 General works
By region or country
United States
95.3 General works
95.35.A-Z By region or state, A-Z
95.4.A-Z Other regions or countries, A-Z
97 Analyses and experiments (General)
Including tables
97.5 Radioisotopes in animal nutrition
97.7 Flavor and odor
97.8 Contamination
98.A-Z Individual feed constituents, components, and feed additives, A-Z
98.A2 Additives (General)
98.A34 Adrenergic beta agonists
98.A38 Amino acid chelates
98.A4 Amino acids
98.A44 Ammonia
98.A5 Antibiotics
98.A9 Azelaic acid
98.C37 Carbohydrates
98.C45 Chromium
Drugs see SF98.M4
98.E58 Enzymes
Fats and oils see SF98.O34
98.F53 Fiber
98.H67 Hormones
98.L54 Lignocellulose
98.L9 Lysine

Feeds and feeding. Animal nutrition
Individual feed constituents, components, and feed additives, A-Z -- Continued

98.M4 Medication
98.M5 Minerals
98.N5 Nitrogen
98.O34 Oils and fats
98.P44 Perchlorates
98.P46 Pesticide residues
98.P5 Phosphorus
98.P64 Polyacrylamide
98.P7 Proteins
98.S2 Salt
98.S4 Selenium
98.S65 Somatotropin
98.T7 Trace elements
98.U7 Urea
98.V5 Vitamins
99.A-Z Individual feeds and substances used as feeds, A-Z
99.A37 Agricultural wastes
99.A5 Alfalfa
Algae, Marine see SF99.M33
99.A54 Animal products
99.A55 Animal waste
99.A6 Apple
99.B25 Bagasse
99.B3 Barley
Broad bean see SF99.F3
99.C3 Cactus
99.C35 Canola meal
99.C37 Cassava
99.C45 Chlorella
99.C55 Clover
99.C57 Coconut palm
99.C58 Cod liver oil
99.C584 Coffee pulp
99.C59 Corn. Maize
99.C6 Cottonseed meal
99.C73 Crop residues
99.D5 Distillers feeds
99.F3 Fava bean
99.F37 Feathers
99.F5 Fishmeal
99.F55 Flaxseed
99.F64 Fodder trees
99.F67 Food waste
99.F8 Fungi

SF

Feeds and feeding. Animal nutrition
Individual feeds and substances used as feeds, A-Z -- Continued

99.G3 Garbage
Grain see SF94.5+
99.H4 Heather
99.L44 Legumes
99.L54 Lignocellulose
99.L58 Live food
Maize see SF99.C59
99.M33 Marine algae
99.M5 Milk
Milo see SF99.S68
99.M6 Molasses
99.M88 Mulberry
99.O28 Oats
99.O4 Oil cake
99.P4 Peanuts
99.P6 Potatoes
99.R5 Rice
99.R52 Rice bran
99.S68 Sorghum
99.S72 Soybean
Including soybean meal
99.S8 Straw
99.S9 Sugar beet
99.S93 Sugarcane
99.T5 Timothy grass
Trees, Fodder see SF99.F64
99.W34 Waste products
99.W35 Water hyacinth
99.W5 Wheat
99.Y4 Yeast

Brands and branding, and other means of identifying
Including cattle brands and earmarks
101 General works
103 Catalogs of brands (General)
For catalogs limited to specific places see SF103.3+
By region or country
United States
103.3 General works
103.4.A-Z By region or state, A-Z
103.5.A-Z Other regions or countries, A-Z

Breeding and breeds
For breeding of particular animals, see the animal
105 General works
105.25.A-SB105.25.Z By region or country, A-Z

Breeding and breeds -- Continued
105.26 Selection indexes
Rare breeds
105.27 General works
105.275.A-Z By region or country, A-Z
105.3 Germplasm
105.5 Artificial insemination
105.7 Ovum transplantation. Embryo transplantation
106 Catalogs of breeders of other than domestic animals. "Wild Beast Merchants"
107 Stock farm catalogs
Cf. SF217 Cattle farm catalogs
109.A-Z Description of individual stock farms, A-Z
Cost, yield, and profit. Accounting
111 General works
(112) Weight tables
see HF5716.C2 etc.
113 Catalogs of sales
113.3 Direct selling
Exhibitions
For works limited to special animals, see the animal, e.g. SF215+ Cattle
Museum exhibits
114.A1 General works
114.A2-Z By region or country, A-Z
Under each country:
.x *General works*
.x2A-.x2Z *Individual museums. By name, A-Z*
Stock shows
117 General works
117.3 Juvenile works
117.5.A-Z International. By place, A-Z
National, state, and local
United States
117.6 General works
117.65.A-Z By region or state, A-Z
Subarrange each state by Table S3a
117.7.A-Z Other countries, A-Z
Subarrange each country by Table S3a
118 Exhibiting and judging
121 Standards of excellence. Livestock champions (General)
140.A-Z Other special topics, A-Z
140.B54 Biotechnology
Captive wild animals see SF408+
140.C37 Carcasses
140.C57 Climatic factors
Cf. SF87 Acclimatization

Other special topics, A-Z -- Continued

140.D35 Data processing

Draft animals see SF180

140.E25 Ecology. Environmental aspects

For local see SF51+

140.E53 Energy consumption

Environmental aspects see SF140.E25

140.F47 Feral animals. Feral livestock

For works limited to special animals, see the animal, e.g. SF450 Feral cats

Cf. SB993.5+ Feral animals injurious and beneficial to plants

Fur-bearing animals see SF402+

140.G73 Greenhouse gases

Laboratory animals see SF405.5+

140.L58 Livestock factories

140.L59 Livestock projects

For local see SF51+

140.L63 Livestock services

For local see SF51+

140.L65 Livestock systems

Including urban livestock production systems

For local see SF51+

Cf. SF140.P38 Pastoral systems

140.M35 Mathematical models

140.M54 Minilivestock

140.P38 Pastoral systems

Including herding

For works limited to special animals, see the animal, e.g. SF401.R4 Reindeer

For local, see SF51+

Cf. S494.5.A47 Agropastoral systems

Pets see SF411+

Radioactive tracers see SF140.R33

140.R33 Radioisotopes. Radioactive tracers

140.S33 Safety measures

140.S55 Simulation methods

Small animal culture see SF409

140.S62 Social aspects

140.S72 Statistical methods

140.S73 Statistical services

140.W37 Water requirements

Zoo animals see SF408+

Working animals
Cf. GV1829+ Circus animals
Cf. HV8025 Animals in police work
Cf. PN1992.8.A58 Animals in television
Cf. PN1995.9.A5 Animals in motion pictures
Cf. UH87+ War use of animals
170 General works
172 Juvenile works
180 Draft animals
Cf. HE153 Transportation
Cf. SF209+ Draft cattle
Cf. SF311+ Draft horses
Cattle
Including cattle ranching
For anatomy see SF767.C3
For physiology see SF768.2.C3
191 Periodicals. Societies. Serials
191.2 Congresses
191.4 Dictionaries. Encyclopedias
191.43 Names
191.5 Breeders' directories
Brands and branding see SF101+
Herdbooks
192.A1-.A3 General
192.A4-Z By region or country, A-Z
By breeds see SF199.A+
Biography (of persons)
194 Collective
194.2.A-Z Individual, A-Z
History
195 General works
196.A-Z By region or country, A-Z
e.g.
196.C2 Canada
197 General works
Including general care of cattle
197.4 Essays and light literature
197.5 Juvenile works
197.7 Study and teaching. Research
197.8 Economic aspects of culture. Costs (General)
Breeds
Cf. SF207 Beef breeds (General)
Cf. SF208 Dairy breeds (General)
198 General works
199.A-Z By breed, A-Z
Cf. SF217 Catalogs
199.A14 Aberdeen-Angus

Cattle
Breeds
By breed, A-Z -- Continued

199.A3 Africander
199.A43 American Brahman
199.A48 Angeln
199.A85 Aubrac
199.A9 Ayrshire
199.B36 Barotse
199.B44 Belgian Blue
199.B56 Blonde d'Aguitaine
199.B67 Boran
199.B7 Brown Swiss
199.C34 Camargue
199.C5 Charolais
199.C54 Chiana
199.C55 Chiangus
199.C74 Criollo
199.D4 Dexter
199.E2 East Prussian
199.F5 Fighting bull
199.F54 Fleckvieh
199.F57 Florida cracker
199.F73 Friesian
199.G34 Galloway
199.G44 Gelbvieh
199.G5 Glan-Donnersberger
199.G62 Gobra zebu
199.G7 Graubundens
199.G74 Grey Tirolean
199.G8 Guernsey
199.H37 Hariana
199.H4 Hereford
199.H44 Hereford, Polled
199.H47 Hérens
199.H7 Holando-Argentino
199.H75 Holstein-Friesian
199.J5 Jersey
199.K45 Kenana
199.K47 Kholmogor
199.K9 Kuhland
199.L48 Limousin
199.L5 Lincoln Red
199.L6 Longhorn
Longhorn, Texas see SF199.T48
199.M38 Maure
199.M54 Milking Shorthorn

Cattle
Breeds
By breed, A-Z -- Continued

199.M57	Mithun
199.M87	Murray grey
199.N19	N'Dama
199.P6	Pinzgauer
199.P64	Polish red and white lowland
	Polled Hereford see SF199.H44
	Polled shorthorn see SF199.S563
199.P9	Prignitzer
199.R35	Red Danish
199.R4	Red-polled
199.S24	Sahiwal
199.S35	Senepol
199.S56	Shorthorn
	Shorthorn, Milking see SF199.M54
199.S563	Shorthorn, Polled
199.S58	Simbrah
199.S6	Simmental
199.S67	SMR
199.S83	Sudanese Fulani
199.T35	Tarentaise
199.T48	Texas longhorn
199.T53	Tharparkar
199.T85	Turino
199.W2	Waldecker
199.W44	Welsh Black
199.Z4	Zebus
	Breeding
201	General works
201.3	Germplasm resources
201.5	Artificial insemination
201.7	Ovum transplantation. Embryo transplantation
202	Miscellaneous
202.5	Behavior
202.7	Handling
	Feeding. Nutrition
	Including feeding for milk, etc.
203	General works
205	Calves, feeding and care
206	Housing and environmental control
	Cf. TH4930 Construction of barns
206.5	Heifers

SF

Cattle -- Continued
207 Beef cattle
Class here general works only
For special aspects and places, see SF195+
For individual breeds see SF199.A+
208 Dairy cattle
Class here general works only
For special aspects and places, see SF195+
For individual breeds see SF199.A+
Draft cattle
Class here general works only
For special aspects and places, see SF195+
For individual breeds see SF199.A+
209 General works
209.5 Ox driving
Cf. HE153 Transportation
211 Dual purpose cattle
Class here general works only
For special aspects and places, see SF195+
For individual breeds see SF199.A+
Water buffalo see SF401.W34
Zebu see SF199.Z4
Cattle shows
Cf. S550+ Agricultural exhibitions
Cf. SF117+ Stock shows
215 General works
215.2 Judging
217 Cattle farm catalogs
219 Cattle sale catalogs
Dairying
Cf. SF208 Dairy cattle
221 Periodicals. Societies. Serials
Including butter and cheese makers' associations
223 Congresses
Documents
United States
Cf. HD9000.9.A+ Government inspection
225.A1-.A5 Federal
225.A6-.W State
227.A-Z Other countries, A-Z
229 Dictionaries. Encyclopedias
Directories
229.5 General works
229.54.A-Z By region or country, A-Z
Biography
229.7.A1 Collective
229.7.A2-Z Individual, A-Z

Cattle
Dairying -- Continued
History
231 General works
By region or country
United States
232.A1 General works
232.A2-Z By region or state, A-Z
233.A-Z Other countries, A-Z
235 Statistics
237 Patents
Legislation
see class K
239 General works
239.5 Juvenile works
240 Miscellaneous (Tables, etc.)
240.7 Vocational guidance
Study and teaching. Research
241 General works
By region or country
United States
243 General works
243.5.A-Z By region or state, A-Z
Under each state:
.x General works
.x2A-.x2Z Local, A-Z
.x3A-.x3Z Special schools or institutions. By place, A-Z
245.A-Z Other regions or countries, A-Z
Under each country:
.x General works
.x2A-.x2Z Local, A-Z
.x3A-.x3Z Special schools or institutions. By place, A-Z
e.g.
India
245.I5 General works
245.I52H3 Haryana
245.I53K3 Karnal, India (City). National Dairy Research Institute
245.8 Economic aspects (General)
Cf. HD9278 Butter marketing
Cf. HD9282+ Milk marketing
246.A-Z Other special aspects of dairying, A-Z
246.C65 Cooperation. Cooperatives
246.D38 Data processing
246.E53 Energy consumption

Cattle
Dairying
Other special aspects of dairying, A-Z -- Continued
246.E55 Environmental aspects
246.H36 Handling of dairy products
246.O74 Organic dairy farming
246.Q3 Quality control
247 Machinery, tools, etc. Dairy engineering
Cf. SF263+ Churns
249 Other animals than cattle (General)
For special animals, see the subject
250 Milking
Cf. SF247 Milking machines
Dairy processing. Dairy products (General)
For special places see SF232.A1+
250.5 General works
Milk and cream
251 Composition, formation and properties
253 Chemistry, analysis and testing (including instruments)
Bacteriology see QR121
Contamination
254.A1 General works
254.A2-Z By contaminant
254.A35 Aflatoxins
254.A6 Antibiotics
254.C66 Copper
254.M93 Mycotoxins
254.P4 Pesticides
254.R3 Radioactive substances
254.V48 Veterinary drug residues
255 Adulteration and inspection
257 Milk hygiene
Cf. HD4501.M5+ Municipal milk supply
Cf. RA602.M54 Public health
Cf. SF254.A1+ Milk contamination
Cf. TX379 Food and nutrition
259 Preparation for use. Pasteurization, condensed milk, etc.
260 Creamery wastes. Filtration, etc.
261 Plant management
Cf. HD9282+ Milk industry
262 Trade publications (Milk dealers)
262.5 Miscellaneous uncataloged pamphlets
Butter
263 Manufacture, composition and properties
265 Chemistry, analysis and testing
Including instruments
266 Creameries

Cattle
Dairy processing. Dairy products (General)
Butter -- Continued
267 Adulteration and inspection
Margarine see TP684.M3
269 Preparation for market
Cf. HD9278 Butter industry
269.5.A-SB269.5.Z By region or country, A-Z
Cheese
Cf. HD9280+ Economic aspects
Cf. TX382 Food
Cf. TX759.5.C48 Cooking
270 Periodicals, societies, congresses, serial collections
270.2 Dictionaries. Encyclopedias
270.3 Directories
270.4 History (General)
271 General works
271.2 Analysis and composition
Microbiology see QR121
271.5 Cheese factories
271.7 Packaging
Cheeses of animals other than cattle
For specific varieties see SF272.A+
271.8 Camel
271.87 Goat
271.9 Sheep
272.A-Z Varieties, A-Z
272.B73 Brie
272.B76 Brined
272.C33 Camembert
272.C5 Cheddar
272.C6 Cottage cheese
272.E32 Edam
272.F47 Feta
272.M35 Manchego
272.M6 Montasio
272.P3 Parmesan
272.P4 Pecorino
272.R6 Roquefort
272.S75 Stilton
272.S9 Swiss cheese
272.W45 Wensleydale
272.5 Process cheese
273 Adulteration
274.A-Z By region or country, A-Z
For specific varieties see SF272.A+
275.A-Z Other products and byproducts, A-Z

	Cattle
	Dairy processing. Dairy products (General)
	Other products and byproducts, A-Z -- Continued
275.A1	General by-products
275.B8	Buttermilk
	Casein see TP1180.C2
275.C84	Cultured milk (General)
	Fermented milk see TP565
275.H65	Honey cream
	Ice cream see TX795.A1+
275.M56	Milkfat
	Including milkfat fractionation
275.W5	Whey
275.Y6	Yogurt
	Horses
	For anatomy see SF765
	For physiology see SF768.2.H67
277	Periodicals. Societies. Serials
277.3	Congresses
278	Dictionaries. Encyclopedias
	Cf. SF321.5 Racing dictionaries
278.3	Names
	Directories
278.5	General works
	By region or country
	United States
278.53	General works
278.54.A-Z	By region or state, A-Z
278.55.A-Z	Other regions or countries, A-Z
	Museums
278.7	General works
278.73.A-Z	By region or country, A-Z
	Under each country:
	.x *General works*
	.x2A-.x2Z *Individual museums. By name, A-Z*
279	Conformation. Color
	Cf. SF765 Veterinary medicine
281	Behavior
	History of culture
283	General works
284.A-Z	By region or country, A-Z
	Horsemen. Horsewomen
284.4	General works
284.42.A-Z	By region or country, A-Z
	Biography
	Cf. SF309.48+ Dressage
	Cf. SF336.A2+ Racing

Horses
Horsemen. Horsewomen
Biography -- Continued
284.5 Collective
284.52.A-Z Individual, A-Z
285 General works
Essays and light literature see SF301
Juvenile works see SF302
Pictorial works see SF303
285.25 Vocational guidance for horse trainers, breeders, etc.
Cf. SF336.5 Horse racing
Study and teaching. Research
Cf. SF310.5 Horsemanship
285.27 General works
285.275.A-Z By region or country, A-Z
Culture and care
Cf. SF951+ Diseases
285.3 General works
285.33 Economic aspects of culture. Costs (General)
285.35 Housing and environmental control
Including stables
Boarding facilities
285.37 General works
285.375.A-Z By region or country, A-Z
285.385 Transportation and travel
Including horse trailering
For travel guides see SF309.254+
285.4 Equipment and supplies
Cf. SF309.9 Riding equipment
Cf. SF909 Horseshoes
285.5 Feeding
285.6 Handling
285.7 Grooming
State studs, stud farms see SF290+
287 Training, breaking
Cf. SF309.48+ Dressage
Cf. SF309.7 Jumping
Cf. SF341 Harness racing
Cf. SF351 Running races
289 The horse in motion. Paces, gaits, etc.
Including trotting, cantering, galloping, etc.
Cf. SF341 Harness racing
Cf. SF351 Running races
289.5 Marking
Including brands
Breeds and breeding
Including stud farms

Horses
Breeds and breeding -- Continued

290.A-Z By region or country, A-Z
291 General works
292 Breeders' directories
293.A-Z By breed or type, A-Z
Including studbooks
Cf. SF315.2.A+ Pony breeds
293.A1 General studbooks, registers
For local see SF290.A+
293.A3 Adayev horse
293.A37 Akhal-Teke
293.A47 American paint horse
293.A5 American saddlebred horse
293.A6 Andalusian horse
293.A63 Anglo-Arab
293.A66 Appalachian singlefoot horse
293.A7 Appaloosa
293.A8 Arabian
293.A84 Ardennes horse
293.A98 Aztec
293.B3 Barbary horse
293.B4 Belgian draft horse
293.B7 Breton
293.C28 Camargue horse
293.C3 Cape horse
293.C45 Chilean
293.C6 Cleveland Bay horse
293.C65 Clydesdale
293.C7 Criollo
293.C72 Crioulo
293.F47 Finnish horse
293.F5 Fjord horse
293.F55 Florida cracker horse
293.F77 Frederiksborg horse
293.F8 French coach-horse
293.F9 Friesian
293.G3 German coach-horse
293.H2 Hackney
293.H3 Haflinger
293.H35 Hanoverian
293.H7 Holstein horse
293.H78 Hucul horse
293.H79 Hungarian
293.H8 Hunter
293.I7 Irish draft horse
293.K47 Kiso horse

Horses
Breeds and breeding
By breed or type, A-Z -- Continued

293.K55 Kladrub horse
293.L5 Lipizzaner
293.M32 Malopolski horse
293.M34 Mangalarga horse
293.M56 Miniature horses
293.M77 Morab horse
293.M8 Morgan
293.M88 Murgese horse
293.M9 Mustang
293.N55 Niĭgmiĭn khongor
293.N66 Nonius horse
293.N67 North Swedish horse
293.N68 Novokirghiz
293.O4 Oldenburger horse
293.O7 Orlov trotter horse
293.P3 Palomino horse
293.P37 Paso fino horse
293.P4 Percheron
293.P45 Peruvian paso horse
293.P5 Pinto horse
293.P65 Posovac horse
293.Q3 Quarter horse
Cf. SF357.57+ Race horses
293.R63 Rocky Mountain horse
293.S12 Saddle horse
Saddlebred horse, American see SF293.A5
293.S45 Selle français horse
293.S56 Shire horse
293.S72 Standardbred horse
293.S8 Suffolk horse
293.T4 Tennessee walking horse
293.T5 Thoroughbred
Cf. SF338 Race horses
293.T7 Tori
293.T75 Trakehner
293.T8 Trotting horse
293.T87 Turkoman horse
293.W32 Waler horse
293.W34 Walking horses
293.W54 Wielkopolski horse
293.Y7 Yomud
294 Record books, blanks, etc.

Horses -- Continued
Horse sports
Cf. GV1010+ Polo
Cf. GV1063.5 Ride and tie
Cf. GV1191+ Tournaments
Cf. GV1833.5+ Rodeos
Cf. SF308.5+ Horsemanship
Cf. SF321+ Horse racing
Cf. SK284+ Fox hunting
Dictionaries and encyclopedias see SF278
294.2 General works
294.23 Juvenile works
By region or country
United States
294.25 General works
294.26.A-Z By region or state, A-Z
294.27.A-Z Other regions or countries, A-Z
294.278 Horse sports sponsorship
Competition horses
294.3 General works
294.32.A-Z Individual horses, A-Z
294.35 Courses. Horse arenas
For courses limited to specific horse sports, see the sport, e.g. SF295.57 Show jumping; SF324+ Racetracks
Horse shows
Including horse show facilities
294.5 General works
294.7 Juvenile works
294.75 Rules
International
294.8.A-Z By place, A-Z
294.85 Olympic games
Cf. SF295.48+ Show jumping
Cf. SF295.7 Three-day event
Cf. SF309.48+ Dressage
National, state, and local
United States
295 General works
295.15.A-Z By region or state, A-Z
Subarrange each state by Table S3a
295.17.A-Z Other countries, A-Z
Subarrange each country by Table S3a
Show horses (General)
295.185 General works
295.187.A-Z Individual show horses, A-Z
295.2 Show riding
Show jumping

Horses
Horse shows
Show jumping -- Continued
295.48 Periodicals. Societies. Serials
295.5 General works
295.525 Juvenile works
Biography (Persons)
295.53 Collective
295.535.A-Z Individual, A-Z
295.54 History
295.55.A-Z By region or country, A-Z
Show jumpers (Horses)
295.56 General works
295.565.A-Z Individual horses, A-Z
295.57 Courses
295.575 Rules
295.58.A-Z Competitive events, A-Z
295.58.P74 Prix des Nations
Cross-country riding
Including cross-country event
Cf. SF359+ Steeplechasing
295.6 General works
295.65 Hunt riding
Cf. SF296.H86 Hunter horse shows
Cf. SK284+ Fox hunting
295.7 Eventing
Including three-day event (Olympic games)
296.A-Z Other competitive events, A-Z
296.A35 Agility trials
296.C87 Cutting horse competitions
Dressage tests see SF309.6
296.E5 Endurance riding
296.E53 English pleasure horse classes
Including Arabian English pleasure horse class
296.G35 Games on horseback
Cf. SF296.P65 Pony Club games
296.G9 Gymkhana games
296.H34 Halter classes
296.H86 Hunter horse shows
Including hunter classes and hunter seat equitation division
Cf. SF295.65 Hunt riding
(296.H87) Hunter seat equitation division
see SF296.H86
Point-to-point racing see SF359.4
296.P65 Pony Club games
296.R4 Reining horse class
Rodeos see GV1833.5+

Horses
Horse shows
Other competitive events, A-Z -- Continued
296.S23 Saddle seat equitation
Show driving see SF305.7+
296.T7 Trail riding. Trail class
Cf. SF309.28 Trail riding for pleasure
296.T75 Trick riding
296.V37 Vaulting
296.W47 Western division and classes
297 Judging
299 Catalogs of sales and stock farms
301 Essays and light literature
Cf. QL795.H7 Stories about wild horses
Cf. SF335.5 Racing
302 Juvenile works
303 Pictorial works
Cf. N7668.H6 Art
Cf. SF309.25 Horsemanship
Cf. SF337 Racehorses
Driving
Cf. GV33 Chariot racing
Cf. HE5746+ Coaching and stagecoach lines
Cf. SF312 Coach horses
304.5 Periodicals. Societies. Serials
305 General works
305.3 History (General)
305.4.A-Z By region or country, A-Z
Show driving
305.7 General works
305.75 Driving horses
305.8.A-Z Competitive events, A-Z
305.8.C65 Combined driving
305.8.D73 Dressage driving
307 Coaching recollections
Horsemanship. Riding
Cf. GT5885+ Customs relating to horsemanship
Cf. RC1220.H67 Sports medicine
Cf. SF289 Paces, gaits, etc.
Cf. SF294.198+ Horse sports
308.5 History (General)
For history by region or country see SF284.A+
309 General works
309.2 Juvenile works
309.25 Pictorial works
Cf. SF303 Horses
Cf. SF337 Racehorses

Horses
Horsemanship. Riding -- Continued
Guidebooks. Vacation guides. Directories
309.254 General works
By region or country
United States
309.255 General works
309.256.A-Z By region or state, A-Z
309.257.A-Z Other regions or countries, A-Z
309.26.A-Z Horsemanship for special classes of persons, A-Z
309.26.H35 Handicapped. People with disabilities
People with disabilities see SF309.26.H35
309.27 Sidesaddle riding
309.28 Trail riding. Pony trekking
For guidebooks see SF309.254+
Cf. SF296.T7 Competitive trail riding
Western riding
309.3 General works
309.34 Western horses
Including training
For western show horses see SF296.W47
School riding
Including dressage
Cf. SF295.2 Show riding
Cf. SF310.A1+ Riding schools
Biography
309.48 Collective
309.482.A-Z Individual, A-Z
309.5 General works
309.57 Haute ecole
309.6 Dressage tests and competitive events
Dressage horses
309.65 Collective
309.653.A-Z Individual, A-Z
309.658 Quadrille
309.7 Jumping
Cf. SF295.48+ Show jumping
309.9 Riding equipment. Bits, saddles, etc.
Cf. SF285.4 Horse equipment
Riding clubs and schools
310.A1 General works

Horses
Horsemanship. Riding
Riding clubs and schools -- Continued
310.A3-Z By region or country, A-Z
Under each country:
.x General works
.x2A-.x2Z Local, A-Z
.x3A-.x3Z Special clubs or schools. By place, A-Z
e.g.
Austria
310.A95 General works
310.A952C35 Carinthia
310.A953V53 Vienna. Spanische Rietschule
310.5 Study and teaching
Cf. SF285.27+ Horses
Draft horses
311 General works
311.3.A-Z By region or country, A-Z
312 Coach horses
Military pack trains see UC300+
Military use of horses see UC600+
Military horses, cavalry see UE460+
Packhorses (Camping) see GV199.7
Ponies
Cf. SF309.28 Pony trekking
315 General works
315.2.A-Z By breed, A-Z
315.2.B3 Basuto
315.2.C35 Cheju
315.2.C4 Chincoteague
315.2.C6 Connemara
315.2.E92 Exmoor
315.2.F34 Faeroes
315.2.H5 Highland
315.2.I3 Iceland
315.2.K47 Kerry bog pony
315.2.K65 Konik
315.2.N49 New Forest
315.2.P68 Pottok
315.2.S5 Shetland
315.2.W38 Welara pony
315.2.W4 Welsh
315.5 Polo ponies
Care of stables see SF285.35
Racing
Cf. HV6718 Racetrack gambling

	Horses
	Racing -- Continued
321	Periodicals. Serials
	Cf. SF323.A1+ Clubs and societies
321.2	Congresses
	Directories
321.4	General works
321.43.A-Z	By region or country, A-Z
321.5	Dictionaries. Encyclopedias
	Including terminology, racing slang, etc.
	Clubs and societies
	Including reports, history, programs, etc.
323.A1	General works
323.A3-Z	Individual clubs and societies. By name, A-Z
	Racetracks
324	General works
	By region or country
	United States
324.3	General works
324.35.A-Z	By region or state, A-Z
324.4.A-Z	Other regions or countries, A-Z
325	Records, calendars, etc.
327	Racing colors
329	Racing rules
	Betting systems, etc.
331	General works
	By region or country
	United States
332	General works
332.5.A-Z	By region or state, A-Z
333.A-Z	Other regions or countries, A-Z
333.4	Claiming races
333.5	Harness racing
334	General works
	History
335.A1	General works
335.A5-Z	Individual countries, A-Z
	e.g.
335.G7	Great Britain
	United States
335.U5	General works
335.U6A-.U6W	By state, A-W
335.5	Essays and light literature
335.6	Juvenile works
	Biography
	Including jockeys, trainers, owners, etc.
336.A2	Collective

Horses
Racing
Biography -- Continued
336.A3-Z Individual, A-Z
336.5 Vocational guidance
337 Illustration of racing horses
Cf. SF309.25 Horsemanship
338 Racehorses
For individual trotters and pacers see SF343.A+
For individual running horses see SF355.A+
For individual steeplechase horses see SF359.5.A+
Harness racing. Trotting and pacing
338.7 Periodicals. Serials
338.73 Congresses
338.76 Dictionaries. Encyclopedias
Societies and clubs
338.8 General works
338.83.A-Z Individual societies and clubs. By name, A-Z
339 General works
339.2 History
339.5.A-Z By region or country, A-Z
Biography see SF336.A2+
339.7 Problems, exercises, examinations
340 Rules
Betting see SF333.5
341 Training of trotters and pacers
343.A-Z Individual trotters and pacers, A-Z
345.A-Z Individual races and series of races, A-Z
345.F68 Fox Stake
345.H35 Hambletonian
345.I58 Interdominion Championship
345.N48 New Zealand Trotting Cup
Running races. Flat racing
General works see SF334
History see SF335.A1+
Betting see SF331+
351 Training of runners
353.A-Z Individual stables, A-Z
355.A-Z Individual running horses, A-Z
355.E34 Eight Belles
356 Claiming races and horses
357.A-Z Individual and special races, A-Z
357.A8 Ascot Gold Cup
Cf. SF335.G7 Royal Ascot
357.B74 Breeders' Cup Championship Day races
Derby Stakes see SF357.E67
357.E67 Epsom Derby

Horses
Racing
Running races. Flat racing
Individual and special races, A-Z -- Continued
Grand National see SF359.7.G7
357.I74 Irish Sweeps Derby
357.J8 July Handicap
357.K4 Kentucky Derby
357.K5 King George VI and Queen Elizabeth Diamond Stakes
357.M4 Melbourne Cup
357.P73 Preakness stakes
357.P75 Prix de l'Arc de Triomphe
357.Q4 Queen's Plate
357.S13 Saint Leger, Chile
357.S14 Saint Leger, Doncaster, England
(357.S8) St. Leger, Chile
see SF357.S13
357.T74 Triple Crown (U.S.)
Quarter racing
357.3 Periodicals. Serials
357.5 General works
357.53 History
357.55.A-Z By region or country, A-Z
Biography see SF336.A2+
Horses
Cf. SF293.Q3 Quarter horse breed
357.57 Collective
357.575.A-Z Individual, A-Z
358.A-Z Individual races, A-Z
Steeplechase and hurdle racing
359 General works
359.2 History
359.3.A-Z By region or country, A-Z
Biography see SF336.A2+
359.4 Point-to-point racing
For individual horses see SF359.5.A+
For individual races see SF359.7.A+
359.5.A-Z Individual horses, A-Z
359.7.A-Z Individual races, A-Z
359.7.C35 Carolina Cup
359.7.C5 Cheltenham Gold Cup
359.7.G7 Grand National Handicap
359.7.G74 Great Pardubice Steeplechase
359.7.L33 Lady Dudley Challenge Cup
359.7.M3 Maryland Hunt Cup
359.7.V55 Virginia Gold Cup
Feral horses. Wild horses

SF

	Horses
	Feral horses. Wild horses -- Continued
360	General works
360.3.A-Z	By region or country, A-Z
360.4	Adoption
	Asses
360.6	General works
360.65.A-Z	By region or country, A-Z
360.7.A-Z	By breed, A-Z
360.7.A53	American mammoth jack stock
	Donkeys
361	General works
361.3.A-Z	By region or country, A-Z
361.4.A-Z	By breed, A-Z
361.4.M54	Miniature donkey
	Wild burros. Feral donkeys
361.7	General works
361.73.A-Z	By region or country, A-Z
362	Mules
	Cf. UC600+ Military use
	Przewalski's horse
363	General works
363.3.A-Z	By region or country, A-Z
	Sheep
	For anatomy see SF767.S5
	For physiology see SF768.2.S5
371	Periodicals. Societies. Serials
371.2	Congresses
371.4	Dictionaries. Encyclopedias
	Directories
371.5	General works
371.52.A-Z	By region or country, A-Z
373.A-Z	By breed, A-Z
373.A33	Adal
373.A54	American Tunis
373.A58	Ansotana
373.A94	Australian merino
373.A96	Awassi
373.B5	Blacktop merino
373.C48	Chamarita
373.C5	Cheviot
373.C8	Coltswold
373.D4	Delaine merino
373.D5	Dickinson merino
373.D7	Dorset horn
373.E3	East Friesian
373.E44	Elliottdale

Sheep
By breed, A-Z -- Continued
373.F3 Fat-tailed
373.G84 Gujarati
373.H17 Hair
373.H2 Hampshire-Down
373.J33 Jacob
373.K3 Karakul
373.M5 Merino
373.N38 Navajo-Churro
373.N67 Northeast Bulgarian fine-wooled
373.O75 Orkhon
373.O9 Oxford downs
373.R3 Rambouillet
373.R6 Romanov
373.S3 Saxon merino
373.S56 Shropshire
373.S7 Southdowns
373.S75 Spanish merino
373.S93 Sudan desert
373.T7 Transbaikol
373.W49 Welsh mountain
373.W5 Wensleydale
373.W9 Württemberg
Shows
374 General works
374.2 Judging
375 General works
375.2 Juvenile works
Biography (of persons)
375.3 Collective
375.32.A-Z Individual, A-Z
History and conditions
375.38 General works
By region or country
United States
375.4.A1 General works
375.4.A2-Z By region or state, A-Z
375.5.A-Z Other regions or countries, A-Z
375.6 Study and teaching. Research
Diseases see SF968+
375.8 Housing and environmental control
375.87 Behavior
376 Feeding
Breeding
376.2 General works
376.25 Artificial insemination

	Sheep -- Continued
376.5	Lambs
376.7	Marketing
376.8	Milk
	For sheep cheese see SF271.9
377	Wool
379	Sheep shearing
	Goats
380	Periodicals. Societies. Serials
380.3	Congresses
380.5	Dictionaries. Encyclopedias
	Directories
380.7	General works
380.73.A-Z	By region or country, A-Z
	Flock books see SF385+
	Shows. Showing
382	General works
382.3	Judging
383	General works
383.3	Essays and light literature
383.35	Juvenile works
	Biography (of persons)
383.37	General works
383.38.A-Z	Individual, A-Z
	By region or country, A-Z
	United States
383.4	General works
383.45.A-Z	By region or state, A-Z
383.5.A-Z	Other regions or countries, A-Z
	Study and teaching. Research
383.7	General works
383.73.A-Z	By region or country, A-Z
384	Housing and environmental control
384.3	Feeding
384.5	Breeding
	Breeds
385	Angora
386.A-Z	Other breeds, A-Z
386.G7	Granada
386.K37	Kashmir
386.N53	Nigerian dwarf
386.N83	Nubian
386.P94	Pygmy
387	Draft goats. Pack goats
388	Milk
	For goat cheese see SF271.87
	Feral goats

Goats
Feral goats -- Continued
389 General works
389.3.A-Z By region or country, A-Z
Swine
For anatomy see SF767.S95
For physiology see SF768.2.S95
391 Periodicals. Societies. Serials
391.3 Congresses
392 Breeders' directories
393.A-Z By breed or type, A-Z
393.B5 Berkshire
393.C4 Cheshire
393.C5 Chester white
393.D34 Danish landrace
393.D9 Duroc
393.E7 Essex
393.H3 Hampshire
393.H45 Hereford
393.L3 Landrace
393.M55 Miniature pigs
Including miniature pet pigs
Cf. SF407.S97 Laboratory animals
393.P7 Poland-China
393.P74 Potbellied pigs
Including pet potbellied pigs
393.T27 Taihu
393.T3 Tamworth
393.V6 Victoria
393.Y6 Yorkshire
394 Shows
395 General works
Including general care of swine
395.4 Essays and light literature
395.5 Juvenile works
395.6 Swine as pets
By region or country
United States
395.8.A1 General works
395.8.A2-Z By region or state, A-Z
396.A-Z Other regions or countries, A-Z
Study and teaching. Research
396.2 General works
396.23.A-Z By region or country, A-Z
Diseases see SF971+
396.3 Housing and environmental control
Including farrowing facilities

Swine -- Continued

396.4 Equipment and supplies

396.5 Feeding. Nutrition

Breeding

396.9 General works

397 Breeders' catalogs

397.2 Marketing

397.3 Economic aspects of culture. Costs (General)

397.4 Carcasses

Feral swine

397.8 General works

397.83.A-Z By region or country, A-Z

Other domesticated and semidomesticated animals

399 General works

400.5 Big game animals

401.A-Z Individual or group, A-Z

401.A34 African buffalo

401.A4 Alpaca

401.A45 American bison

(401.B56) Bison, American

see SF401.A45

401.C2 Camel

401.C25 Cheetahs

401.D3 Deer

401.E3 Elephants

Cf. SF408.6.E44 Zoo animals

401.E4 Elk

Ferret see SK293

401.G85 Guinea pigs

Cf. SF459.G9 Pets

401.L35 Lama (Genus)

401.L6 Llamas

401.M8 Muskox

401.P34 Paca

401.R4 Reindeer

401.R54 Rhinoceroses

401.V5 Vicuña

401.W34 Water buffalo

401.W54 Wild boar

401.Y3 Yak

Fur-bearing animals

Including fur farming

Cf. HD9944 Fur trade

Cf. SK283+ Trapping

Cf. TS1060+ Fur manufacture

402 Periodicals. Societies. Serials

402.3 Congresses

	Fur-bearing animals -- Continued
403	General works
	By region or country
	United States
403.4.A2	General works
403.4.A3-Z	By region or state, A-Z
403.5.A-Z	Other regions or countries, A-Z
405.A-Z	Individual, A-Z
405.B4	Beaver
405.C45	Chinchilla
405.C6	Coypu
405.F8	Fox
405.M3	Marten
405.M6	Mink
405.M7	Muskrat
405.R3	Raccoon
405.S3	Sable
405.S6	Skunk
	Laboratory animals
	Cf. QL55 Zoology
405.5	Periodicals. Societies. Serials
405.6	Breeders' directories
406	General breeding and care
406.2	Feeding
406.3	Housing and environmental control
406.4	Safety measures
	Diseases see SF996.5
406.7	Transportation
407.A-Z	Individual, A-Z
407.A45	Amphibians
407.B53	Birds
407.C37	Cats
407.D6	Dogs
407.F39	Ferret
407.F5	Fish
407.F74	Frogs
407.G85	Guinea pigs
407.G95	Gypsy moths
407.H35	Hamsters
407.I58	Invertebrates
407.J3	Japanese quail
407.M37	Marine invertebrates
407.M5	Mice
407.M65	Mollusks
407.P7	Primates
407.R33	Rabbits
407.R38	Rats

Laboratory animals
Individual, A-Z -- Continued

407.R6 Rodents
407.R8 Ruminants
407.S4 Sea birds
407.S62 Snails
407.S97 Swine
407.Z42 Zebra danio

Zoo animals. Captive wild animals
Including captive mammals
Cf. QL77.5 Zoology
Cf. SF456+ Aquarium animals
Cf. SF462.5+ Captive wild birds
Cf. SF515+ Captive reptiles

408 Culture and care
408.3 Breeding
408.4 Feeding
408.45 Housing and environmental control
408.6.A-Z By animal, A-Z
408.6.A54 Alligators
408.6.A56 Antelopes
408.6.A64 Apes
408.6.B35 Bandicoots (Marsupialia)
Including individual species
408.6.B38 Bats
408.6.B43 Bears
Including individual species
Cf. SF408.6.P64 Polar bear
408.6.C47 Cetacea
408.6.D54 Dik-diks
Including individual species
408.6.D64 Dolphins
Including individual species
408.6.E44 Elephants
Cf. SF401.E3 Semidomesticated animals
408.6.F44 Felidae
408.6.G37 Gazelles
Including individual species
408.6.G57 Giraffe
408.6.H57 Hippopotamus
408.6.I53 Indian rhinoceros
408.6.I55 Invertebrates
408.6.K35 Kangaroos
408.6.K54 Killer whale
408.6.L54 Lions
408.6.M37 Marine mammals

Zoo animals. Captive wild animals
By animal, A-Z -- Continued
408.6.O74 Otters
Including individual species, e.g., Oriental small-clawed otters
408.6.P64 Polar bear
408.6.P74 Primates
408.6.P93 Pygmy hippopotamus
408.6.R45 Rhinoceroses
Including individual species
408.6.S32 Sea lions
408.6.S35 Seals
408.6.S63 Snakes
Class here works limited to snakes in zoos
Cf. SF459.S5 Pets
Cf. SF515.5.S64 General culture and captive snakes
408.6.T53 Tigers
408.6.U54 Ungulates
408.6.W46 Wetas
Including individual species
409 Small animal culture
Pets
Cf. D+ for pets of presidents, statesmen, politicians, etc., e.g. E176.48 for pets of United States presidents in general
411 Periodicals. Societies. Serials
411.3 Names
History and conditions
411.35 General works
411.36.A-Z By region or country, A-Z
Pet breeders, owners, etc.
411.4 General works
411.43.A-Z By region or country, A-Z
Biography
411.44 Collective
411.45.A-Z Individual, A-Z
411.47 Psychology
411.5 General works
412 Shows
412.5 Behavior
412.7 Training
413 Culture and care
Cf. SF981+ Diseases
413.5 Equipment and supplies
Including handicraft
413.7 Breeding
414 Feeding
414.2 Housing and environmental control
414.3 Boarding facilities

Pets -- Continued
414.34 Pet sitting
414.5 Cemeteries
Marketing. Pet shops
For marketing of particular pets, see the pet, e.g. SF434.5+ Dogs
414.7 General works
415 Catalogs, etc.
415.45 Travel
415.5 Transportation
416 Essays and popular works
416.2 Juvenile works
416.5 Pictorial works
416.6 Study and teaching. Research
Dogs
For anatomy see SF767.D6
For physiology see SF768.2.D6
Cf. SF459.C68 Coydogs
Cf. SF459.W62 Wolfdogs
421 Periodicals. Societies. Serials
422 Dictionaries. Encyclopedias
422.3 Names
Communication of information
422.33 General works
422.334 Information services
422.336 Computer network resources
Including the Internet
Directories
422.35 General works
422.36.A-Z By region or country, A-Z
History and conditions
422.5 General works
422.6.A-Z By region or country, A-Z
Dog breeders, owners, etc.
422.7 General works
422.73.A-Z By region or country, A-Z
Biography
422.8 Collective
422.82.A-Z Individual, A-Z
422.86 Psychology
423 Pedigree books
Class here general works only
For particular breeds see SF429.A+

Pets
Dogs -- Continued
424 Dog sports
Class here general works only
For dogfighting see GV1109
For individual sports see SF425.85.A+
For dog racing see SF439.5+
For hunting see SK1+
Cf. SF427.45 Games
Dog shows and competitive events
Including conformation or bench shows
425 General works
425.13 Juvenile works
Including Junior Showmanship
425.14.A-Z International. By place, A-Z
National, state and local. By region or country
United States
425.15 General works
425.16.A-Z By region or state, A-Z
Subarrange each state by Table S3a
425.18.A-Z Other regions or countries, A-Z
Subarrange each country by Table S3a
425.2 Judging. Standards
425.3 Show dogs
425.4 Agility trials
Field trials and stakes
425.5 General works
425.53 Earthdog tests
425.55 Lure field trials
425.6 Pointing breed hunting tests
425.7 Obedience trials and classes
425.8 Sheep dog trials
425.85.A-Z Other sports and competitive events, A-Z
425.85.D36 Dancing
425.85.F56 Flyball
Racing see SF439.5+
425.85.R35 Rally
425.85.S35 Schutzhund
Cf. SF428.78 Schutzhund dogs
425.85.S38 Scootering
425.85.S57 Skijoring
426 General works
426.2 Essays and light literature
For stories about particular breeds see SF429.A+
426.5 Juvenile works
Pictorial works see SF430
426.55 Vocational guidance for dog trainers, breeders, etc.

Pets
Dogs -- Continued
427 Culture and care
Cf. SF991+ Diseases
427.15 Equipment and supplies
Including handicraft
427.2 Breeding
427.4 Feeding
427.43 Housing and environmental control
Cf. SF428 Kennels
427.45 Exercise and amusements
Including games, parks, and parties
427.455 Hiking and camping
427.456 Boating
Travel. Vacation guides. Guidebooks
Class here works on traveling or vacationing with dogs
427.457 General works
By region or country
United States
427.4573 General works
427.4574.A-Z By region or state, A-Z
427.4576.A-Z Other regions or countries, A-Z
427.46 Dog walking
427.48 Cleaning up
Grooming
427.5 General works
427.55 Dog grooming industry
Training see SF431
427.7 Dog day care
428 Kennels
Working dogs
428.2 General works
Cattle dogs see SF428.6
Herding dogs see SF428.6
428.5 Hunting dogs. Bird dogs
Including pointing dogs
Livestock protection dogs see SF428.6
Police dogs see HV8025
428.55 Rescue dogs
Including water rescue dogs
Seeing-eye dogs see HV1780+
428.6 Sheep dogs. Cattle dogs. Herding dogs. Livestock protection dogs
Cf. SF425.8 Sheep dog trials
428.7 Sled dogs
Cf. SF440.15 Sled dog racing

Pets
Dogs
Working dogs -- Continued
Search dogs
Cf. HV8025 Police dogs
Cf. SF428.55 Rescue dogs

428.73 General works
428.75 Tracking dogs
428.78 Schutzhund dogs
Cf. SF425.85.S35 Schutzhund (Dog sport)
428.8 Watchdogs
428.85 Fighting dogs
Cf. GV1109 Dogfighting
429.A-Z By breed, A-Z
429.A4 Afghan hound
429.A45 Africanis
429.A58 Ainu dogs
429.A6 Airedale terrier
429.A63 Akbash dogs
429.A65 Akita dogs
429.A67 Alaskan Malamute
429.A69 American Eskimo
429.A7 American foxhound
429.A72 American pit bull terrier
429.A73 American Staffordshire terrier
429.A735 American water spaniel
429.A74 Anatolian shepherd dog
429.A75 Argentine Dogo
429.A77 Australian cattle dog
429.A78 Australian kelpie
429.A79 Australian shepherd dog
429.A8 Australian terriers
429.A93 Azawakh
429.B15 Basenjis
429.B156 Basset fauve de Bretagne
Basset griffon Vendéen, Petit see SF429.P36
429.B2 Basset hounds
429.B3 Beagle
429.B32 Bearded collie
429.B325 Beauceron
429.B33 Bedlington terriers
429.B4 Belgian sheep dog
429.B42 Belgian tervuren
429.B45 Bergamasco
429.B47 Bernese mountain dog
429.B52 Bichon frise
429.B56 Black and tan coonhound

SF

Pets
Dogs
By breed, A-Z -- Continued

429.I7 Irish setters
429.I8 Irish terriers
429.I83 Irish water spaniels
429.I85 Irish wolfhounds
429.I89 Italian greyhound
429.J27 Jack Russell terrier
429.J29 Japanese chin
429.J3 Japanese spaniels
429.K37 Karelian bear dog
429.K4 Keeshonds
(429.K45) Kelpie
see SF429.A78
429.K5 Kerry blue terriers
429.K65 Komondors
429.K76 Kromfohrländer
429.K88 Kuvasz
429.L29 Labradoodle
429.L3 Labrador retriever
429.L35 Lakeland terriers
429.L45 Leonberger dog
429.L5 Lhasa apso
429.L68 Löwchen
429.L87 Lurcher
429.M25 Maltese dog
429.M3 Manchester terriers
429.M34 Maremma sheepdog
429.M36 Mastiff breeds. Mastiff
429.M52 Miniature dachshunds
429.M56 Miniature pinscher
429.M57 Miniature poodle. Toy poodle
429.M58 Miniature schnauzer
429.M67 Morkie
429.N33 Neapolitan mastiff
429.N4 Newfoundland dog
429.N56 Norfolk terrier
429.N57 Northern breeds
429.N6 Norwegian elkhound
429.N65 Norwich terriers
429.N68 Nova Scotia duck tolling retriever
429.O4 Old English sheepdog
429.O77 Otter hound
429.P2 Papillon
429.P3 Pekingese dog
429.P33 Pembroke Welsh corgi

Pets
Dogs
By breed, A-Z -- Continued

429.P35 Perro de presa canario
429.P36 Petit basset griffon Vendéen
429.P43 Pharaoh hound
Pinschers
Doberman pinscher see SF429.D6
German pinscher see SF429.G367
Miniature pinscher see SF429.M56
429.P58 Pit bull terriers
429.P66 Plott hound
429.P7 Pointer
Cf. SF428.5 Pointing dogs
429.P75 Polish lowland sheepdog
429.P8 Pomeranian dog
429.P85 Poodles
Including standard poodle
For miniature and toy poodles see SF429.M57
429.P87 Portuguese water dog
429.P9 Pug
429.P92 Puggle
429.P93 Puli
429.P95 P'ungsan dog
429.P97 Pyrenean mastiff
Racing greyhound see SF429.G8
429.R35 Rat terrier
429.R4 Retrievers
429.R5 Rhodesian ridgeback
429.R7 Rottweiler dogs
Russian wolfhound see SF429.B67
429.S3 Saint Bernard dog
429.S33 Saluki
429.S35 Samoyeds
429.S354 Sapsal dog
429.S36 Schipperke
429.S37 Schnauzers
(429.S375) Miniature schnauzer
see SF429.M58
429.S378 Schnoodle
429.S39 Scottish deerhound
429.S4 Scottish terrier
429.S45 Sealyham terriers
429.S47 Sennenhunde
429.S5 Setters
429.S62 Shetland sheepdog
429.S63 Shiba dogs

SF

Pets
Dogs
By breed, A-Z -- Continued

429.S64 Shih tzu
429.S645 Shikoku dogs
429.S65 Siberian husky
429.S653 Sighthounds
429.S66 Silky terriers
429.S67 Skye terriers
429.S68 Sloughi
Smooth collie see SF429.C6
429.S69 Soft coated wheaten terrier
429.S7 Spaniels
429.S72 Spanish water dog
429.S74 Spinone
429.S75 Spitz dogs
429.S85 Staffordshire bull terrier
Standard poodle see SF429.P85
429.S88 Sussex spaniel
429.S94 Swedish vallhund
429.T3 Terriers
(429.T35) Tervuren
see SF429.B42
429.T48 Tibetan mastiff
429.T5 Tibetan spaniel
429.T52 Tibetan terrier
429.T7 Toy dogs
429.T73 Toy fox terrier
Toy poodle see SF429.M57
429.V5 Vizsla
429.W33 Weimaraners
Welsh corgi, Cardigan see SF429.C34
Welsh corgi, Pembroke see SF429.P33
429.W37 Welsh springer spaniel
429.W38 Welsh terrier
429.W4 West Highland white terrier
429.W5 Whippet
Cf. SF440.14 Whippet racing
429.W52 White German shepherd dog
429.W55 Wire fox terrier
429.W57 Wirehaired pointing griffon
429.X6 Xoloitzcuintli
429.Y57 Yorkie poo
429.Y6 Yorkshire terrier
430 Pictorial works

Pets
Dogs -- Continued
431 Training
Cf. SF425+ Training for dog shows and trials
Cf. SF428.2+ Training of particular types of dogs
432 Locomotion
433 Behavior
Including behavior therapy
Marketing. Dog industry
434.5 General works
434.7.A-Z By region or country, A-Z
435 Catalogs
Dog racing
439.5 General works
440 Greyhound racing
Cf. SF429.G8 Racing greyhound
440.14 Whippet racing
Cf. SF429.W5 Whippet
440.15 Sled dog racing
Cf. SF428.7 Sled dogs
440.2 Betting
Cats
441 Periodicals. Societies. Serials
442 General works
442.2 Dictionaries. Encyclopedias
442.4 Names
History and conditions
442.6 General works
442.63.A-Z By region or country, A-Z
Cat breeders, owners, etc.
442.7 General works
442.73.A-Z By region or country, A-Z
Biography
442.8 Collective
442.82.A-Z Individual, A-Z
442.86 Psychology
443 Pedigree books
Class here general works only
For particular breeds see SF449.A+
Shows. Showing
445 General works
445.2 Juvenile works
445.3.A-Z International. By place, A-Z
National, state, and local. By region or country
United States
445.32 General works

	Pets
	Cats
	Shows. Showing
	National, state, and local. By region or country
	United States -- Continued
445.33.A-Z	By region or state, A-Z
	Subarrange each country by Table S3a
445.35.A-Z	Other regions or countries, A-Z
	Subarrange each country by Table S3a
445.37	Judging. Standards
445.5	Essays and light literature
445.7	Juvenile works
446	Pictorial works
446.5	Behavior
	Including behavior therapy
446.6	Training
446.7	Exercises and amusements
	Including games
447	Culture and care
	Cf. HV4743 Animal welfare, animal protection, animal rights, etc.
	Cf. SF985+ Diseases
	Equipment and supplies
	Including handicraft
447.3	General works
447.34	Litter boxes
447.5	Breeding
447.6	Feeding
447.65	Grooming
447.8	Working cats
449.A-Z	By breed or type, A-Z
	Including pedigree books
449.A28	Abyssinian
449.A44	American curl
449.A45	American shorthair
449.A47	American wirehair
	Angora see SF449.T87
449.B34	Balinese
449.B45	Bengal
449.B5	Birman
449.B55	Black
449.B65	Bombay
449.B74	British shorthair
449.B8	Burmese
449.C34	Calico
449.C45	Chartreux
449.C47	Chausie

Pets
Cats
By breed or type, A-Z -- Continued
Colorpoint see SF449.H55
449.E39 Egyptian maus
449.E93 Exotic shorthair
449.G73 Gray
449.H53 Havana brown
449.H55 Himalayan
449.J37 Japanese bobtail
449.K67 Korat cat
449.L65 Longhair cats
449.M34 Maine coon cat
449.M36 Manx
449.M38 Marmalade
449.N65 Norwegian forest
449.O35 Ocicat
449.O73 Oriental shorthair
449.P4 Persian
449.P59 Pixie-Bob
449.R34 Ragdoll
449.R4 Rex
449.R86 Russian Blue
449.S24 Safari
449.S28 Savannah
449.S35 Scottish fold
449.S5 Siamese
449.S65 Somali
449.S68 Sphynx
449.T32 Tabby
449.T65 Tonkinese
449.T69 Toyger
449.T87 Turkish Angora
450 Feral cats
Rabbits and hares
Cf. SB994.R15 Agricultural zoology
451 Periodicals. Societies. Serials
453 General works
453.2 Juvenile works
453.25 Essays and light literature
By region or country
United States
453.4 General works
453.45.A-Z By region or state, A-Z
453.5.A-Z Other regions or countries, A-Z
Shows. Showing
453.7 General works

Pets
Rabbits and hares
Shows. Showing -- Continued
453.76 Judging. Standards
453.8 Housing and environmental control
454 Feeding
454.2 Breeding
455.A-Z By breed, species, or group, A-Z
455.A4 American checkered giant
455.A5 Angora
455.B4 Belgian hare
455.C5 Chinchilla
455.D8 Dutch rabbits
455.D85 Dwarf rabbits
455.J33 Jackrabbits
455.L4 Lepus timidus
455.L64 Lop
455.R4 Rex rabbits
Fishes. Aquarium animals
Including tropical fish
Cf. QL78+ Public aquariums
456 Periodicals. Societies. Serials
456.5 Dictionaries. Encyclopedias
456.8 Shows. Showing
457 General works
457.1 Marine aquarium culture
Including marine aquarium animals, coral reef and marine tropical fishes, and captive marine invertebrates
For individual species, families, or groups see SF458.A+
457.25 Juvenile works
457.3 Aquariums and furnishings
457.5 Environment (Water, temperature, light, etc.)
457.7 Plants, snails, etc., for the aquarium
Cf. SB423+ Aquatic plants
457.75 Feeding
457.85 Collecting technique
457.9 Breeding
For particular varieties see SF458.A+
458.A-Z By variety, species, family, or group, A-Z
458.A45 Amphiprion. Anemonefishes
Anemonefishes see SF458.A45
458.A5 Angelfishes
Including freshwater and marine angelfishes
458.B3 Barbs
458.B4 Betta
Carp, Ornamental see SF458.K64

Pets
Fishes. Aquarium animals
By variety, species, family, or group, A-Z -- Continued

458.C38 Catfishes
458.C5 Cichlids
458.C64 Corals
Coral reef fishes see SF457.1
458.C65 Corydoras
458.C94 Cyprinodontidae
458.D5 Discus
Freshwater angelfishes see SF458.A5
458.F75 Freshwater stingrays
458.G6 Goldfish
458.G65 Gouramis
458.G8 Guppies
458.K54 Killifishes
458.K64 Koi
458.L26 Labyrinth fishes
458.L58 Livebearing fishes
458.L63 Loaches
Marine angelfishes see SF458.A5
458.M65 Morays
458.O73 Orchid dottyback
Ornamental carp see SF458.K64
458.O76 Ornamental shrimps
458.O83 Oscar
458.P57 Piranhas
458.P63 Poeciliidae
458.P66 Pomacentridae
458.R35 Rainbowfish
458.S34 Scalare
458.S37 Scorpionfishes
458.S43 Sea horses
Siamese fighting fish see SF458.B4
458.S53 Sharks
Shrimps, Ornamental see SF458.O76
Stingrays, Freshwater see SF458.F75
458.T4 Tetras
458.T75 Triops longicaudatus
Tropical fish see SF456+
458.W73 Wrasses
458.X58 Xiphophorus
Including swordtails and platies
458.5 Diseases and pests
For diseases of particular varieties see SF458.A+
Marketing. Ornamental fish trade
458.8 General works

Pets
Fishes. Aquarium animals
Marketing. Ornamental fish trade -- Continued
458.83.A-Z By region or country, A-Z
By variety, species, etc. see SF458.A+
459.A-Z Other animals, A-Z
Cf. SF460+ Birds
459.A4 Alligators
Cf. SF515.5.A44 Alligator farming
459.A45 Amphibians
459.A47 Ants
Aquatic animals see SF458.A+
459.B37 Bats
459.B43 Beetles
Including individual species and genera
For ladybugs see SF459.L33
459.B87 Butterflies
Cf. SF562.B8 Butterfly farming
459.C36 Capybaras
459.C38 Caterpillars
459.C39 Cephalopoda
459.C45 Chameleons
Including individual species and genera
459.C47 Chimpanzees
459.C48 Chinchillas
459.C5 Chipmunks
459.C68 Coydogs
Crabs, Hermit see SF459.H47
459.C75 Crickets
459.D4 Deer
Including individual species and genera
459.D43 Degus
459.E37 Earthworms
459.E95 European wildcats
459.F47 Ferrets
Cf. SK293 Ferreting
459.F68 Foxes
459.F83 Frogs
Including individual species and genera
Cf. SF459.T35 Tadpoles
459.G35 Geckos
Including individual species and genera
459.G4 Gerbils
Including Mongolian gerbil
459.G53 Gibbons
459.G6 Gorillas
459.G7 Grasshoppers

Pets

Other animals, A-Z -- Continued

459.G9 Guinea pigs (Cavies)

Cf. SF401.G85 General culture

459.H3 Hamsters

459.H43 Hedgehogs

459.H47 Hermit crabs

Including land hermit crabs and individual species and genera of hermit crabs

459.I38 Iguanas

Including individual species and genera

459.I5 Insects

459.I85 Isopoda

Including wood lice

459.L33 Ladybugs

Land hermit crabs see SF459.H47

459.L4 Leopards

459.L47 Lions

459.L5 Lizards

Including individual species and genera

For geckos see SF459.G35

For iguanas see SF459.I38

Cf. SF515.5.L58 General culture

459.L52 Llamas

459.M5 Mice

459.M54 Millipedes

Miniature pigs see SF393.M55

459.M58 Mollusks

459.M6 Monkeys

Including individual species and genera

459.M97 Myriapoda

459.N48 Newts

459.O2 Ocelots

459.O74 Orangutans

459.O87 Otters

Potbellied pigs see SF393.P74

459.P64 Prairie dogs

459.P7 Primates

459.P85 Pumas

459.R22 Raccoons

459.R3 Rats

459.R4 Reptiles

459.R63 Rodents

459.S32 Salamanders

459.S35 Scorpions

459.S38 Skinks

Including individual species and genera

Pets
Other animals, A-Z -- Continued
459.S4 Skunks
Slugs see SF459.S48
459.S48 Snails. Slugs (Mollusks)
459.S5 Snakes
Including individual species and genera
Cf. SF408.6.S63 Snakes in zoos
Cf. SF515.5.S64 General culture and captive snakes
459.S64 Spiders
459.S74 Stick insects
459.S83 Sugar gliders
Swine see SF395.6
459.T35 Tadpoles
459.T37 Tarantulas
459.T46 Tigers
459.T54 Toads
Including individual species and genera
Cf. SF459.T35 Tadpoles
459.T8 Turtles
Including individual species and genera
Wildcats, European see SF459.E95
459.W62 Wolfdogs
459.W63 Wolves
Wood lice (Crustaceans) see SF459.I85
459.W66 Worms
Birds. Cage birds
Cf. QL671+ Ornithology
460 Periodicals. Societies. Serials
460.3 Collected works (nonserial)
460.4 Congresses
460.6 Dictionaries. Encyclopedias
461 General works
461.3 Essays and light literature
461.35 Juvenile works
461.37 Pictorial works
History and conditions
461.4 General works
461.43.A-Z By region or country, A-Z
461.5 Shows. Showing
461.6 Behavior
461.65 Training
461.7 Housing and environmental control
461.75 Feeding
461.8 Breeding
Wild birds
462.5 General works

Birds. Cage birds
Wild birds -- Continued
Wild bird trade
462.6 General works
462.63.A-Z By region or country, A-Z
By variety, species, etc.
see SF462.8, SF463+ etc.
462.8 Talking birds
Canaries
463 General works
463.4 Housing and environmental control
463.5 Feeding
463.6 Breeding
463.7.A-Z By breed, A-Z
463.7.B67 Border fancy
463.7.C64 Color
463.7.G55 Gloster fancy
463.7.R64 Roller
463.7.Y67 Yorkshire
Pigeons
464.5 Periodicals. Societies. Serials
464.7 Congresses
465 General works
465.3 Essays and light literature
465.35 Juvenile works
465.5 Shows. Showing
466 Feeding
467 Squabs
469 Homing, racing, and carrier pigeons
470.A-Z By breed or type, A-Z
470.C64 Color pigeons
470.K56 King pigeons
470.P68 Pouter pigeons
470.T78 Tumbler pigeons
470.T8 Turbit
470.W55 White pigeons
Including white racing homer
471 Flock books and trials
472 Miscellaneous
473.A-Z Other pet and captive birds, A-Z
473.A87 Australian finches
(473.A88) Australian parakeets
see SF473.B76
473.B76 Broad-tailed parrots
473.B8 Budgerigars
473.C6 Cockatiel
473.C63 Cockatoos

Birds. Cage birds
Other pet and captive birds, A-Z -- Continued

473.C64 Colius
473.C65 Conures
473.C73 Cranes
473.C76 Crows
473.D6 Doves
473.F5 Finches
473.G68 Gouldian finch
473.G74 Gray-cheeked parakeet
473.H39 Hawks
473.H84 Hummingbirds
473.K57 Kiwis
473.L57 Lories
473.L6 Lovebirds
473.M33 Macaws
473.M65 Monk parakeet
473.M85 Mute swan
473.M9 Mynahs
473.N5 Nightingales
473.O85 Owls
473.P24 Parrot finches
473.P3 Parrots
Including individual species
473.P46 Penguins
473.Q34 Quails
(473.S45) Senegal parrot
see SF473.P3
473.S6 Shama
473.S64 Softbills
473.S9 Starlings
473.T48 Thrushes
473.T8 Turtledove
473.W4 Weaverbirds
473.Y44 Yellowhead
473.Z42 Zebra finch

Aviaries see QL677.8

Poultry
Including chickens
Cf. HD9437+ Poultry industry

481 Periodicals. Societies. Serials
481.2 Congresses
481.25 Directories
Cf. SF493 Breeders' directories
481.3 Dictionaries. Encyclopedias
481.6 Vocational guidance

Study and teaching. Research

	Poultry
	Study and teaching. Research -- Continued
481.7	General works
481.75.A-Z	By region or country, A-Z
	History see SF487.7
	Exhibitions
483	General works
483.3.A-Z	International. By place, A-Z
	National, state, and local. By region or country
	United States
483.4	General works
483.43.A-Z	By region or state, A-Z
	Subarrange each state by Table S3a
483.45.A-Z	Other regions or countries, A-Z
	Subarrange each country by Table S3a
484	Supplies
485	Standards of excellence and judging in general
	Housing and environmental control see SF494.5
487	General works
	Including general care of poultry
487.3	Essays and light literature
487.5	Juvenile works
487.7	History (General)
	By region or country
	United States
487.8.A1	General works
487.8.A2-Z	By region or state, A-Z
488.A-Z	Other regions or countries, A-Z
489.A-Z	By breed, A-Z
	Including pedigree books
489.A6	Ancona
489.A65	Andalusian
	Including Blue Andalusian
489.A68	Araucana
489.A8	Australorp
489.B2	Bantams
	Blue Andalusian see SF489.A65
489.B8	Brahma
489.C2	Campine
489.C55	Cochin bantam
489.C6	Cornish
489.D67	Dominique
489.D7	Dorking
	Gamecock see SF502.8+
489.H2	Hamburg
489.H7	Houdan
489.L5	Leghorn

Poultry
By breed, A-Z -- Continued
489.M6 Minorca
Old English Game see SF502.8+
489.O8 Orpington
489.P7 Plymouth Rock
489.R6 Rhode Island red
489.S4 Sebright bantam
489.S8 Sussex
489.W9 Wyandotte
Eggs
Cf. HD9284 Egg trade
Cf. SF481+ Egg production
490 General works
490.3 Juvenile works
Preparation for market. Handling
490.5 General works
490.53 Candling
490.54 Cleaning
490.56 Storage
490.57 Packing and packaging
490.7 Grading. Standards. Quality
490.73 Inspection
490.8 Processing. Products
Including preservation
491 Catalogs of dealers
Breeding
492 General works
493 Breeders' directories
493.2 Germplasm resources
493.3 Artificial insemination
493.5 Behavior
Physiology see SF768.2.P6
Diseases see SF994+
494 Feeding
494.5 Housing and environmental control
Cf. TH4930 Construction
Hatcheries
Including incubation, brooding, etc.
495 General works
496.A-Z By region or country, A-Z
497 Incubator catalogs
498 Poultry sexing
498.4 Chicks
Including feeding and care
498.7 Broilers
For local see SF487.8+

	Poultry -- Continued
498.8	Fryers
499	Capons and caponizing
	Cf. SF889 Castration
499.5	Dubbing
	Egg preservation see SF490.8
502	Economic aspects of culture (General). Marketing
	For local see SF487.8+
	Processing see TS1968
	Game fowls and cockfighting
	Including Old English Game
502.8	Periodicals. Societies. Serials
502.82	Congresses
503	General works
	Biography
503.4	Collective
503.42.A-Z	Individual, A-Z
	History and conditions
503.5	General works
503.52.A-Z	By region or country, A-Z
	Ducks and geese
	Cf. SF510.D8 Wild ducks
504.7	Periodicals. Societies. Serials
504.75	Congresses
505	General works
505.3	Juvenile works
505.34	Essays and light literature
	By region or country
	United States
505.4	General works
505.43.A-Z	By region or state, A-Z
505.44.A-Z	Other regions or countries, A-Z
505.5	Shows. Showing
505.55	Housing and environmental control
505.57	Feeding
505.6	Breeding
505.63.A-Z	By breed, species, or group, A-Z
505.63.B74	Brown teal
505.63.C34	Call duck
506	Guinea fowl
507	Turkeys
	Game birds
508	General works
509	Pheasants
510.A-Z	Other, A-Z
510.D8	Ducks
	Cf. SF504.7+ Domestic ducks

	Game birds
	Other, A-Z -- Continued
510.H68	Houbara
510.P3	Partridges
510.P7	Prairie chickens
510.Q2	Quail
510.W3	Waterfowl
	Cf. SF512.5 Ornamental waterfowl
(510.5)	Emus
	see SF511.5.E46
(510.6)	Greater rhea
	see SF511.5.G74
	Ratites. Ostrich
511	General works
511.3.A-Z	By region or country, A-Z
511.5.A-Z	Individual and groups, A-Z
511.5.E46	Emus
511.5.G74	Greater rhea
	Ornamental birds
	Cf. SF460+ Cage birds
512	General works
512.5	Water birds. Ornamental waterfowl
513.A-Z	Individual, A-Z
513.J8	Jungle cock
513.P4	Peafowl
	Pheasants see SF509
	Reptiles
	Cf. SF459.R4 Pets
515	General works
515.5.A-Z	Individual, A-Z
515.5.A44	Alligators
	Cf. SF459.A4 Alligators as pets
	Boas see SF515.5.B64
515.5.B64	Boidae
	Including boas and pythons
515.5.C75	Crocodiles
515.5.D45	Dendrobatidae
515.5.G37	Garter snakes
515.5.G43	Geckos
515.5.I38	Iguanas
515.5.L58	Lizards
	Cf. SF459.L5 Pets
515.5.M65	Monitor lizards
515.5.N47	Nerodia
515.5.N48	Newts
	Pythons see SF515.5.B64
515.5.R37	Rattlesnakes

	Reptiles
	Individual, A-Z -- Continued
515.5.S64	Snakes
	Cf. SF408.6.S63 Snakes in zoos
	Cf. SF459.S5 General culture and captive snakes
515.5.T8	Tuatara
	Beneficial insects and insect culture
517	General works
517.3.A-Z	By region or country, A-Z
518	Insect rearing
	Cf. QL461+ Zoology
	Cf. SB933.6 Sterilization control
	Cf. SF459.I5 Insects as pets
	Bee culture
	Cf. QL563+ Zoology
521	Periodicals. Societies. Serials
521.2	Congresses
522	Documents
522.3	Dictionaries. Encyclopedias
	General works
522.5	Early works to 1800
523	1800-
523.3	Essays and light literature
523.5	Juvenile works
523.7	Pictorial works
	Biography
523.8	Collective
523.82.A-Z	Individual, A-Z
	History and conditions
524	General works
	By region or country
	United States
524.5	General works
524.52.A-Z	By region or state, A-Z
531.A-Z	Other regions or countries, A-Z
	Study and teaching. Research
531.3	General works
531.35	Audiovisual aids
	Exhibitions
531.4.A-Z	International. By place, A-Z
531.42.A-Z	National and local. By country, A-Z
	Subarrange each country by Table S3a
	Breeding
531.5	General works
531.55	Queen rearing
531.6	Swarming
531.7	Wintering

Beneficial insects and insect culture
Bee culture -- Continued

532 Hives and appliances
533 Catalogs of beekeeper's supplies
Honey plants. Botany for beekeepers
535 General works
535.2.A-Z By region or country, A-Z
535.5 Supplemental feeding
537 Bee hunting
Cf. QL568.A6 Zoology
Diseases and pests
538 General works
538.3.A-Z By region or country, A-Z
538.5.A-Z By individual or type of disease or pest, A-Z
538.5.A37 Africanized honeybee
Cf. SF539.5+ Culture
538.5.A44 American foulbrood
538.5.B72 Braula coeca
538.5.C65 Colony collapse disorder
538.5.D95 Dysentery
538.5.E87 European foulbrood
(538.5.F68) Foul brood, American
see SF538.5.A44
(538.5.F69) Foul brood, European
see SF538.5.E87
538.5.M55 Mildew
538.5.M57 Mites
538.5.N67 Nosema apis
538.5.P65 Poisoning
Including pesticide toxicolocy
538.5.S23 Sacbrood
538.5.V37 Varroa disease. Varroa jacobsoni
539 Honey and other hive products
Cf. HD9120 Honey industry
Africanized honeybee
Cf. SF538.5.A37 Honeybee pest
539.5 General works
539.6.A-Z By region or country, A-Z
539.8.A-Z Other bees, A-Z
539.8.A65 Apis cerana
(539.8.C47) Apis cerana
see SF539.8.A65
539.8.M44 Melipona
539.8.O73 Orchard mason bee

Beneficial insects and insect culture -- Continued
Sericulture. Silk culture
Class here works on the culture of Bombyx more and silkworms (General)
Cf. SF559.5+ other silkworms
Cf. HD9910+ Silk industry

541 Periodicals. Societies. Serials
541.6 Dictionaries. Encyclopedias
542 General works
542.5 Juvenile works
Study and teaching. Research
542.7 General works
542.75.A-Z By region or country, A-Z
Subarrange each country by Table S3a
History and conditions
543 General works
545 United States
547 England
549 France
551 Germany
553.A-Z Other regions or countries, A-Z
554 Breeding
555 Diseases
557 Mulberry culture
559 Catalogs of silk cultural implements
Non-mulberry silkworms and sericulture
559.5 General works
560.A-Z Individual silkworms, A-Z
560.A36 Ailanthus moth
560.C45 Chinese oak silkworm
560.M84 Muga moth
560.O18 Oak tasar silkworm
560.Y34 Yamamai
561 Lac-insects
Cf. HD9769.L3+ Lac industry
Cf. QL527.K44 Zoology
Cf. TP938 Varnishes. Shellac
562.A-Z Other insects, A-Z
562.A58 Ants
562.A63 Aphantorhaphopsis samarensis
562.B43 Beetles
562.B58 Boll weevil
Brown mopane worm see SF562.M56
562.B8 Butterflies
Cf. SF459.B87 Pets
562.C45 Chinese wax scale insect
562.C48 Chrysoperla carnea

Beneficial insects and insect culture
Other insects, A-Z -- Continued

562.C6	Cochineal
562.E43	Elaeidobius kamerunicus
	Ericerus pela see SF562.C45
(562.I52)	Imbrasia belina see SF562.M56
562.L33	Lacewings
562.L34	Ladybugs
562.L46	Lepidoptera
562.M56	Mopane worm Including brown mopane worm
562.M58	Mosquitoes
562.M6	Moths
562.O74	Orius
562.P64	Polyphagidae
562.T75	Trichogramma
	Insects injurious to animals
	General works see SF810.A3
	Special, A-Z see SF810.A4+
597.A-Z	Other invertebrate animals, A-Z
597.E3	Earthworms
597.S6	Snails
	Veterinary medicine For veterinary microbiology (General) see SF780.2 For bacteriology (General) see SF780.3 Cf. HD9996 Veterinary supplies Cf. SF995.84+ Zoo veterinarians
	Periodicals. Societies. Serials
600	International bureaus, etc.
601	American and British
602	French
603	German
604	Other
	Veterinary hospitals
604.4	Periodicals. Societies. Serials
604.5	General works
604.55	Juvenile works
	By region or country
	United States
604.6	General works
604.62.A-Z	By region or state, A-Z *Under each state:* *.x* *General works* *.x2A-.x2Z* *Individual hospitals. By name, A-Z*

Veterinary medicine
Veterinary hospitals
By region or country -- Continued
604.63.A-Z Other regions or countries, A-Z
Under each country:
.x General works
.x2A-.x2Z Individual hospitals. By name, A-Z
604.7 Architectural planning and construction
Including designs and plans
605 Congresses
Exhibitions
606.A1 General works
606.A2-Z By region or country
Under each country:
.x General works
.x2A-.x2Z Special. By name, A-Z
607 Collections
609 Dictionaries. Encyclopedias
610 Nomenclature. Terminology. Abbreviations
Communication in veterinary medicine
610.5 General works
610.6 Information services
610.7 Computer network resources
Including the Internet
610.8 Veterinary literature
611 Directories
Biography
612 Collective
613.A-Z Individual, A-Z
History and conditions
615 General works
621-723 By region or country (Table S1)
Add number in table to SF600
724 Tropics
Veterinary public health
Including preventive medicine, zoonosis control, and general quarantine
Cf. SF757+ Veterinary hygiene
740 General works
By region or country see SF621+
General works
743 Early works to 1800
745 1800-
Alternative veterinary medicine. Holistic veterinary medicine
745.5 General works
746 Homeopathic veterinary medicine
747 Addresses, essays, lectures

SF

Veterinary medicine -- Continued

748 Handbooks, manuals, etc.

Manuals for the non-professional

751 United States and Canada

753 Great Britain

755 Other

756 Juvenile works

756.28 Vocational guidance

Study and teaching. Research

Including schools and research institutions and laboratories

756.3 General works

756.34.A-Z International institutions. By name, A-Z

By region or country

United States

756.35 General works

756.36.A-Z By region or state, A-Z

Under each state:

.x	*General works*
.x2A-.x2Z	*Individual schools and research institutions. By name, A-Z*

756.37.A-Z Other regions or countries, A-Z

Under each country:

.x	*General works*
.x2A-.x2Z	*Individual schools and research institutions. By name, A-Z*

756.39 Veterinary ethics

756.394 Euthanasia

Economics of veterinary practice

756.4 General works

Employment surveys, manpower requirements, distribution and utilization of veterinarians and veterinary personnel

756.46 General works

By region or country

United States

756.47 General works

756.475.A-Z By region or state, A-Z

756.48.A-Z Other regions or countries, A-Z

Veterinary genetics

For hereditary aspects of particular diseases see SF781+

Cf. SF757.23+ Veterinary immunogenetics

756.5 General works

756.6 Veterinary cytogenetics

756.65 Genome mapping

756.7 Veterinary ethology

For behavior of special classes or breeds of animals, see the class or breed, e.g. Horse behavior, SF281; Arabian horse behavior, SF293.A8

Veterinary medicine -- Continued
Veterinary psychopathology
756.8 General works
756.83 Animal behavior therapy
For behavior therapy of special classes or breeds of animals, see the class or breed, e. g. Behavior therapy for dogs SF433, Behavior therapy for American pit bull terrier SF429.A72
Veterinary psychopharmacology. Veterinary psychotropic drugs
756.84 General works
756.85 Psychotropic plants
Veterinary hygiene
757 General works
By region or country see SF621+
757.15 Veterinary disinfection
Veterinary immunology
Cf. SF910.I45 Immunologic diseases in animals
757.2 General works
Veterinary immunogenetics
757.23 General works
757.234 Histocompatibility
757.25 Veterinary cytology
Cf. SF756.6 Veterinary cytogenetics
757.3 Veterinary histology
Cf. SF769.25 Veterinary histopathology
757.5 Veterinary toxicology
757.8 Veterinary radiology. Veterinary nuclear medicine. Veterinary radiography
758 Miscellaneous
759 Tables, examinations, questions, etc.
760.A-Z Special aspects of the subject as a whole, A-Z
760.A54 Animal handling
760.A55 Animal immobilization
Cf. QL62.5 Zoology
760.C55 Climatology
760.E4 Electronic data processing
760.E44 Electronics
Handling, Animal see SF760.A54
Immobilization, Animal see SF760.A55
760.L43 Leadership
760.R44 Reporting of diseases
760.S64 Specialities. Specialization
760.S73 Statistical methods
Veterinary anatomy
For radiographic atlases see SF757.8
761 General works

SF

Veterinary medicine
Veterinary anatomy -- Continued
762 Laboratory manuals. Veterinary dissection
765 Horse
Cf. SF279 Conformation
767.A-Z Other, A-Z
767.B57 Birds
Including cage birds
767.C28 Camels
767.C29 Cats
767.C3 Cattle
767.D6 Dogs
767.P6 Poultry
767.S5 Sheep
767.S95 Swine
767.W38 Water buffalo
767.5 Veterinary embryology
Veterinary physiology
768 General works
768.2.A-Z By animal, A-Z
768.2.C27 Camels
768.2.C3 Cattle
768.2.D6 Dogs
768.2.H67 Horses
768.2.P6 Poultry
768.2.R8 Ruminants
768.2.S5 Sheep
768.2.S95 Swine
768.3 Veterinary endocrinology
768.5 Veterinary geriatrics
Veterinary pathology
Including post-mortem examinations
Cf. SF772.6+ Veterinary clinical pathology
769 General works
769.25 Veterinary histopathology
769.3 Veterinary clinical biochemistry
769.4 Veterinary pathophysiology
769.44 Paleopathology
769.47 Veterinary forensic medicine
769.5 Veterinary hematology
Cf. SF772.67 Blood examination
Diagnosis
771 General works
Biopsy see SF772.65
772.5 Physical diagnosis
772.55 Endoscopy
Radiodiagnosis see SF757.8

Veterinary medicine
Diagnosis -- Continued
772.58 Ultrasonography
Laboratory diagnosis. Veterinary clinical pathology
772.6 General works
772.65 Biopsy
Chemical examination. Veterinary clinical chemistry
772.66 General works
772.665 Tables. Reference values
772.67 Blood examination
Cf. SF769.5 Veterinary hematology
772.7 Feces examination
773 Urine examination
774 Other special methods
Animal health technology
774.4 General works
774.5 Veterinary nursing
778 Veterinary emergencies. Veterinary critical care. First aid for animals
Cf. SF914.3+ Veterinary surgical emergencies. Veterinary traumatology
Laws. Veterinary jurisprudence
see class K
780.2 Veterinary microbiology
780.3 Veterinary bacteriology
780.4 Veterinary virology
Deficiency diseases see SF854+
Veterinary parasitology see SF810.A3+
780.6 Veterinary protozoology
Including Apicomplexa
Cf. QR251+ Pathogenic protozoa
780.7 Veterinary mycology
780.9 Veterinary epidemiology. Epizootiology
Communicable diseases of animals
For special microbial diseases see SF784+
For special parasitic diseases see SF810.A4+
For special diseases associated with a specific animal see SF951+
781 General works
Special diseases
784 Actinomycosis
787 Anthrax
790 Azoturia
791 Babesiosis
792 Coccidiosis
792.5 Dermatophilosis
793 Foot-and-mouth disease

	Veterinary medicine
	Communicable diseases of animals
	Special diseases -- Continued
796	Glanders
	Hemorrhagic septicemia see SF802
797	Hydrophobia. Rabies
799	Meningitis
	Piroplasmosis see SF791
	Rabies see SF797
802	Septicemia
	Including hemorrhagic septicemia
804	Tetanus
	Texas fever see SF967.B17
807	Trypanosomiasis
	Including tsetse-fly disease
808	Tuberculosis
809.A-Z	Other, A-Z
809.A44	Akabane disease
809.A86	Aspergillosis
809.A94	Aujeszky's disease
809.B55	Bluetongue
809.B67	Borrelia infections
809.B8	Brucella infections
809.C45	Chlamydia infections
809.C6	Clostridium infections
809.D87	Dysentery
809.E62	Encephalitis
809.E63	Enterobacteriaceae infections
809.E64	Enterovirus infections
809.E7	Equine encephalomyelitis
809.E82	Escherichia coli infections
809.F87	Fusobacterium infections
809.H4	Heartwater
809.H45	Hemmorrhagic fever
809.H47	Herpesvirus diseases
(809.J6)	Johne's disease see SF809.P375
809.L4	Leptospirosis
809.L5	Listeriosis
809.M9	Mycoplasma infections
809.N63	Nocardia infections
809.P37	Paramyxovirus infections
809.P375	Paratuberculosis
809.P38	Pasteurella infections
(809.P8)	Pseudorabies see SF809.A94
809.R52	Rickettsial diseases

Veterinary medicine
Communicable diseases of animals
Special diseases
Other, A-Z -- Continued

809.R55 Ringworm
809.S24 Salmonella infections
809.S6 Spirochaeta and spirochetosis
809.S72 Staphyloccal infections
809.T5 Theileria infections
Tick-borne diseases see SF809.T5
Tinea see SF809.R55
809.T6 Toxoplasmosis
809.V52 Vibrio infections
809.Y47 Yersinia enterocolitica infections

Veterinary parasitology
For parasites and pests of special classes of animals see SF951+

810.A3 General works
810.A4-Z By parasite or pest, A-Z
Apicomplexa see SF780.6
810.A5 Ascaridae
810.B4 Besnoitiosis
810.B6 Blowflies
810.C3 Capillaria
810.C5 Cestodes
810.D4 Dermatobia
810.D48 Dicrocoelium
810.D5 Dictyocaulus
810.E8 Eurytrema
810.F3 Fasciola
810.F47 Fleas
810.F5 Flies
Fungi see SF780.7
810.H3 Haemosporidia
810.H44 Helminths
810.H6 Horn fly
810.H8 Hydatids
810.L47 Lice
810.L8 Lungworms
810.M5 Mites
810.N4 Nematodes
810.O6 Onchocerca
Protozoa see SF780.6
810.S26 Sarcoptes
810.S3 Screwworm
Tapeworms see SF810.C5

Veterinary medicine
Veterinary parasitology
By parasite or pest, A-Z -- Continued
810.T5 Ticks
Including tick-borne diseases (General)
810.T69 Trematodes
810.T7 Trichina and trichinosis
810.T73 Trichomonas
810.T75 Trichosurus vulpecula
Tsetse fly see SF807
Predatory animals and their control
Cf. QL758 Predation
810.5 General works
810.6.A-Z By region or country, A-Z
810.7.A-Z By predator, A-Z
810.7.B58 Black bear
810.7.B73 Brown bear
810.7.B76 Brown tree snake
810.7.C88 Coyote
810.7.D56 Dingo
810.7.D65 Dogs
810.7.E74 Ermine
810.7.R43 Red fox
810.7.T76 Trimeresurus flavoviridis
810.7.W65 Wolves
Veterinary medicine of special organs, regions, and systems
For diseases of special classes of animals see SF951+
811 Cardiovascular system
831 Respiratory system
Nutritional system
851 General works
852 Mouth
Deficiency diseases
854 General works
855.A-Z Special deficiencies, A-Z
855.I75 Iron
855.M34 Magnesium
855.P67 Potassium
855.P76 Protein
855.S44 Selenium
855.T7 Trace elements
855.V58 Vitamins
Including individual vitamin deficiencies
Teeth. Dentistry
867 General works
869 Age determination by teeth

Veterinary medicine
Veterinary medicine of special organs, regions, and systems -- Continued
Urinary and reproductive organs. Theriogenology
Including urogenital organs
871 General works
887 Obstetrics
Cf. SF105+ Breeding
889 Castration
Cf. SF499 Caponizing
890 Mammary glands
Cf. SF967.U3 Cattle
891 Eyes, ears, throat, etc.
895 Nervous system
Musculoskeletal system and skin
Including skin glands
Cf. SF910.5 Veterinary orthopedics
901 General works
Feet
906 General works
Horse's foot and horseshoeing
Including hoof diseases
Cf. UC640+ Military horseshoeing
907 General works
909 Horseshoes, trade publications
910.A-Z Other diseases and conditions, A-Z
For diseases of special classes of animals see SF951+
Acid-base imbalances see SF910.W38
910.A35 Acid-forming emissions
Aging see SF768.5
910.B45 Bloat
Cancer see SF910.T8
910.H86 Hypocalcemia
910.I45 Immunologic diseases
910.L4 Leukemia
910.L8 Loco-weed disease
910.M48 Metabolic disorders
910.P34 Pain
910.S5 Shock
910.T47 Tetany
910.T8 Tumors
Including cancer
910.W38 Water-electrolyte imbalances. Acid-base imbalances
910.5 Veterinary orthopedics
Cf. SF901+ Bones, joints, muscles, and skin

Veterinary medicine -- Continued
Veterinary surgery
For surgery of special classes of animals see SF951+
Cf. RD29.5.A+ Experimental surgery on laboratory animals
911 General works
912 Dehorning
Fractures see SF914.4
Wounds and injuries see SF914.3+
913 Surgical instruments
Including catalogs
914 Anesthesia
914.2 Veterinary endoscopic surgery
Veterinary surgical emergencies. Veterinary traumatology
Cf. SF910.S5 Shock
914.3 General works
914.4 Fractures
Cf. SF959.F78 Fractures in horses
914.5 Veterinary acupuncture
Veterinary pharmacology
Cf. SF98.M4 Medicated feeds
Cf. SF756.84+ Veterinary psychopharmacology
915 General works
916.5 Formularies. Collected prescriptions
917 Veterinary drugs
918.A-Z Special, A-Z
918.A25 Adrenergic alpha blockers
918.A27 Adrenergic beta agonists
918.A45 Anthelmintics
918.A48 Anti-infective agents
918.A5 Antibiotics
918.B5 Biologicals
918.C45 Chlorfenvinphos
918.F87 Furosemide
918.H47 Herbs
Cf. SF756.85 Psychotropic plants
918.H75 Hormones
918.I83 Ivermectin
918.N5 Nicotine solutions
918.N65 Nonsteroidal anti-inflammatory agents
918.P3 Parbendazole
918.P5 Phenothiazine
918.P75 Procaine
918.T5 Thiazolylbenzimidazole
918.V32 Vaccines
Methods of drug administration
919 General works

Veterinary medicine
Veterinary pharmacology
Methods of drug administration -- Continued

919.5.A-Z Special, A-Z
919.5.B55 Blood transfusion
919.5.C65 Controlled release
919.5.I5 Inhalation
919.5.I53 Injection
925 Veterinary physical medicine
Diseases of special classes of animals
Horses
951 General works
956 Sports medicine
959.A-Z Diseases and pests, A-Z
959.A3 African horse sickness
959.A6 Anemia, Infectious
959.A76 Arteritis, Viral
959.A78 Arthritis
959.A8 Ascaris equorum
959.B32 Babesiosis
959.B6 Botflies
959.B65 Bowed tendon
959.B78 Brucellosis
959.C376 Cardiovascular diseases
Including heart diseases
Cerebral meningitis see SF959.M4
959.C6 Colic
959.D6 Dourine
959.E5 Encephalomyelitis
Equine infectious anemia see SF959.A6
Equine viral arteritis see SF959.A76
959.E93 Eye diseases
959.F5 Filariasis
959.F6 Fistula
959.F78 Fractures
Generative organs diseases see SF959.U73
Glanders see SF796
Heart diseases see SF959.C376
959.H45 Herpesvirus diseases
Hoof diseases see SF907+
959.H9 Hyperparathyroidism
959.H94 Hyphomycosis
Infectious anemia see SF959.A6
959.J64 Joint diseases
959.K5 Kimberley horse disease
959.L25 Lameness
959.L3 Laminitis

Veterinary medicine
Diseases of special classes of animals
Horses
Diseases and pests, A-Z -- Continued

959.L42 Leg injuries
959.M4 Meningitis
959.M66 Mouth diseases. Teeth diseases
959.N39 Navicular disease
959.N45 Neonatal diseases
959.N47 Nervous system diseases
959.P37 Parasites and pests
Piroplasmosis see SF959.B32
959.R47 Respiratory diseases
959.S54 Skin diseases
959.S6 Spavin
959.S65 Spinal cord disease
959.S8 Strongylidae
(959.T43) Teeth diseases
see SF959.M66
959.T47 Tendon injuries
959.T7 Trypanosomiasis
959.U73 Urinary and reproductive diseases
959.V57 Virus diseases (General)

Cattle

961 General works
962 Blackleg
963 Mange
964 Contagious pleuropneumonia
966 Rinderpest
967.A-Z Other, A-Z
967.A2 Acetonemia
African coast fever see SF967.E3
African trypanosomiasis see SF967.T78
967.A6 Anaplasmosis
967.B17 Babesiosis
967.B64 Boophilus microplus
Bovine leukosis see SF967.L4
Bovine spongiform encephalopathy see SF967.S63
Bovine viral diarrhea see SF967.M78
967.B7 Brucellosis
967.C47 Chlamydia infections
967.C5 Cholera
967.C6 Coccidiosis
967.C64 Colibacillosis
Communicable diseases see SF961
967.C96 Cysticerosis
967.D4 Deficiency diseases

Veterinary medicine
Diseases of special classes of animals
Cattle
Other, A-Z -- Continued

967.D52 Diarrhea
Including neonatal diarrhea
Cf. SF967.M78 Bovine viral diarrhea
967.D53 Dictyocaulus viviparus
967.D9 Dyspepsia
967.E3 East coast fever
967.E5 Emphysema, Pulmonary
967.E65 Epizootic catarrh
967.F37 Fascioliasis
967.F55 Fluorosis
967.G65 Granular vaginitis
967.G7 Grass tetany
967.H3 Haematuria
967.H44 Hemorrhagic septicemia
967.H65 Hoof diseases
Hydrophobia see SF967.R3
967.I48 Infectious bovine rhinotracheitis
Infectious diseases see SF961
Infertility see SF967.S75
(967.J6) Johne's disease
see SF967.P33
967.K47 Keratoconjunctivitis
967.L3 Lameness
967.L4 Leukemia
967.L7 Liver diseases
967.L8 Lumpy skin disease
967.M3 Mastitis
967.M5 Milk fever
967.M78 Mucosal diseases
Including bovine viral diarrhea
967.M8 Muscular dystrophy
967.O6 Onchocerciasis
Osteophytosis, Spinal see SF967.S6
967.P3 Parasites and pests
967.P33 Paratuberculosis
Piroplasmosis see SF967.B17
967.R3 Rabies
967.R47 Respiratory diseases
967.R5 Rickets
Rhinotracheitis, Infectious bovine see SF967.I48
967.S3 Scabies
967.S57 Simulium arcticum
Skin disease, Lumpy see SF967.L8

Veterinary medicine
Diseases of special classes of animals
Cattle
Other, A-Z -- Continued

967.S6 Spinal osteophytosis
967.S63 Spongiform encephalopathy
967.S75 Sterility. Infertility
967.S8 Stomatitis
Tetany, Grass see SF967.G7
967.T44 Theileriosis
Cf. SF967.E3 East coast fever
967.T47 Three-day sickness
967.T52 Ticks
967.T7 Trichomoniasis
967.T78 Trypanosomiasis
967.T8 Tuberculosis
967.U3 Udder diseases
967.U8 Uterine diseases
Vaginitis, Granular see SF967.G65
967.V5 Vibriosis
Viral diarrhea, Bovine see SF967.M78
967.W3 Warble-flies
967.W35 Warts

Sheep and goats
968 General works
969.A-Z Diseases and pests, A-Z
Adenomatosis, Pulmonary see SF969.P8
969.A94 Aujeszky's disease
969.B32 Babesiosis
969.B5 Blowflies
969.B54 Bluetongue
969.B58 Border disease
969.B6 Botflies
969.B78 Brucellosis
969.C65 Contagious agalactia
969.D9 Dysentery
969.E5 Enterotoxemia
969.F6 Foot rot
969.K47 Keratoconjunctivitis
969.L5 Lice
969.L55 Liver-fluke
969.L56 Liver-rot
969.L6 Locomotor ataxia
969.L65 Louping ill
969.M34 Maedi-visna
969.N44 Nematodes
969.N45 Nematodirus

Veterinary medicine
Diseases of special classes of animals
Sheep and goats
Diseases and pests, A-Z -- Continued

969.P3 Parasites and pests
969.P34 Paratuberculosis
969.P34 Paratuberculosis
969.P47 Peste des petits ruminants
Piroplasmosis see SF969.B32
969.P74 Psoroptic scabies
969.P8 Pulmonary adenomatosis
969.S2 Scabies
969.S3 Scrapie
969.S6 Smallpox
969.T8 Tularemia

Swine

971 General works
973 Classical swine fever
977.A-Z Other, A-Z
977.A4 African swine fever
977.A94 Aujeszky's disease
977.B7 Brucellosis
977.C55 Clostridial enteritis
977.C67 Corynebacterium diseases
977.D4 Deficiency diseases
977.D9 Dystentery
977.E3 Edema
977.E7 Erysipelas
977.E83 Escherichia coli infections
Exanthema, Vesicular see SF977.V3
Gastroenteritis, Transmissible see SF977.T7
977.L5 Liver diseases
977.M9 Muscle necrosis
977.M94 Mycoplasma infections
977.P3 Parasites and pests
(977.P5) Plague
see SF973
977.P6 Pneumonia
977.P66 Poisoning
Stomatitis, Vesicular see SF977.V4
977.T4 Teschen disease
977.T7 Transmissible gastroenteritis
977.V28 Vesicular disease
977.V3 Vesicular exanthema
977.V4 Vesicular stomatitis
977.V57 Virus diseases

Pets

Veterinary medicine
Diseases of special classes of animals
Pets -- Continued
981 General works
Cats
985 General works
986.A-Z Diseases and pests, A-Z
986.B56 Blindness. Blind cats
986.C33 Cancer
986.C37 Cat flea
986.E93 Eye diseases
986.G37 Gastroenteritis
986.I55 Immunodeficiency virus infection
986.L48 Leukemia
986.P37 Parasites
Reproductive diseases see SF986.U74
986.S55 Skin diseases
986.U74 Urinary and reproductive diseases
Dogs
991 General works
991.6 Sports medicine
992.A-Z Diseases and pests, A-Z
992.A44 Allergy
992.A5 Anemia
992.A77 Arthritis
992.B55 Blacktongue
992.B56 Blindness. Blind dogs
992.B57 Blood diseases
992.C35 Cancer
992.C37 Cardiopulmonary diseases. Cardiovascular diseases
Including heart diseases
Cardiovascular diseases see SF992.C37
992.D33 Deafness. Deaf dogs
992.D46 Disabilities (General). Dogs with disabilities
992.D5 Distemper
992.E53 Endocrine diseases
992.E57 Epilepsy
992.E92 Eye diseases
992.G38 Gastrointestinal diseases
Generative organs diseases see SF992.U75
992.G45 Genetic disorders
Heart diseases see SF992.C37
992.H4 Heartworm disease
992.H56 Hip dysplasia
992.J64 Joint diseases
992.K53 Kidney diseases
992.L46 Leptospirosis

Veterinary medicine
Diseases of special classes of animals
Pets
Dogs
Diseases and pests, A-Z -- Continued

992.L5 Liver diseases
992.L94 Lymphomas
992.M68 Mouth diseases. Teeth diseases
992.M86 Musculoskeletal system diseases
992.N3 Nervous system diseases
992.N88 Nutrition disorders
992.O74 Otitis
992.P3 Parasites and pests
992.P64 Poisoning
992.R3 Rabies
Reproductive diseases see SF992.U75
992.R47 Respiratory diseases
992.S55 Skin diseases
Including pyoderma
Teeth diseases see SF992.M68
992.U75 Urinary and reproductive diseases

Avian diseases
994 General works
Diseases of special classes of birds
994.2.A-Z Cage birds, A-Z
994.2.A1 General
994.2.B8 Budgerigars
994.2.C3 Canaries
994.2.P37 Parrots
994.2.T7 Tropical birds
994.4.A-Z Game birds, A-Z
994.4.A1 General
994.4.G7 Grouse
994.4.M3 Mallard
994.4.R5 Ring-necked pheasant
994.4.U6 Upland game birds
994.4.W3 Waterfowl
Birds of prey
994.5 General works
994.52.A-Z Individual species, A-Z
Charadriiformes see SF995.55
Ciconiiformes see SF995.55
Passeriformes. Songbirds
994.56 General works
994.563.A-Z By family, A-Z
Class individual species with the family
994.563.C34 Callaeidae

SF

Veterinary medicine
Diseases of special classes of animals
Avian diseases
Diseases of special classes of birds -- Continued

994.57 Penguins
994.6 Pigeons
Poultry
Including chickens
995 General works
995.2 Ducks. Geese
995.4 Turkeys
Ratites
995.5 General works
995.52.A-Z Individual species or groups, A-Z
995.52.K58 Kiwis
995.55 Waders. Wading birds
Including Charadriiformes and Ciconiiformes
995.6.A-Z By disease or pest, A-Z
Class here general works including poultry (general) and chickens
For special birds, see the type of bird
995.6.A6 Anemia
995.6.B32 Bacterial diseases
Beak and feather disease, Psittacine see SF995.6.P75
995.6.B66 Botulism
995.6.C4 Chicken cholera
Cholera see SF995.6.C4
995.6.C6 Coccidiosis
995.6.D4 Deficiency diseases
995.6.E5 Encephalomyelitis
995.6.F3 Fatty liver syndrome
(995.6.F59) Fowl plague
see SF995.6.I6
995.6.F595 Fowl pox
995.6.F6 Fowl typhoid
995.6.I6 Influenza
995.6.L4 Leukosis
Liver syndrome, Fatty see SF995.6.F3
Lymphomatosis see SF995.6.M33
995.6.M3 Malaria
995.6.M32 Mallophaga
995.6.M33 Marek's disease
995.6.M5 Mites
995.6.N37 Nematoda
995.6.N4 Newcastle disease
Cf. QR189.5.N48 Vaccines
995.6.O7 Ornithosis

Veterinary medicine
Diseases of special classes of animals
Avian diseases
By disease or pest, A-Z -- Continued

995.6.P3	Paralysis
995.6.P35	Parasites
995.6.P4	Perosis
	Plague see SF995.6.I6
995.6.P5	Plasmodium
995.6.P75	Psittacine beak and feather disease
995.6.P8	Pullorum disease
995.6.S3	Salmonella infections
995.6.S75	Stress
995.6.T8	Tuberculosis
995.6.T85	Tumors
	Typhoid see SF995.6.F6
995.6.V55	Virus diseases
	Bees see SF538+
	Zoo animals
	Zoo veterinarians
995.84	General works
995.85	Juvenile works
995.86.A-Z	By region or country, A-Z
	Biography
995.87	Collective
995.88.A-Z	Individual, A-Z
996	General works
	Wild animals
	Wildlife veterinarians
	Biography
996.35	Collective
996.36.A-Z	Individual, A-Z
996.4	General works
996.45	Wildlife rehabilitation Cf. QL83.2 Wildlife rescue
996.5	Laboratory animals Including laboratory rabbits and rodents
997.3	Fur-bearing animals
997.5.A-Z	Other animals or groups of animals, A-Z Including individual diseases occurring in particular animals, e.g., Myxomatosis, SF997.5.R2
997.5.A43	American bison
997.5.A45	Amphibians
997.5.A63	Apes
997.5.A65	Aquatic animals
997.5.B38	Bats
997.5.B43	Bears

Veterinary medicine
Diseases of special classes of animals
Other animals or groups of animals, A-Z -- Continued

997.5.B8 Buffaloes
997.5.C3 Camelidae. Camels
997.5.C37 Caribou
997.5.C46 Cervidae
Including chronic wasting disease
997.5.C5 Chinchillas
997.5.C65 Corals
997.5.D4 Deer
997.5.E4 Elephants
997.5.E74 Ermine
997.5.E95 Exotic animals
997.5.F47 Ferret
Fishes see SH171+
Fishes, Aquarium see SF458.5
997.5.F76 Frogs
997.5.G65 Gorilla
997.5.G84 Guinea pigs
997.5.H43 Hedgehogs
997.5.I5 Invertebrates
Laboratory animals see SF996.5
997.5.L35 Lama (Genus)
997.5.M33 Marine fauna
997.5.M35 Marine mammals
997.5.M4 Mice
997.5.M5 Minks
997.5.M8 Muskrats
997.5.N44 Nematoda
997.5.P7 Primates
997.5.R2 Rabbits
Including individual species
Including myxomatosis
Cf. SF996.5 Laboratory rabbit diseases
997.5.R3 Rats
997.5.R35 Reindeer
997.5.R4 Reptiles
997.5.R64 Rodents
Cf. SF996.5 Laboratory rodent diseases
997.5.R86 Ruminants
997.5.S65 Snakes
Including individual species and genera
997.5.T73 Trichosurus vulpecula
997.5.T87 Turtles
997.5.U5 Ungulata

Veterinary medicine
Diseases of special classes of animals
Other animals or groups of animals, A-Z -- Continued
997.5.W64 Wombats
Including individual species
Zoo animals see SF996
Quarantine, inspection, etc. see SF740+
1100 Miscellaneous pamphlets

Aquaculture. Fisheries. Angling
Cf. HD9450+ Aquaculture industry, fish trade, fishery products industry
Cf. QL614+ Fishes
1 Periodicals. Societies. Serials
3 Congresses
Documents
Class here general documents (reports of departments, bureaus, etc.) and special documents of general character not limited to a subject elsewhere provided for
United States
11.A1-.A5 Federal
11.A6-Z State
Other countries
see SH223+
19 Collections
Biography
20.A1 Collective
20.A2-Z Individual, A-Z
Aquaculture
Periodicals, societies, and serials see SH1
Congresses see SH3
20.3 Dictionaries. Encyclopedias
20.34 Terminology. Abbreviations. Notation
20.5 Directories
21 History (General)
By region or country
For classification of species see SH167.A+
For classification of species of shellfish see SH365+
North America
33 General works
United States
34 General works
35.A1-.A5 Regions
35.A47 Southwest
35.A5 Pacific coast
35.A6-.W By state, A-W
e.g.
35.H3 Hawaii
36 Great Lakes
Canada
37 General works
37.5.A-Z By region or province, A-Z
38 Latin America
39 Mexico
Central America
41 General works

Aquaculture
By region or country
Central America -- Continued
41.5.A-Z By region or country, A-Z
West Indies
42 General works
42.5.A-Z By island or group of islands, A-Z
South America
43 General works
45 Argentina
47 Bolivia
49 Brazil
51 Chile
53 Colombia
55 Ecuador
56 Guyana. British Guiana
57 Suriname. Dutch Guiana
58 French Guiana
59 Paraguay
61 Peru
63 Uruguay
65 Venezuela
Europe
67 General works
69 Great Britain
71 Austria
73 Belgium
75 Denmark
77 France
79 Germany
81 Greece
83 Netherlands
85 Italy
87 Norway
89 Portugal
91 Russia. Soviet Union. Former Soviet republics
92 Russia (Federation)
For Russia in Asia see SH115
93 Spain
95 Sweden
97 Switzerland
99 Turkey
101.A-Z Other regions or countries, A-Z
e.g.
101.F5 Finland
101.P7 Poland
Asia

Aquaculture
By region or country
Asia -- Continued
103 General works
105 China
105.5 Taiwan
107 India
109 Japan
111 Iran
113 Asia Minor
115 Russia in Asia. Siberia. Russian Far East
117.A-Z Other divisions of Asia, A-Z
e.g.
117.S8 Straits Settlements
Africa
121 General works
123 Egypt
125.A-Z Other divisions of Africa, A-Z
Indian Ocean islands
129.5 General works
130.A-Z By island or group of islands, A-Z
130.M38 Mayotte
131 Australia and New Zealand
133.A-Z Pacific islands. Oceania
133.A1 General works
133.A2-Z By island or group of islands, A-Z
Hawaii see SH35.H3
134.A-Z Atlantic Ocean islands, A-Z
134.6 Tropics
135 General works
For aquarium culture see SF456+
For general culture by country see SH33+
For culture of individual species or groups see SH167.A+
136.A-Z Special aspects of aquaculture as a whole, A-Z
136.B56 Biotechnology
136.Q37 Quarantine
136.S87 Surveys
Class here works on surveying methods
For works on the results of surveying see SH21
136.S88 Sustainable aquaculture
Aquacultural engineering
137 General works
137.3 Cage aquaculture
137.33 Capture-based aquaculture
137.37 Poly-aquaculture

Aquaculture -- Continued

137.4 Pond aquaculture

Including ponds

Cf. SH157.85.F52 Fish ponds

138 Mariculture

For general culture by country see SH33+

Cf. SH163 Saltwater fish culture

141 Urban aquaculture

Fish culture

Cf. QH545.F52 Effect on plants and animals

Dictionaries and encyclopedias see SH201

Statistics

Serial documents

For United States, see SH11

For other countries, see SH223+

Separate documents, nonofficial serials and monographs see SH33+; SH219+

151 General works

Local see SH33+

153 Miscellaneous

Study and teaching. Research

153.5 General works

153.53.A-Z By region or country, A-Z

153.7 Economic aspects. Finance

154 Water requirements

155 Equipment

Cf. SH155.8 Incubators

Cf. SH157.6 Fish shocking equipment

155.5 Breeding. Selection

Cf. SF457.9 Aquarium fish breeding

155.6 Artificial spawning. Stripping

155.7 Induced spawning

Natural spawning see QL639.2

155.8 Incubation. Incubators. Fish hatcheries

156 Feeding

For special kinds of fish see SH167.A+

156.8 Tagging and marking

156.9 Anesthesia in marking and transport

157 Transportation

157.5 Stocking

For stocking particular waters see SH33+

157.6 Electrofishing in culture and management

Cf. SH344.6.E4 Commercial fishing methods

157.7 Fish control. Piscicides

Habitat improvement

157.8 General works

157.85.A-Z By type of improvement, A-Z

	Aquaculture
	Fish culture
	Habitat improvement
	By type of improvement, A-Z -- Continued
157.85.A7	Artificial reefs
157.85.A73	Artificial structures
157.85.D47	Destratification of lakes and reservoirs
157.85.F49	Fish aggregation devices
157.85.F52	Fish ponds
157.85.F54	Fish screens
157.85.F56	Fishways
157.85.L34	Lake renewal
	Ponds see SH157.85.F52
157.85.S75	Streamflow augmentation
159	Freshwater culture
163	Saltwater culture
(165)	Reproduction, care, etc. see SH151
167.A-Z	Individual species and groups of fish, A-Z Cf. SF458.A+ Aquarium fishes
167.A65	American smelt. Rainbow smelt
167.A7	Anadromous fish
	Atlantic herring see SH167.H5
167.A74	Atlantic salmon
167.A88	Ayu
167.B3	Bass
167.C3	Carp
167.C35	Catfish
167.C42	Channel bass. Red drum
167.C44	Channel catfish
167.C47	Chinook salmon
167.C6	Cod
167.C87	Cutthroat trout
167.C9	Cyprinidae
167.E3	Eels
	European perch see SH167.P4
167.F55	Flatfishes
167.G53	Giant perch
	Goldfish see SF458.G6
	Gray mullets see SH167.M84
	Guppies see SF458.G8
167.G86	Groupers
167.H5	Herring Including Atlantic herring and Pacific herring
167.K37	Kareius bicoloratus
167.L6	Loaches
167.L65	Longfin tilapia

	Aquaculture
	Fish culture
	Individual species and groups of fish, A-Z -- Continued
167.M5	Milkfish
167.M82	Mudfishes
167.M84	Mullets
167.N54	Nile tilapia
	Pacific herring see SH167.H5
167.P34	Pagrosomus auratus
167.P4	Perch
	Including European perch and yellow perch
167.P5	Pike
167.P6	Pike perch
167.P7	Pompano
167.R34	Rainbow trout
	Red drum see SH167.C42
167.S13	Sablefish
167.S17	Salmon
167.S18	Salmonidae
167.S26	Scatophagus argus
167.S33	Sea bass
167.S5	Shad
(167.S65)	Stizostedion vitreum
	see SH167.W34
167.S68	Striped bass
167.S7	Sturgeons
167.T54	Tilapia
	Tropical fish see SF457
167.T86	Trout
	Trout, Rainbow see SH167.R34
167.T88	Tuna
167.T9	Turbot
167.W34	Walleye
	Yellow perch see SH167.P4
	Diseases and adverse factors
	Including fish kills
	Cf. SF458.5 Aquarium fish diseases
	Cf. SH157.7 Fish control
171	General works
173	Dams. Hydroelectric power plants
173.5	Water levels. Streamflow
	Cf. SH157.85.S75 Streamflow augmentation
174	Pollution. Water quality
	Aquatic pests
	Cf. TD427.A68 Water pollution
174.5	General works
174.7	Fish pests

SH

Aquaculture
Fish culture
Diseases and adverse factors -- Continued

175 Parasites
176 Predators
177.A-Z Individual diseases, pollutants, parasites, predators, etc., A-Z
177.A34 Acid mine drainage
177.A4 Aeromonas
177.A44 Aggregate industry
177.A46 Algal blooms
Including dinoflagellate blooms, red tide, etc.
177.A55 Amphipoda
177.B33 Bacterial kidney disease
177.C37 Ceratomyxa shasta
177.C4 Cestodes
177.C415 Chloramine-T
177.C43 Chlorine
177.C44 Chlorocatechols
177.C45 Ciliates
177.C48 Coal washing wastes
177.C49 Columnaris diseases
177.C5 Copepods
177.C6 Cormorants
177.C78 Cryptobia
177.C83 Cyanides
177.D48 Detergents
177.D52 Dichlorophenoxyacetic acid
Dinoflagellate blooms see SH177.A46
Dissolved oxygen see SH177.O95
Electric powerplants see SH173
177.F57 Fire-extinguishing agents
177.F59 Fish hatchery discharge
Forest fire-fighting chemicals see SH177.F57
177.F8 Fungi
177.F85 Furunculosis
177.G3 Gas bubble disease
Gonyaulax see SH177.A46
Gymnodinium see SH177.A46
177.G8 Gyrodactylus
177.H4 Heavy metals
177.H45 Helminths
Hemorrhagic septicemia, Viral see SH177.V55
Hydroelectric plants see SH173
Hydrostatic pressure see SH177.P7
Infusoria see SH177.C45
Insecticides see SH177.P44

Aquaculture
Fish culture
Diseases and adverse factors
Individual diseases, pollutants, parasites, predators, etc., A-Z -- Continued

177.I74 Iron
177.L3 Lampreys
177.L63 Logging
177.M45 Mercury
177.M47 Metals
177.M48 Methoxychlor
177.N52 Nickel
177.O53 Oil pollution
177.O54 Oil sands wastewater
177.O95 Oxygen stress
PCB see SH177.P65
Paper mills see SH177.W64
177.P4 Peat industry
177.P44 Pesticides
177.P45 Phenols
177.P47 Phosphorus
177.P49 Phytoplankton
Cf. SH177.A46 Algal blooms
177.P65 Polychlorinated biphenyls
177.P7 Pressure
Including underwater explosions
Pulp mills see SH177.W64
(177.R4) Red tide
see SH177.A46
Reservoir drawdown see SH173.5
177.S24 Saprolegniaceae
177.S43 Sediments
177.S45 Selenium
Septicemia, Viral hemorrhagic see SH177.V55
177.S68 Sound
177.S7 Sporozoans
Streamflow see SH173.5
177.S75 Stress
Tapeworms see SH177.C4
177.T45 Thermal stress
177.T7 Trematodes
177.T86 Tumors
Underwater explosions see SH177.P7
177.V35 Vanadium
177.V55 Viral hemorrhagic septicemia
177.V57 Viruses
Water levels see SH173.5

Aquaculture
Fish culture
Diseases and adverse factors
Individual diseases, pollutants, parasites, predators, etc., A-Z -- Continued
Water quality see SH174
177.W55 Whirling disease
177.W64 Wood pulp industry
177.X35 Xanathates
177.Z5 Zinc
179.A-Z Diseases and pests of individual species, A-Z
For diseases of individual aquarium fish see SF458.A+
179.B6 Black bass
179.C3 Carp
179.C32 Catfish
Channel catfish see SH179.C32
179.E45 Eels
179.H3 Halibut
179.O94 Oysters
179.P42 Penaeidae
179.P44 Platichthys flesus
179.R33 Rainbow trout
179.S28 Salmon
179.S3 Salmonidae
179.S5 Shellfish
179.S8 Sturgeon
179.T35 Tilapia
179.T8 Trout
Mariculture see SH138
Shellfish culture see SH365+
185 Frog culture
187 Leech culture
Sponge culture see SH396
Turtle culture, Freshwater see SH191.T5
Turtle culture, Saltwater see SH399.T9
191.A-Z Other (not fish or shellfish), A-Z
Freshwater turtles see SH191.T5
191.P55 Plankton
191.T5 Terrapin. Freshwater turtles
Turtle, Freshwater see SH191.T5
Fisheries
Cf. QH545.F53 Influence in the environment
201 Dictionaries. Encyclopedias
203 Directories
Biography see SH20.A1+

Fisheries -- Continued
211 History
For history in a particular ocean or sea see SH213+
For history in a particular region or country see SH219+
By oceans and seas
For fisheries by a particular country or off the coast of a particular country see SH219+
Atlantic Ocean
Cf. SH319.5.A+ Atlantic Ocean islands
213 General works
North Atlantic
213.2 General works
Eastern North Atlantic
Including the coast of Europe (General)
213.3 General works
213.32 Greenland Sea
213.34 Norwegian Sea
213.35 Baltic Sea
213.36 Kattegat. Skagerrak
213.37 North Sea
213.38 English Channel
213.39 Irish Sea
Mediterranean Sea
213.4 General works
213.42 Adriatic Sea
213.44 Aegean Sea
213.46 Black Sea
Caspian Sea see SH284.C27
Western North Atlantic
Including the coast of North America (General)
Cf. SH221.5.A75 Atlantic Coast (U.S.)
213.5 General works
213.52 Baffin Bay
213.53 Davis Strait
Newfoundland Banks see SH225+
213.56 Gulf of Mexico
213.58 Caribbean Sea
Central Atlantic. Tropical Atlantic
213.6 General works
213.62 Eastern Central Atlantic
213.65 Western Central Atlantic
South Atlantic
213.7 General works
213.715 Argentine Sea
Eastern South Atlantic
Including the coast of Africa (General)
213.72 General works

Fisheries
By oceans and seas
Atlantic Ocean
South Atlantic
Eastern South Atlantic -- Continued
213.75 Gulf of Guinea
213.77 Western South Atlantic
Including the coast of South America (General)
Pacific Ocean
Cf. SH319.A2+ Pacific Ocean islands
214 General works
North Pacific
214.2 General works
214.3 Bering Sea
Eastern North Pacific
Including the coast of North America (General)
214.4 General works
214.45 Gulf of Alaska
Western North Pacific
Including the coast of Asia (General)
214.5 General works
214.52 Okhotsk Sea
214.53 Japan Sea
214.54 Yellow Sea
214.55 East China Sea
214.56 South China Sea
214.58 Philippine Sea
Central Pacific. Tropical Pacific
214.6 General works
214.62 Eastern Central Pacific
214.65 Western Central Pacific
South Pacific
214.7 General works
214.8 Eastern South Pacific
Including the coast of South America (General)
Western South Pacific
Including Australasia
214.9 General works
214.92 Java Sea
214.94 Coral Sea
214.96 Tasman Sea
215 Indo-Pacific
Indian Ocean
Cf. SH319.2.A+ Indian Ocean islands
216 General works
North Indian Ocean
216.2 General works

Fisheries
By oceans and seas
Indian Ocean
North Indian Ocean -- Continued
Arabian Sea
216.3 General works
216.32 Persian Gulf
216.34 Red Sea
216.36 Gulf of Aden
Bay of Bengal
216.4 General works
216.45 Andaman Sea
South Indian Ocean
216.5 General works
216.55 Mozambique Channel
Arctic Ocean see SH320
Antarctic Ocean see SH320.5
By region or country
North America
219 General works
North Pacific fisheries (North Pacific Ocean) see SH214.2+
North Pacific fisheries (North Pacific region of the United States) see SH221.5.N65
Great Lakes fishery
219.6 General works
219.7.A-Z By lake, A-Z
For fishery of a particular state see SH222.A+
For fishery of a particular province see SH224.A+
United States
For documents see SH11+
221 General works
221.5.A-Z Regions, A-Z
Atlantic Coast (Middle Atlantic States) see SH221.5.M53
221.5.A75 Atlantic Coast (U.S.)
221.5.C45 Charleston Bump Region
221.5.C48 Chesapeake Bay
221.5.C63 Colorado River (Colo.-Mexico)
221.5.C64 Columbia River
221.5.D44 Delaware Bay (Del. and N.Y.)
Great Lakes see SH219.6+
221.5.G75 Gulf States
221.5.H83 Hudson River
221.5.M35 Maine, Gulf of
221.5.M53 Middle Atlantic States
221.5.M58 Mississippi River

Fisheries
By region or country
United States
Regions, A-Z -- Continued

221.5.N4 New England
221.5.N63 Northeastern States
221.5.N65 Northwest, Pacific
221.5.P32 Pacific Coast
Pacific Northwest see SH221.5.N65
221.5.R37 Raritan Bay (N.J. and N.Y.)
221.5.S68 Southern States
221.5.Y45 Yellowstone National Park
222.A-.W States, A-W
Hawaii see SH319.H3
Canada
Class here only descriptive and technical works
223 General works
224.A-Z Provinces, A-Z
Grand Banks fisheries
225 General works
226 To 1763
227 1763-1818
229 1819-
231 Mexico
Including Yucatán Peninsula
Central America
232.A1 General works
232.A2-Z By region or country, A-Z
West Indies
233.A1 General works
233.A2-Z By island or group of islands, A-Z
South America
234 General works
234.5 Amazon River. Amazonia
235 Argentina
235.5 Bolivia
236 Brazil
237 Chile
239 Colombia
241 Ecuador
Guianas
242 Guyana
243 Suriname
244 French Guiana
245 Paraguay
247 Peru
249 Uruguay

Fisheries
By region or country
South America -- Continued
251 Venezuela
Europe
253 General works
254.A-Z Regions of Europe, A-Z
254.E87 European Economic Community countries
Great Britain
255 General works
England
257 General works
258.A-Z Local, A-Z
258.5 Wales
Scotland
259 General works
260.A-Z Local, A-Z
Ireland
261 General works
262.A-Z Local, A-Z
Austria
263 General works
264.A-Z Local, A-Z
Belgium
265 General works
266.A-Z Local, A-Z
Denmark
267 General works
268.A-Z Local, A-Z
268.G83 Greenland
France
269 General works
270.A-Z Local, A-Z
Germany
271 General works
272.A-Z Local, A-Z
Greece
273 General works
274.A-Z Local, A-Z
Netherlands
275 General works
276.A-Z Local, A-Z
Italy
277 General works
278.A-Z Local, A-Z
Norway
279 General works

Fisheries
By region or country
Europe
Norway -- Continued
280.A-Z Local, A-Z
Portugal
281 General works
282.A-Z Local, A-Z
Russia. Soviet Union. Russia (Federation)
Cf. SH293.F5 Finland
Cf. SH293.P7 Poland
Cf. SH305+ Siberia
283 General works
284.A-Z Local, A-Z
284.C27 Caspian Sea
Spain
285 General works
286.A-Z Local, A-Z
Sweden
287 General works
288.A-Z Local, A-Z
Switzerland
289 General works
290.A-Z Local, A-Z
Turkey
291 General works
292.A-Z Local, A-Z
293.A-Z Other countries of Europe, A-Z
e.g.
293.F5 Finland
293.P7 Poland
Asia
295 General works
China
297 General works
298.A-Z Local, A-Z
For Hong Kong see SH298.3
298.3 Hong Kong
298.5 Taiwan
India
299 General works
300.A-Z Local, A-Z
Japan
301 General works
302.A-Z Local, A-Z
302.5 Korea
Including South Korea

	Fisheries
	By region or country
	Asia -- Continued
302.7	North Korea
	Iran
303	General works
304.A-Z	Local, A-Z
	Siberia
305	General works
306.A-Z	Local, A-Z
307.A-Z	Other divisions of Asia, A-Z
	e.g.
307.F3	Far Eastern Republic
307.P5	Philippine Islands
	Africa
311	General works
312.A-Z	Regions of Africa, A-Z
	Egypt
313	General works
314.A-Z	Local, A-Z
315.A-Z	Other African countries, A-Z
	Australasia
316	General works
	Australia
317	General works
318.A-Z	Local, A-Z
318.5	New Zealand
	Pacific islands. Oceania
319.A2	General works
319.A3-Z	By island or group of islands, A-Z
319.C66	Cook Islands
319.F5	Fiji Islands
319.F73	French Polynesia
319.G88	Guam
319.H3	Hawaii
319.K5	Kiribati
319.M37	Marshall Islands
319.M5	Micronesia
319.N49	New Caledonia
319.P34	Palau
	Samoa see SH319.W45
319.S65	Solomon Islands
319.T65	Tonga
319.V35	Vanuatu
319.W45	Western Samoa. Samoa
319.2.A-Z	Indian Ocean islands, A-Z
319.5.A-Z	Atlantic Ocean islands, A-Z

Fisheries
By region or country
Atlantic Ocean islands, A-Z -- Continued
319.5.B45 Bermuda
319.5.C37 Cape Verde
320 Arctic regions
Cf. SH268.G83 Greenland
320.5 Antarctic regions
321 Tropics
Cf. SH213.6+ Tropical Atlantic Ocean
Cf. SH214.6+ Tropical Pacific Ocean
322 Developing countries
327.5 Fishery resources
For particular waters see SH213+
For particular fish, etc. see SH346+
Cf. SH343.5 Exploratory fishing
Bycatches
For particular fisheries see SH346+
For particular waters see SH213+
For particular regions or countries see SH219+
327.6 General works
327.65.A-Z By type of bycatch, A-Z
327.65.B68 Bottlenose dolphin
327.65.C65 Common dolphin
327.65.H35 Harbor porpoise
327.65.H43 Hector's dolphin
327.65.H64 Hooker's sea lion
327.65.M33 Marbled murrelet
327.65.M35 Marine mammals
327.65.N47 New Zealand fur seal
327.65.S4 Sea birds
327.65.S42 Sea turtles
327.65.S43 Seals
327.65.S65 Sooty shearwater
327.65.S75 Striped dolphin
327.7 Fishery conservation
For particular waters see SH213+
For particular fish, etc. see SH346+
Fishery management. Fishery policy
For particular waters see SH213+
For particular fish, etc. see SH346+
Cf. SH334 Economic aspects
328 General works
329.A-Z Special topics, A-Z
329.A66 Aquatic habitat classification
329.A67 Aquatic parks and reserves
329.C57 Citizen participation

Fisheries
Fishery management. Fishery policy
Special topics, A-Z -- Continued

329.C6 Co-management
329.E93 Evaluation
329.F56 Fish stock assessment
329.F563 Fish stock identification
329.F57 Fish stocking
329.F59 Fisheries inspectors
329.I53 Individual fishing quotas
Inspectors see SH329.F59
329.L53 Licensing. Limited entry
329.M35 Marine parks and reserves. Marine protected areas
329.M66 Monitoring
329.O94 Overfishing
329.S53 Small-scale fisheries
329.S87 Sustainable fisheries
331 General works
331.15 Juvenile works
331.2 Addresses, essays, lectures
331.5.A-Z Special aspects as a whole, A-Z
331.5.C65 Computer programs
Data collecting see SH331.5.S75
Economic aspects see SH334
(331.5.F57) Fish stock assessment
see SH329.F56
331.5.G46 Geographic information systems
331.5.M48 Mathematical models
Cf. QL618.3 Fish population dynamics
Mathematics see SH331.5.M48
331.5.M58 Metric conversion tables
Safety measures see SH343.9
331.5.S74 Statistical methods
331.5.S75 Statistical services
331.9 Vocational guidance
Study and teaching. Research
Cf. SH343.4 Fishery research vessels
332 General works
332.2.A-Z By region or country, A-Z
(333) Special aspects of fisheries
see SH331.5
334 Economic aspects. Finance
For particular waters see SH213+
For particular fish, etc. see SH346+
Cf. HD9450+ Fishery products industry
Fishery technology
Cf. VM431 Fishing boats

SH

Fisheries
Fishery technology -- Continued
334.5 Periodicals. Societies. Serials
334.55 Congresses
334.7 General works
Local see SH219+
Fishery processing
Including shellfish processing
Cf. RA602.F5 Public health aspects of fish as food
Cf. TX612.F5 Preserving and storing fish for home consumption
334.9 Periodicals. Societies. Serials
334.95 Congresses
335 General works
Local see SH219+
Plant management
335.4 General works
335.5.A-Z Special topics, A-Z
335.5.C6 Costs
335.5.E65 Equipment
335.5.F57 Fire prevention
335.5.I5 Inspection
335.5.L3 Labor productivity
335.5.Q35 Quality control
335.5.S2 Sanitation
335.5.S9 Standards
335.6 Fishery processing ships
335.7 Composition and analysis
Cf. TX556.5 Nutritional analysis
335.8 By-products (General)
For specific by-products see SH336.A+
336.A-Z By method, product, etc., A-Z
For particular species see SH336.5.A+
336.A5 Antibiotics
336.A57 Antioxidants
336.C3 Canning
336.D7 Drying
336.F45 Fermentation
336.F52 Fish protein concentrate
336.F55 Fishmeal
336.F7 Freezing
Cf. SH344.8.R4 Freezing at sea
336.R3 Radiation
336.S3 Salting
336.S6 Smoking
336.S94 Surimi
336.5.A-Z By fish, A-Z

Fisheries
Fishery processing
By fish, A-Z -- Continued
336.5.B66 Bonito
336.5.C63 Cod
336.5.C73 Crabs
336.5.H47 Herring
336.5.K75 Krill
336.5.M3 Mackerel
336.5.S24 Salmon
336.5.S36 Scombridae
336.5.S53 Shark
Shellfish (General) see SH334.9+
336.5.S56 Shrimp
336.5.T85 Tuna
337 Packing, transportation, and storage
Cf. SH344.8.R4 Fishing boat refrigeration
337.5 Fishing port facilities
For particular ports see SH213+
Museums and exhibitions
338 Organization; classification and preparation of exhibits
339.A-Z Museums. By place, A-Z
341.A-Z Exhibitions. By place, A-Z
e.g.
341.I6 International fishery exhibitions. By date of exhibition
343.A-Z Exhibits of individual countries. By country, A-Z
Subarrange by place of exhibition
e.g.
343.C5B5 China at Berlin, 1880
343.C5L8 China at London, 1883
343.2 Fishery oceanography. Hydrologic factors
343.3 Fishery meteorology. Climatic factors
343.4 Fishery research vessels
Cf. VM431 Construction
343.5 Exploratory fishing
For works on exploratory fishing in particular waters see SH219+
343.8 Navigation
Cf. SH344.8.B6 Fishing boats
343.9 Safety measures
Methods and gear
For individual species see SH346+
Cf. HD9488+ Fishing equipment industry
344 General works
344.15 Gear selectivity
344.17 Electronic monitoring
Detection of fish

Fisheries
Methods and gear
Detection of fish -- Continued
344.2 General works
344.23.A-Z By method, A-Z
344.23.E3 Echo sounding
344.23.S6 Sonar. Echo ranging
Attraction of fish
344.4 General works
344.43.A-Z By method, A-Z
344.43.L5 Light
Catching of fish
General works see SH344
344.6.A-Z By method, A-Z
344.6.C67 Cormorants
344.6.D73 Dredging
344.6.D74 Drift net fishing
344.6.E4 Electrofishing
Cf. SH157.6 Fishery management
344.6.G5 Gillnetting
344.6.L5 Lift net fishing
344.6.L64 Longlining
344.6.P68 Pound net fishing
344.6.P8 Pump fishing
344.6.P85 Purse seining
344.6.R56 Ring seines
344.6.S4 Seining
344.6.T67 Trap fishing
344.6.T7 Trawling
344.8.A-Z Miscellaneous equipment and supplies, A-Z
344.8.B46 Bird-scaring lines
Boat refrigeration see SH344.8.R4
344.8.B6 Boats
Cf. HD9489.B63+ Fishing boat industry
Cf. HE566.F57 Fishing boat registers
Cf. SH335.6 Fishery processing ships
Cf. SH343.4 Fishery research vessels
Cf. SH343.8 Navigation
Cf. SH452.9.B58 Sport fishing boats
Cf. VM431 Construction
344.8.B93 Bycatch excluder devices
Fishing port facilities see SH337.5
344.8.H6 Hooks
344.8.N4 Nets
For particular nets see SH344.6.A+
344.8.P55 Plastics
344.8.R4 Refrigeration at sea

Fisheries -- Continued
Fishery for individual species
Salmon

346 General works
347 Great Britain
348 United States
349 Canada
350.A-Z Other, A-Z
351.A-Z Other species or groups, A-Z
351.A42 Albacore
351.A44 Alosa
351.A5 Anchovy
351.A54 Anglerfish
351.A58 Anguilla dieffenbachii
351.A72 Arctic char
351.A73 Arctic grayling
351.A74 Argentine hake
351.A82 Atka mackerel
351.A823 Atlantic cod
Atlantic croaker see SH351.C75
Atlantic herring see SH351.H5
351.A83 Atlantic menhaden
351.A84 Atlantic sturgeon
351.B27 Baitfish
351.B29 Bass, Channel. Red drum
351.B3 Bass, Striped
351.B53 Black sea bass
351.B56 Bluefin tuna
351.B57 Bluefish
351.B6 Bonito
351.B74 Broadband anchovy
351.B84 Bull trout
351.C28 Capelin
351.C3 Carp
351.C4 Catfish
Channel bass see SH351.B29
351.C47 Ciscoes
351.C5 Cod
351.C55 Copper redhorse
351.C75 Croaker, Atlantic
351.D3 Dace, European
351.D57 Dipturus
Including individual species
351.D6 Dogfish
351.D63 Dolly Varden
351.E4 Eels
351.E43 Elasmobranch fisheries

Fisheries
Fishery for individual species
Other species or groups, A-Z -- Continued

351.E44 Electrona carlsbergi
351.E65 Epigonus telescopus
351.E85 European pollack
351.E87 European seabass
351.F5 Flatfish
Flounder see SH351.F5
351.F67 Forage fishes
351.F68 Fourwing flyingfish
351.G35 Galaxias. Whitebait
351.G46 Genypterus blacodes
Gooseflesh see SH351.A54
351.G76 Groundfish
351.G78 Grunts
351.G84 Gulf menhaden
351.H18 Haddock
351.H185 Hake
351.H195 Halfbeaks
351.H2 Halibut
351.H5 Herring
Including Atlantic herring and Pacific herring
351.H67 Hoki
351.L33 Lake sturgeon
351.L35 Lampreys
351.L5 Lingcod
351.L85 Lumpfish
Lutianidae see SH351.S75
351.M2 Mackerel
351.M3 Marlin
351.M4 Meagre
351.M5 Menhaden
351.M57 Merluccius capensis
351.M63 Micropogonias furnieri
351.M88 Mullet
351.M886 Murray cod
351.M89 Muskellunge
351.N54 Nile perch
351.O7 Orange roughy
351.P25 Pacific halibut
Pacific herring see SH351.H5
351.P27 Pacific ocean perch
351.P3 Pacific saury
351.P33 Paddlefish
351.P37 Parapercis colias
351.P38 Patagonian toothfish

	Fisheries
	Fishery for individual species
	Other species or groups, A-Z -- Continued
351.P6	Plaice
351.P83	Puffers
	Red drum see SH351.B29
351.R43	Red porgy
351.R58	River sardine
351.R6	Roach
351.S15	Sablefish
	Salmon see SH346+
351.S27	Sandy sprat
351.S29	Sardinella lemuru
351.S3	Sardines
	Saury, Pacific see SH351.P3
	Seabass, White see SH351.W45
	Seriola see SH351.Y44
351.S5	Shad
351.S6	Sharks
351.S613	Shortspine thornyhead
351.S617	Silver hake
351.S62	Skate
351.S64	Skipjack tuna
351.S7	Smelt
351.S75	Snapper
	Sole see SH351.F5
351.S755	Southern blue whiting
351.S76	Spiny dogfish
	Sprat see SH351.H5
351.S77	Steelhead
	Stizostedion vitreum see SH351.W3
	Striped bass see SH351.B3
351.S787	Striped marlin
351.S788	Stripped weakfish
351.S79	Sturgeon
351.S8	Swordfish
351.T37	Tarpon
351.T38	Tautog
351.T46	Thaleichthys pacificus
351.T5	Tile fish
351.T68	Totoaba
351.T8	Tuna
351.W3	Walleye
351.W32	Walleye pollock
351.W45	White seabass
	Whitebait, New Zealand see SH351.G35
351.W73	Wreckfish

Fisheries
Fishery for individual species
Other species or groups, A-Z -- Continued
351.Y43 Yellowfin tuna
351.Y44 Yellowtail
Seal fisheries. Fur sealing
360 General works
By region or country
361 United States
362 Canada
363.A-Z Other regions or countries, A-Z
364 Sea otter
Shellfish fisheries. Shellfish culture
Cf. HD9471+ Shellfish industry
Cf. RA602.S6 Public health
Cf. SH179.S5 Diseases and pests
Cf. SH334.9+ Processing
Cf. SH335.5.S2 Sanitation in shellfish processing plants
Cf. SH400.4+ Shellfish gathering for personal food
By region or country
United States
365.A1 Periodicals. Societies. Serials
365.A3 General works
365.A4-Z By region or state, A-Z
367.A-Z Other regions or countries, A-Z
370.A1 Periodicals. Societies. Serials
370.A2-Z General works
Mollusks
Oysters
371 General works
Special countries see SH365+
371.3.A-Z By species or group, A-Z
371.3.A44 American oyster
371.3.C72 Crassostrea
371.3.O77 Ostrea
371.3.O78 Ostrea angasi
371.3.P32 Pacific oyster
Abalones
371.5 General works
371.52.A-Z By region or country, A-Z
371.54.A-Z By species or group, A-Z
371.54.B58 Blacklip abalone
371.54.H34 Haliotis midae
371.54.P38 Paua
371.54.P56 Pinto abalone
371.54.R63 Roe's abalone
371.54.W48 White abalone

Fisheries
Shellfish fisheries. Shellfish culture
Mollusks -- Continued
Scallops
372 General works
372.2.A-Z By region or country, A-Z
372.3.A-Z By species or group, A-Z
372.3.A84 Atlantic calico scallop
372.3.B39 Bay scallop
372.3.C72 Crassadoma gigantea
372.3.I33 Iceland scallop
372.3.P38 Patagonian scallop
372.3.P58 Placopecten magellanicus
372.3.S28 Saucer scallop
372.3.W42 Weathervane scallop
Sea mussels
372.5 General works
372.52.A-Z By region or country, A-Z
372.54.A-Z By species or group, A-Z
372.54.M97 Mytilus edulis
Clams
373 General works
373.2.A-Z By region or country, A-Z
373.3.A-Z By species or group, A-Z
373.3.A53 Anadara ovalis
373.3.A97 Austrovenus stutchburyi
373.3.C63 Cockles
373.3.G53 Giant clams
373.3.M36 Manila clam
373.3.N63 Noetia ponderosa
373.3.P33 Pacific geoduck
373.3.P34 Pacific razor clam
Conchs
373.5 General works
373.52.A-Z By region or country, A-Z
373.6.A-Z By species or group, A-Z
373.6.Q43 Queen conch
Octopuses
374 General works
374.2.A-Z By region or country, A-Z
374.3.A-Z By species or group, A-Z
374.3.C65 Common octopus
374.3.N67 North Pacific giant octopus
Squid
374.5 General works
374.52.A-Z By region or country, A-Z
374.6.A-Z By species or group, A-Z

	Fisheries
	Shellfish fisheries. Shellfish culture
	Mollusks
	Squid
	By species or group, A-Z -- Continued
374.6.L64	Loligo
374.6.L65	Loligo opalescens
374.6.O55	Ommastrephes bartramii
	Pearl fisheries. Pearl oyster culture
375	General works
376	Special
377.A-Z	Local, A-Z
377.5	Mother of pearl
	Freshwater mollusks (Mussels, pearls, etc.)
378	General works
379.A-Z	By region or country, A-Z
379.2.A-Z	By species or group, A-Z
379.5	Crushed shell
	Crustaceans
	For freshwater crustaceans see SH380.9+
379.6	General works
379.65.A-Z	By region or country, A-Z
	Lobsters
	Including spiny or rock lobsters
380	General works
380.2.A-Z	By region or country, A-Z
380.25.A-Z	By species or group, A-Z
380.25.A45	American lobster
380.25.C37	Caribbean spiny lobster
380.25.J37	Jasus edwardsii
380.25.S39	Scyllaridae
380.25.W47	Western rock lobster
	Crabs
	Cf. SH336.5.C73 Processing
	Cf. SH400.5.C7 Crabbing
380.4	General works
380.45.A-Z	By region or country, A-Z
380.47.A-Z	By species or group, A-Z
380.47.A43	Alaskan king crab
380.47.B58	Blue crab
380.47.B585	Blue king crab
380.47.B59	Blue swimming crab
380.47.C34	Callinectes
380.47.C35	Callinectes arcuatus
380.47.C36	Cancer pagurus
380.47.D86	Dungeness crab
380.47.M46	Menippe mercenaria

Fisheries
Shellfish fisheries. Shellfish culture
Crustaceans
Crabs
By species or group, A-Z -- Continued
380.47.S66 Snow crab
380.47.T36 Tanner crabs
Shrimps
Including freshwater shrimps
380.6 General works
380.62.A-Z By region or country, A-Z
380.64.A-Z By species or group, A-Z
380.64.G73 Green tiger prawn
380.64.M33 Macrobrachium rosenbergii
380.64.P36 Pandalus
380.64.P37 Pandalus borealis
380.64.P38 Pandalus jordani
380.64.P45 Penaeidae
380.64.P46 Penaeus
380.64.P47 Penaeus aztecus
380.64.P48 Penaeus duorarum
380.64.P485 Penaeus indicus
380.64.P49 Penaeus monodon
380.64.S66 Spot shrimp
380.64.W42 Western king prawn
380.64.W45 Whiteleg shrimp
Krill
Cf. SH336.5.K75 Processing
380.7 General works
380.72.A-Z By region or country, A-Z
Freshwater crustaceans (Crayfish, etc.)
For freshwater shrimps see SH380.6+
380.9 General works
380.92.A-Z By region or country, A-Z
380.94.A-Z By species or group, A-Z
380.94.A88 Astacus astacus
380.94.C48 Cherax cainii
Freshwater shrimps see SH380.6+
380.94.P33 Pacifastacus leniusculus
Shrimps see SH380.6+
380.94.Y32 Yabbies
Whaling
381.A1 Periodicals. Societies. Serials
381.A15 Congresses
381.A2-Z General works
381.5 Juvenile works

Fisheries
Whaling -- Continued
381.7 Whaling ships
Cf. VM465 Construction
By oceans and seas
For whaling by a particular country see SH383.2+
382 Arctic
382.2 North Atlantic
382.3 South Atlantic
382.5 Antarctic
382.6 South Pacific
382.7 North Pacific
History and conditions
383 General works
By nationality of industry
For whaling carried on in particular waters but not associated with a particular country see SH382+
383.2 United States
383.5.A-Z Other countries, A-Z
384.A-Z By whale species or group, A-Z
384.B55 Blue whale
384.B67 Bowhead whale
384.G7 Gray whale
384.H84 Humpback whale
384.M54 Minke whale
384.S66 Sperm whale
384.W48 White whale
385 Whalebone
387 Porpoises. Dolphins
Algae and algae culture
Including cyanobacteria and freshwater algae culture
Cf. QK564+ Botany
388.7 Periodicals. Societies. Serials
388.75 Congresses
389 General works
389.4.A-Z By region or country, A-Z
389.6 Utilization (General)
Marine algae. Seaweed
390.A1 Periodicals. Societies. Serials
390.A15 Congresses
390.A2-Z General works
390.5.A-Z By region or country, A-Z
390.7 Utilization (General)
391.A-Z By species or group, A-Z
391.C47 Chlorella
391.C5 Chondrus crispus
391.E93 Eucheuma

Fisheries
Algae and algae culture
By species or group, A-Z -- Continued
391.G44 Gelidium sesquipedale
391.G5 Giant kelp
391.K44 Kelps
391.L33 Laminaria digitata
391.L35 Laminaria hyperborea
391.L38 Laminaria saccharina
391.M3 Macrocystis integrifolia
Macrocystis pyrifera see SH391.G5
391.N47 Nereocystis luetkeana
391.N65 Nori
391.S67 Spirulina
391.5 Harvesting
393 Seagrasses
Seaweed see SH390+
396 Sponge fisheries
399.A-Z Other fisheries, A-Z
Algae see SH388.7+
399.C6 Coral
399.S32 Sea urchins
Sea turtles see SH399.T9
399.T8 Trepang
399.T9 Turtles, Marine
399.W65 Worms, Marine
Seafood gathering
For commercial harvest and culture see SH1+
400 General works
Saltwater angling see SH457+
Shellfish gathering
400.4 General works
400.5.A-Z By type of shellfish, A-Z
400.5.C53 Clams
400.5.C7 Crabs
400.6.A-Z Other, A-Z
400.8.A-Z By region or country, A-Z
Angling
Cf. TX612.F5 Preservation and handling of fish for home consumption
Cf. TX747+ Preparation and cooking of fish
401 Periodicals. Societies. Serials
Fishing clubs
403.A1 General works
403.A2-Z Individual
405 Fishing resorts, camps, hotels, marinas, etc.
For facilities of a particular country or place see SH461+

SH

	Angling -- Continued
407	Congresses
411	Dictionaries. Encyclopedias
412	Guidebooks (General). Vacation guides
	Biography
414	Collective
415.A-Z	Individual, A-Z
421	History
	General works, essays and light literature
431	To 1653
	Walton. The compleat angler
433.A	Editions. By imprint date
	Subarrange by appending date to .A, e.g. SH433.A1975
433.A4-Z	Translations. By language, A-Z
	Subarrange by translator, e.g. SH433.F7C45, French language translation by Chasse
435	Waltoniana
437	1654-1800
	1801-
439	English
441	American
443	Other
445	Juvenile works
446.A-Z	Special aspects, A-Z
446.B3	Backpack fishing
446.D74	Dressing of fishes
	Equipment. Tackle
	Cf. HD9489.T33+ Tackle industry
447	General works
448	Natural bait. Live bait
	Lures
449	General works
451	Flies. Fly tying
451.2	Plugs
451.3	Decoys
451.4	Soft baits. Soft plastic baits. Soft plastic lures
	Rods
452	General works
452.2	Rod wrapping
	Reels
452.5	General works
452.6	Spinning reels
452.9.A-Z	Other, A-Z
452.9.B58	Boats
	Cf. VM320+ Small craft construction
452.9.B6	Bobbers
452.9.C74	Creels

Angling
Equipment. Tackle
Other, A-Z -- Continued
Floats see SH452.9.B6
452.9.K6 Knots
452.9.L43 Leaders
452.9.R5 Rigs
Sinkers see SH452.9.W43
Terminal tackle see SH452.9.R5
452.9.W43 Weights. Sinkers
453 Catalogs of equipment
Casting
454 General works
Bait casting see SH454.4
Fly casting
454.2 General works
454.25 Spey casting
454.4 Plug casting
454.6 Spin casting
454.7 Surf casting
454.9 Tournament casting
455 Records, score books, etc.
Fish mounting see QL618.6
455.2 Tournament fishing
Methods of angling
Class here general works on the special methods listed
For works on several methods see SH431+
For special methods in a particular place see SH461+
For special methods for special fish (whether or not of a particular place) see SH681+
455.4 Bait (natural) fishing. Still fishing
455.45 Ice fishing
(455.5) Plug fishing
see SH456.3
455.6 Bottom fishing
Lure fishing
455.8 General works
Fly fishing
456 General works
456.12 Dapping
456.15 Nymph fishing
456.2 Saltwater fly fishing
456.25 Streamer fly fishing
456.27 Tenkara fly fishing
456.3 Plug fishing
456.5 Spin fishing. Spin-cast fishing
Saltwater fishing

Angling
Methods of angling
Saltwater fishing -- Continued
457 General works
457.2 Surf fishing
457.3 Flats fishing
457.4 Reef fishing
457.5 Big game fishing
457.7 Trolling
Including general and freshwater
For big game trolling see SH457.5
458 Spear fishing
459 Bowfishing
Angling in special countries
America
461 General works
462 North America
United States
463 General works
464.A-Z By region, A-Z
e.g.
464.W4 West
465 Alabama
467 Alaska
469 Arizona
471 Arkansas
473 California
475 Colorado
477 Connecticut
479 Delaware
481 District of Columbia
483 Florida
485 Georgia
Hawaii see SH679.H3
487 Idaho
489 Illinois
491 Indian Territory
493 Indiana
495 Iowa
497 Kansas
499 Kentucky
501 Louisiana
503 Maine
505 Maryland
507 Massachusetts
509 Michigan
511 Minnesota

Angling
Angling in special countries
America
United States -- Continued

513 Mississippi
515 Missouri
517 Montana
519 Nebraska
521 Nevada
523 New Hampshire
525 New Jersey
527 New Mexico
529 New York
531 North Carolina
533 North Dakota
535 Ohio
537 Oklahoma
539 Oregon
541 Pennsylvania
543 Rhode Island
545 South Carolina
547 South Dakota
549 Tennessee
551 Texas
553 Utah
555 Vermont
557 Virginia
559 Washington
561 West Virginia
563 Wisconsin
565 Wyoming

Canada
571 General works
572.A-Z Special provinces, A-Z
573 Mexico

Central America
575 General works
576.A-Z Special countries, A-Z

West Indies
577 General works
578.A-Z Special countries, A-Z

South America
579 General works
581 Argentina
583 Bolivia
585 Brazil
587 Chile

Angling
Angling in special countries
America
South America -- Continued
589 Colombia
591 Ecuador
592 Guyana
593 Suriname
594 French Guiana
595 Paraguay
597 Peru
599 Uruguay
601 Venezuela
Europe
603 General works
Great Britain
605 General works
606 England
607 Wales
609 Scotland
611 Northern Ireland
612 Ireland
613 Austria
615 Belgium
617 Denmark
619 France
621 Germany
623 Greece
625 Netherlands
627 Italy
629 Norway
631 Portugal
633 Russia. Soviet Union. Russia (Federation)
Cf. SH665 Russia in Asia. Siberia. Russian Far East
Cf. SH667.A+ Central Asia
635 Spain
637 Sweden
639 Switzerland
641 Turkey
643.A-Z Other regions or countries, A-Z
e.g.
643.L25 Lapland
643.M43 Mediterranean Region
643.S35 Scandinavia
Asia
651 General works
653 China

Angling
Angling in special countries
Asia -- Continued
655 India
657 Sri Lanka
659 Japan
661 Iran
663 Asia Minor
665 Russia in Asia. Siberia. Russian Far East
667.A-Z Other divisions of Asia, A-Z
669 Arctic and Antarctic regions
Africa
671 General works
673 Egypt
675.A-Z Other divisions of Africa, A-Z
677 Australia
678 New Zealand
679.A-Z Pacific islands, A-Z
e.g.
679.H3 Hawaii
679.2.A-Z Indian Ocean islands, A-Z
Angling for special kinds of fish
681 Bass (Freshwater)
Including black bass, largemouth bass, smallmouth bass, etc.
Salmon
684 General works
Atlantic salmon (Salmo)
685 General works
685.2 Ouananiche
Pacific salmon (Oncorhynchus)
686 General works
686.2 Chinook
686.3 Chum
686.4 Coho (Silver)
686.5 Pink
Sockeye
686.6 General works
686.7 Kokanee
Trout (Salmo)
687 General works
Brook trout see SH689.3
Brown
687.2 General works
687.3 Sea
687.4 Cutthroat
687.5 Golden
Rainbow

Angling
Angling for special kinds of fish
Trout (Salmo)
Rainbow -- Continued
687.6 General works
687.7 Steelhead
688.A-Z By region or country, A-Z
Char (Salvelinus)
689 General works
689.2 Arctic char
689.3 Brook trout
689.4 Bull trout
689.5 Dolly Varden
689.7 Lake trout
691.A-Z Other, A-Z
691.A52 American shad
691.A54 American smelt. Rainbow smelt
Arctic char see SH689.2
691.A73 Arctic grayling
Atlantic cod see SH691.C6
691.A85 Atlantic herring
691.A9 Ayu
691.B3 Barbel
691.B52 Billfish
691.B55 Bluefish
691.B56 Bluegill
691.B6 Bonefish
691.B7 Bream
691.B87 Burbot
691.C25 Carangidae
691.C3 Carp
691.C35 Catfishes
691.C5 Channel bass. Red drum
691.C54 Chub
691.C58 Coarse fish
691.C6 Cod
691.C73 Crappie
(691.D5) Dicentrarchus labrax
see SH691.E87
691.D6 Dolphinfish
Dorado, Freshwater see SH691.S3
Dorado, Saltwater see SH691.D6
691.E4 Eels
691.E87 European seabass
691.F5 Flatfishes
691.F83 Fugu
691.G7 Grayling

Angling
Angling for special kinds of fish
Other, A-Z -- Continued

691.H3	Halibut
691.L35	Lake whitefish
691.M25	Mackerel
691.M3	Mahseer
691.M78	Mullet
691.M8	Muskellunge
	Pacific halibut see SH691.H3
691.P35	Panfish
691.P37	Peacock bass
691.P4	Perch
691.P45	Permit
691.P55	Pickerel
691.P6	Pike
	Rainbow smelt see SH691.A54
	Red drum see SH691.C5
691.R6	Roach
691.S24	Sailfish
691.S3	Salminus
691.S35	Sea basses
691.S38	Shad
691.S4	Shark
691.S45	Sheatfish
691.S55	Skates
(691.S62)	Smallmouth bass see SH681
691.S64	Snook
691.S66	Spotted seatrout
691.S7	Striped bass
691.S72	Sturgeon
691.S76	Sunfish
691.S8	Swordfish
691.T2	Tarpon
691.T4	Tench
691.T65	Tope
691.T8	Tuna
691.W3	Walleye
691.W4	Weakfish
691.W47	Western Australian salmon
691.Z35	Zander

Hunting sports
Class here works on hunting and fishing combined
For works that are predominantly on fishing see SH401+
Cf. GT5810+ Customs relative to hunting

1 Periodicals. Societies. Congresses
3 Hunting clubs
7 Almanacs, etc.
9 Collections
11 Dictionaries. Encyclopedias
11.5 Communication in hunting sports
12 Directories
Guidebooks
13 General
By region or country see SK40+
Philosophy
14 General works
14.3 Ethical aspects
Biography
15 Collective
17.A-Z Individual, A-Z
History
21 General works
By region or country see SK40+
25 Early works to 1800
General works, light literature, etc.
For anthologies, see PN, PQ, PR, PS, etc.
31 English
33 American
35 Other
35.5 Juvenile works
Bowhunting
Cf. SK273.5 Bows and arrows
36 General works
36.15 Crossbow hunting
36.2 Dressing and skinning
Cf. TS1960+ Commercial butchering
Cf. TX751 Game cooking
36.3 Flying
36.7 Poaching
36.9 Other (not A-Z)
Shooting
Cf. GV1151+ Sports and games
Cf. SK274+ Guns and rifles
Cf. UD330+ Military firing
37 General works
38 Rifle hunting
39 Shotgun hunting

Shooting -- Continued
39.2 Muzzleloader huntng
39.3 Handgun huntng
39.5 Safety measures. Accidents
By region or country
North America
40 General works
United States
41 General works
43 The South
45 The West
47 Alabama
49 Alaska
51 Arizona
53 Arkansas
55 California
57 Colorado
59 Connecticut
61 Delaware
63 District of Columbia
65 Florida
67 Georgia
69 Idaho
71 Illinois
73 Indian Territory
75 Indiana
77 Iowa
79 Kansas
81 Kentucky
83 Louisiana
85 Maine
87 Maryland
89 Massachusetts
91 Michigan
93 Minnesota
95 Mississippi
97 Missouri
99 Montana
101 Nebraska
103 Nevada
105 New Hampshire
107 New Jersey
109 New Mexico
111 New York
113 North Carolina
114 North Dakota
115 Ohio

By region or country
North America
United States -- Continued
117 Oklahoma
119 Oregon
121 Pennsylvania
123 Rhode Island
125 South Carolina
127 South Dakota
129 Tennessee
131 Texas
133 Utah
135 Vermont
137 Virginia
141 Washington
142 West Virginia
143 Wisconsin
145 Wyoming
Canada
151 General works
152.A-Z By province, A-Z
153 Mexico
155 Central America
157 West Indies
South America
Including Latin America in general
159 General works
161 Argentina
163 Bolivia
165 Brazil
167 Chile
169 Colombia
171 Ecuador
173 Guianas
175 Paraguay
177 Peru
179 Uruguay
181 Venezuela
Europe
183 General works
Great Britain. England
185 General works
186.A-Z Local, A-Z
187 Wales
189 Scotland
191 Ireland
Austria

By region or country
Europe
Austria -- Continued
193 General works
194.A-Z Local, A-Z
195 Belgium
197 Denmark
France
199 General works
200.A-Z Local, A-Z
Germany
201 General works
202.A-Z Local, A-Z
202.Z9 Colonies
203 Greece
Cf. DE61.H86 Greco-Roman antiquities
205 Holland
207 Italy
Cf. DE61.H86 Greco-Roman antiquities
Scandinavia
208 General works
Denmark see SK197
208.5 Iceland
209 Norway
210 Sweden
211 Portugal
213 Russia. Soviet Union. Russia (Federation)
Cf. SK245 Russia in Asia. Siberia. Russian Far East
Cf. SK247.A+ Central Asia
215 Spain
219 Switzerland
221 Turkey
223.A-Z Other European countries, A-Z
Asia
231 General works
233 China
India
235 General works
236.A-Z Local, A-Z
237 Sri Lanka
239 Japan
241 Iran
243 Turkey. Asia Minor
245 Russia in Asia. Siberia. Russian Far East
247.A-Z Other divisions of Asia, A-Z
Africa
251 General works

By region or country
Africa -- Continued
252 Roosevelt expedition, 1909-1910
255.A-Z Divisions, A-Z
For Northern, Central, or South Africa see SK251
261 Australia
262 New Zealand
265 Arctic and Antarctic regions
Including Greenland
267.A-Z Pacific islands, A-Z
268.A-Z Indian Ocean islands, A-Z
269 Handbooks, tables, etc.
271 Illustrations of hunting (Hunting scenes, etc.)
Equipment
For hunting dogs see SF421+
273 General works
273.5 Bows and arrows
Including arrowheads, broadheads, etc.
Hunting guns
Cf. GV1177 Target shooting
Cf. SK37+ Hunting
Cf. TS535+ Manufacture
274 General works
274.15 Hunting pouches
Rifles
Cf. SK38 Rifle hunting
Cf. TS536.4+ Manufacture
274.2 General works
274.3 Ballistics
274.4 Sights
Shotguns
Cf. SK39 Shotgun hunting
Cf. TS536.8 Manufacture
274.5 General works
274.6 Ballistics
Cf. TS538.3 Handloading
274.63 Shot (Pellets)
274.7 Pistols
274.8 Air guns
274.85 Spears
275 Catalogs
Museums and collections
276.A1 General works
276.A2-Z By region or country
Under each country:
.x *General works*
.x2A-.x2Z *Special. By name, A-Z*

277 Trophies and records
Cf. QL63 Taxidermy
281 Special methods and types of hunting
Cf. SK36+ Bowhunting
Cf. SK36.7 Poaching
Cf. SK319 Netting
Cf. SK321 Falconry
281.3 Bolos
281.5 Game calling
282 Tracking
Cf. QL768 Animal tracks and signs
Trapping and snaring
Including the trapping of fur-bearing animals
For special animals, see the animal, e.g. Fox hunting, SK284+
283 General works
283.2 Equipment
Including catalogs
283.6.A-Z By region or country, A-Z
283.8 Dressing and skinning
Cf. TS1960+ Commercial butchering
Fox hunting
Cf. SF293.H8 Hunters (Horses)
Cf. SF295.65 Hunt riding
Cf. SF429.F6 Foxhounds
284 Periodicals. Societies. Serials
285 General works
286 Biography
287.A-Z By region or country, A-Z
Under each country:
.x *General works*
.x2A-.x2Z *Local, A-Z*
.x3A-.x3Z *Individual hunts, A-Z*
Coursing
For coursing trials see SF425+
291 General works
292.A-Z By prey, A-Z
292.C6 Coyote
292.H3 Hare
292.S7 Stag
293 Ferreting
Including culture
Big game
For general works on big game hunting see SK31+
295 Bears
Including individual species
297 American bison
299 Chamois

SK

Big game -- Continued
301 Deer
302 Moose
303 Elk (Wapiti)
305.A-Z Other, A-Z
305.A35 African buffalo
Antelope, Pronghorn see SK305.P76
305.A6 Antelopes
305.A74 Argali
305.B45 Bighorn sheep
Bison see SK297
305.C3 Caribou
305.C64 Collared peccary
305.C7 Crocodiles
305.D34 Dall sheep
305.E3 Elephants
Feral swine see SK305.W5
305.I24 Ibex
305.J3 Jaguar
305.K3 Kangaroo
305.L4 Leopard
305.L5 Lion
305.L8 Lynx
Mountain goat see SK305.R62
305.M6 Mountain sheep
305.P76 Pronghorn
305.P8 Puma
305.R4 Reindeer
305.R5 Rhinoceros
305.R62 Rocky Mountain goat. Mountain goat
305.S64 Spectacled caiman
305.T5 Tiger
305.W25 Wallabies
305.W3 Walrus
305.W5 Wild boar. Feral swine
305.W6 Wolves
Bird hunting. Fowling
General works
311 British works
313 American (U.S.) works
315 Other general works
316.A-Z By region or country, A-Z
Great Britain see SK311
United States see SK313
317 Shooting preserves
319 Trapping, netting, liming
321 Hawking, falconry

Bird hunting. Fowling -- Continued
Land birds
323 General works
324.A-Z By region or country, A-Z
For English and American works see SK323
325.A-Z Individual birds, A-Z
325.B3 Band-tailed pigeon
325.C7 Crow
325.G7 Grouse
325.M65 Mourning dove
325.P3 Partridge
325.P5 Pheasant
325.P55 Pigeon
325.P7 Prairie chickens
325.P83 Ptarmigans
325.Q2 Quail
325.S35 Sandhill crane
325.T8 Turkeys
325.W7 Woodcock
Bay birds
327 General works
329.A-Z Individual birds, A-Z
329.R3 Rail
329.S6 Snipe
Waterfowl
331 General works
333.A-Z Individual waterfowl, A-Z
333.D8 Ducks
333.G6 Goose
335 Decoys
Cf. NK4890.5 Decorative arts
Cf. TT199.75 Handicraft
336 Varmint hunting (General)
For hunting of individual varmints, see the animal, e.g. Coyotes, SK341.C65
337 Predator hunting
Small game hunting
340 General works
341.A-Z Individual small game, A-Z
341.B4 Beaver
341.C6 Coon
341.C65 Coyote
341.E74 Ermine
341.H3 Hare
341.M3 Marmot
For American marmot see SK341.W6
341.M33 Martens

Small game hunting
Individual small game, A-Z -- Continued

341.M55 Mink
341.M87 Muskrats
341.O8 Otter
Cf. SH364 Sea otter
341.P4 Peccary
341.R2 Rabbit
Raccoon see SK341.C6
Rats see SB994.R2
341.S23 Sable
341.S5 Snakes
Including rattlesnakes
341.S7 Squirrel
341.W6 Woodchuck

Wildlife management. Game protection

351 Periodicals. Societies. Serials
352 Congresses
(353) General works
see SK355
Biography
354.A1 Collective
354.A2-Z Individual
354.2 Juvenile works
355 General works
356.A-Z Special aspects of wildlife management as a whole, A-Z
356.C65 Contraception
356.V53 Video recording
356.W54 Wildlife habitat improvement
For local see SK361+
Cf. QL81.5+ Wildlife conservation
357 Game preserves, refuges, etc.
By region or country
Including annual reports, etc., of game commissioners
For fish and game or game and fish commissioners, etc. see SH11+
United States
Including United States and Canada
361 General works
365 Alabama
367 Alaska
369 Arizona
371 Arkansas
373 California
375 Colorado
377 Connecticut
379 Delaware

Wildlife management. Game protection
By region or country
United States -- Continued

381 District of Columbia
383 Florida
385 Georgia
Hawaii see SK578.H3
387 Idaho
389 Illinois
391 Indian Territory
393 Indiana
395 Iowa
397 Kansas
399 Kentucky
401 Louisiana
403 Maine
405 Maryland
407 Massachusetts
409 Michigan
411 Minnesota
413 Mississippi
415 Missouri
417 Montana
419 Nebraska
421 Nevada
423 New Hampshire
425 New Jersey
427 New Mexico
429 New York
431 North Carolina
433 North Dakota
435 Ohio
437 Oklahoma
439 Oregon
441 Pennsylvania
443 Rhode Island
445 South Carolina
447 South Dakota
449 Tennessee
451 Texas
453 Utah
455 Vermont
457 Virginia
459 Washington
461 West Virginia
463 Wisconsin
465 Wyoming

Wildlife management. Game protection
By region or country -- Continued
Canada
470 General works
471.A-Z By region or province, A-Z
473 Mexico
475 Central America
477 West Indies
South America
479 General works
481 Argentina
483 Bolivia
485 Brazil
487 Chile
489 Colombia
491 Ecuador
492 Guyana
493 Suriname
494 French Guiana
495 Paraguay
497 Peru
499 Uruguay
501 Venezuela
Europe
503 General works
Great Britain
505 General works
507 Wales
509 Scotland
511 Ireland
513 Austria
515 Belgium
517 Denmark
519 France
521 Germany
523 Greece
525 Holland
527 Italy
529 Norway
531 Portugal
533 Soviet Union
535 Spain
537 Sweden
539 Switzerland
541 Turkey
543.A-Z Other European countries, A-Z
Asia

Wildlife management. Game protection
By region or country
Asia -- Continued
553 China
555 India
557 Sri Lanka
559 Japan
561 Iran
563 Philippines
565 Siberia
567.A-Z Other divisions of Asia, A-Z
Africa
571 General works
573 Egypt
575.A-Z Other divisions of Africa, A-Z
577 Australia
577.5 New Zealand
578.A-Z Pacific islands, A-Z
578.H3 Hawaii
579 Arctic and Antarctic
579.5 Northern Hemisphere
Wild animal trade
Cf. QL81.5+ Wildlife conservation
590 Periodicals. Societies. Serials
590.3 Congresses
Biography
590.6 Collective
590.65.A-Z Individual, A-Z
591 General works
592.A-Z By region or country, A-Z
593.A-Z By animal, A-Z
593.B4 Bears
Birds see SF462.6+
593.R47 Reptiles
593.S66 Snow leopard
593.T54 Tiger
Camping. Outdoor life see GV191.2+
Wildlife-related recreation
Cf. SK1+ Hunting
Cf. QL59 Wildlife attracting
Cf. QL60 Wildlife watching
Cf. SH401+ Fishing
Cf. TR729.W54 Wildlife photography
650 Periodicals. Societies. Serials
652 Congresses
655 General works
By region or country

Wildlife-related recreation
By region or country -- Continued
United States
660 General works
662.A-Z By region or state, A-Z
664.A-Z Other regions or countries, A-Z

21	America
22	North America
23	United States
24.A-.W	States, A-W
	e.g.
24.H3	Hawaii
26-27	Canada (Table S3)
28-29	Mexico (Table S3)
30-31	Central America (Table S3)
32-33	West Indies (Table S3)
34	South America
	Including Latin America in general
36-37	Argentina (Table S3)
38-39	Bolivia (Table S3)
41-42	Brazil (Table S3)
43-44	Chile (Table S3)
45-46	Colombia (Table S3)
47-48	Ecuador (Table S3)
49	Guianas
50.3-.4	French Guiana (Table S3)
50.5-.6	Guyana. British Guiana (Table S3)
50.7-.8	Suriname. Dutch Guiana (Table S3)
51	Paraguay
52	Peru
53	Uruguay
54	Venezuela
	Atlantic islands
54.5	General works
54.6.A-Z	By island or group of islands, A-Z
55	Europe
57-58	Great Britain. England (Table S3)
59-60	Wales (Table S3)
61-62	Scotland (Table S3)
62.5-.6	Northern Ireland (Table S3)
63-64	Ireland (Table S3)
65-66	Austria (Table S3)
67-68	Belgium (Table S3)
69-70	Denmark (Table S3)
71-72	France (Table S3)
73-74	Germany (Table S3)
75-76	Greece (Table S3)
77-78	Holland (Table S3)
79-80	Italy (Table S3)
81-82	Norway (Table S3)
83-84	Portugal (Table S3)
85-86	Russia. Soviet Union. Russia (Federation) (Table S3)
	Cf. S1 109 Russia in Asia. Siberia

TABLES

	Europe -- Continued
87-88	Spain (Table S3)
89-90	Sweden (Table S3)
91-92	Switzerland (Table S3)
93-94	Turkey (Table S3)
95.A-Z	Other regions or countries, A-Z
99	Asia
101-102	China (Table S3)
103-104	India (Table S3)
105-106	Japan (Table S3)
107-108	Iran (Table S3)
109	Russia in Asia. Siberia
110	Central Asia
111	Turkey in Asia
112	Asia Minor
113.A-Z	Other regions or countries, A-Z
	e.g.
113.T3	Taiwan
115	Africa
117-118	Egypt (Table S3)
119.A-Z	Other regions or countries, A-Z
	Indian Ocean islands
119.5	General works
119.6.A-Z	By island or group of islands, A-Z
121-122	Australia (Table S3)
122.2	New Zealand
122.8	Pacific Area
	Pacific islands. Oceania
122.9	General works
123.A-Z	By island or group of islands, A-Z

	America
	North America
1-2	Canada (Table S3)
3-4	Mexico (Table S3)
5-6	Central America (Table S3)
7-8	West Indies (Table S3)
	South America
	Including Latin America in general
9	General works
11-12	Argentina (Table S3)
13-14	Bolivia (Table S3)
15-16	Brazil (Table S3)
17-18	Chile (Table S3)
19-20	Colombia (Table S3)
21-22	Ecuador (Table S3)
	Guianas
23	General works
24.3-.4	French Guiana (Table S3)
24.5-.6	Guyana. British Guiana (Table S3)
24.7-.8	Suriname. Dutch Guiana (Table S3)
25-26	Paraguay (Table S3)
27-28	Peru (Table S3)
29-30	Uruguay (Table S3)
31-32	Venezuela (Table S3)
	Atlantic islands
32.5	General works
32.6.A-Z	By island or group of islands, A-Z
	Europe
33	General works
35-36	Great Britain. England (Table S3)
37-38	Wales (Table S3)
39-40	Scotland (Table S3)
40.5-.6	Northern Ireland (Table S3)
41-42	Ireland (Table S3)
43-44	Austria (Table S3)
45-46	Belgium (Table S3)
47-48	Denmark (Table S3)
49-50	France (Table S3)
51-52	Germany (Table S3)
53-54	Greece (Table S3)
55-56	Holland (Table S3)
57-58	Italy (Table S3)
59-60	Norway (Table S3)
61-62	Portugal (Table S3)
63-64	Russia. Soviet Union. Russia (Federation) (Table S3)
	Cf. S2 87+ Russia in Asia. Siberia
65-66	Spain (Table S3)

	Europe -- Continued
67-68	Sweden (Table S3)
69-70	Switzerland (Table S3)
71-72	Turkey (Table S3)
73.A-Z	Other regions or countries, A-Z
	Asia
75	General works
77-78	China (Table S3)
79-80	India (Table S3)
81-82	Japan (Table S3)
83-84	Iran (Table S3)
85-86	Philippines (Table S3)
87-88	Russia in Asia. Siberia (Table S3)
88.5-.6	Central Asia (Table S3)
89-90	Turkey in Asia (Table S3)
91.A-Z	Other regions or countries, A-Z
	e.g.
91.T3	Taiwan
	Africa
93	General works
95-96	Egypt (Table S3)
98.A-Z	Other regions or countries, A-Z
	Indian Ocean islands
98.5	General works
98.6.A-Z	By island or group of islands, A-Z
99-100	Australia (Table S3)
100.2	New Zealand
	Pacific Area
100.8	General works
	Pacific islands. Oceania
100.9	General works
101.A-Z	By island or group of islands, A-Z

1	General works
2.A-Z	Local, A-Z

.x	General works
.x2A-.x2Z	Local, A-Z

1	General works
2.A-Z	Local, A-Z
2.5.A-Z	Special schools or universities. By name, A-Z

.x	General works
.x2A-.x2Z	Local, A-Z
.x3A-.x3Z	Special schools or universities. By name, A-Z

INDEX

B

Birch, Paper
  Forest trees: SD397.P28
Birch, Yellow
  Forest trees: SD397.Y44
Bird dogs: SF428.5
Bird hunting: SK311+
Bird-scaring lines
  Fishery equipment and supplies:
    SH344.8.B46
Bird trade, Wild: SF462.6+
Birds
  Agricultural zoology: SB995+
  Animal culture: SF460+
  Laboratory animal culture: SF407.B53
  Veterinary anatomy: SF767.B57
Birds, Cage
  Animal culture: SF460+
  Diseases: SF994.2.A+
  Veterinary anatomy: SF767.B57
Birds, Game
  Animal culture: SF508+
  Diseases: SF994.4.A+
Birds of prey
  Diseases: SF994.5+
Birds, Ornamental
  Animal culture: SF512+
Birds, Talking
  Animal culture: SF462.8
Birds, Tropical
  Diseases: SF994.2.T7
Birds, Water
  Ornamental birds: SF512.5
Birds, Wild
  Animal culture: SF462.5+
Birman
  Cat breeds: SF449.B5
Birthflowers
  Ornamental plants: SB413.B57
Bison, American
  Animal culture: SF401.A45
  Big game hunting: SK297
  Diseases: SF997.5.A43
Bits
  Horsemanship: SF309.9
Black
  Cat breeds: SF449.B55
Black and tan coonhound
  Dog breeds: SF429.B56
Black bass
  Angling: SH681
  Diseases: SH179.B6
Black bear
  Predatory animals: SF810.7.B58
Black cherry
  Forest trees: SD397.B514
Black cutworm
  Economic entomology: SB945.B44
Black grama grass: SB201.B47
Black locust
  Forest trees: SD397.B516
Black oak, California
  Forest trees: SD397.C33
Black pepper
  Spice and condiment plants:
    SB307.P5
Black pine, Japanese
  Ornamental plants: SB413.J32
Black poplar
  Forest trees: SD397.B52
Black poplar, Hybrid
  Forest trees: SD397.H93
Black rot
  Plant pathology: SB741.B6
Black Russian terrier
  Dog breeds: SF429.B58
Black sea bass
  Fisheries: SH351.B53
Black spruce
  Forest trees: SD397.B53
Black walnut
  Forest trees: SD397.W2
Black willow
  Forest trees: SD397.B54
Blackberries
  Fruit culture: SB386.B6
Blackleg
  Cattle diseases: SF962
Blacklip abalone
  Fisheries: SH371.54.B58
Blacktongue
  Diseases and pests of dogs:
    SF992.B55

Brook trout
  Angling: SH689.3
Broom snakeweed
  Weeds, parasitic plants, etc.: SB615.B74
Broom, Spanish
  Economic plants: SB317.S7
Broomcorn
  Economic plants: SB317.B8
Brown bear
  Predatory animals: SF810.7.B73
Brown mopane worm
  Insect culture: SF562.M56
Brown planthopper
  Economic entomology: SB945.B89
Brown Swiss
  Cattle breeds: SF199.B7
Brown teal
  Duck breeds: SF505.63.B74
Brown tree snake
  Predatory animals: SF810.7.B76
Brown trout
  Angling: SH687.2+
Browntail moth
  Economic entomology: SB945.B9
Brucella infections
  Veterinary medicine: SF809.B8
Brucellosis
  Cattle diseases: SF967.B7
  Horse diseases: SF959.B78
  Sheep and goats: SF969.B78
  Swine diseases: SF977.B7
Brugmansia
  Ornamental plants: SB413.B76
Brussels griffon
  Dog breeds: SF429.B79
Brussels sprouts
  Plant pests and diseases: SB608.B78
  Vegetable culture: SB351.B7
Buckeye, Yellow
  Forest trees: SD397.Y442
Buckthorn, Sea
  Fruit culture: SB386.S4
  Plant pests and diseases: SB608.S42
Buckwheat
  Grain and cereals: SB191.B9
Budding
  Fruit culture: SB359.45
  Plant propagation: SB123.65
Budgerigars
  Diseases: SF994.2.B8
  Pet and captive birds: SF473.B8
Budworm, Spruce
  Economic entomology: SB945.S7
Budworm, Western spruce
  Economic entomology: SB945.W539
Buffalo, African
  Animal culture: SF401.A34
  Big game hunting: SK305.A35
Buffalo grass: SB201.B9
Buffalo, Water
  Animal culture: SF401.W34
  Veterinary anatomy: SF767.W38
Buffaloes
  Diseases: SF997.5.B8
Buffelgrass: SB201.B93
Bufo marinus
  Agricultural zoology: SB998.B82
Buildings, Farm: S770+
Buildings, Locating
  Agriculture (General): S563
Bulb industry
  Ornamental plants: SB425.3+
Bulbophyllum
  Flowers and flower culture: SB409.8.B84
Bulbs
  Ornamental plants: SB425+
  Plant pests and diseases: SB608.B85
Bulgarian fine-wooled, Northeast
  Sheep breeds: SF373.N67
Bull, Fighting
  Cattle breeds: SF199.F5
Bull terrier
  Dog breeds: SF429.B8
Bull terrier, American pit
  Dog breeds: SF429.A72
Bull terrier, Staffordshire
  Dog breeds: SF429.S85
Bull terriers, Pit
  Dog breeds: SF429.P58
Bull trout
  Angling: SH689.4

Bull trout
  Fisheries: SH351.B84
Bulldogs
  Dog breeds: SF429.B85
Bulldogs, French
  Dog breeds: SF429.F8
Bullmastiff
  Dog breeds: SF429.B86
Burbot
  Angling: SH691.B87
Burmese
  Cat breeds: SF449.B8
Burning of land: S608
Burros, Wild
  Animal culture: SF361.7+
Burrowing nematode
  Agricultural zoology: SB998.B85
Business and agriculture: S560+
Butter
  Dairy products: SF263+
Butter and cheese makers' associations: SF221
Butterflies
  Insect culture: SF562.B8
  Pets: SF459.B87
Butterfly bushes
  Ornamental plants: SB413.B86
Buttermilk
  Dairy products: SF275.B8
Butternut
  Forest trees: SD397.B88
  Plant pests and diseases: SB608.B88
By-products
  Dairy: SF275.A1
  Fishery processing: SH335.8
  Forest exploitation and utilization: SD543+
Bycatch excluder devices
  Fishery equipment and supplies: SH344.8.B93
Bycatches
  Fisheries: SH327.6+
Bypyridinium compounds
  Plant pesticides: SB952.B5
Byzantine gardens: SB457.547

C

Cabbage
  Implements and machinery for: S715.C33
  Plant pests and diseases: SB608.C14, SB608.C28
  Vegetable culture: SB331
Cabbage, Chinese
  Vegetable culture: SB351.C53
Cabbage maggot
  Economic entomology: SB945.C24
Cacao
  Alkaloidal plants: SB267+
  Fertilizers: S667.C33
  Plant pests and diseases: SB608.C17
Cacao pod borer
  Economic entomology: SB945.C26
Cactus
  Animal nutrition: SF99.C3
  Economic plants: SB317.C2
  Forage and feed crops: SB207.C2
  Ornamental plants: SB438+
  Plant pests and diseases: SB608.C18
Cactus industry: SB438.3+
Cactus marketing: SB438.3+
Caesalpinia
  Forest trees: SD397.C3
Cage aquaculture: SH137.3
Cage birds
  Animal culture: SF460+
  Diseases: SF994.2.A+
  Veterinary anatomy: SF767.B57
Cairn terrier
  Dog breeds: SF429.C3
Cake, Oil
  Animal nutrition: SF99.O4
Cala lily
  Plant pests and diseases: SB608.C2
Calabrese
  Vegetable culture: SB333
Calamus margaritae
  Economic plants: SB317.C24
Calcium
  Soil chemistry: S592.6.C3
Calendars
  Horse racing: SF325

Caribbean spiny lobster
  Fisheries: SH380.25.C37
Caribou
  Big game hunting: SK305.C3
  Diseases: SF997.5.C37
Caringidae
  Angling: SH691.C25
Carnation
  Flowers and flower culture: SB413.C3
  Plant pests and diseases: SB608.C3
Carnauba palm
  Oil-bearing and wax plants:
    SB299.C28
Carnivorous plants
  Ornamental plants: SB432.7
Caroa
  Textile and fiber plants: SB261.N4
Carob
  Economic plants: SB317.C255
Carolina Cup
  Horse racing: SF359.7.C35
Carp
  Angling: SH691.C3
  Diseases: SH179.C3
  Fish culture: SH167.C3
  Fisheries: SH351.C3
Carp, Ornamental
  Aquarium fishes: SF458.K64
Carrier pigeons
  Animal culture: SF469
Carrots
  Plant pests and diseases: SB608.C32
  Vegetable culture: SB351.C3
Cartography
  Agriculture: S494.5.C3
Carts
  Farm machinery: S713.5
Carver, George Washington: S417.A+
Caryota
  Economic plants: SB317.C26
Cascara
  Medicinal plants: SB295.C4
Cases, Wardian: SB417
Cashew
  Fruit culture: SB401.C3
Cassava
  Plant pests and diseases: SB608.C33
Cassava
  Root and tuber crops: SB211.C3
Cassava as feed: SF99.C37
Cassia
  Forest trees: SD397.C34
Casting
  Angling: SH454+
Casting, Bait
  Angling: SH454.4
Casting, Fly
  Angling: SH454.2+
Casting, Plug
  Angling: SH454.4
Casting, Spey: SH454.25
Casting, Spin
  Angling: SH454.6
Casting, Surf
  Angling: SH454.7
Casting, Tournament
  Angling: SH454.9
Castor oil plant
  Oil-bearing and wax plants:
    SB299.C3
Castration
  Veterinary medicine: SF889
Casuarina
  Forest trees: SD397.C344
Casuarina cunninghamiana
  Plant pests and diseases: SB608.C34
Cat breeders: SF442.7+
Cat flea
  Diseases and pests of cats:
    SF986.C37
Cat owners: SF442.7+
Cat shows: SF445+
Catahoula leopard dogs
  Dog breeds: SF429.C35
Catalogs, Florists': SB445
Catalogs, Fruit plant: SB362.3
Catalogs, Fruit seed: SB362.3
Catalogs of sales and stock farms
  Horses: SF299
Catalogs, Vegetable plant: SB320.27
Catalogs, Vegetable seed: SB320.27
Catalpa
  Forest trees: SD397.C35

Catasetums
Flowers and flower culture: SB409.8.C36
Catch crops: SB283.5+
Catching of fish
Fisheries: SH344.582+
Caterpillar, Florida tent
Economic entomology: SB945.F7
Caterpillars
Pets: SF459.C38
Caterpillars, Tent
Economic entomology: SB945.T36
Catfish
Diseases: SH179.C32
Fish culture: SH167.C35
Fisheries: SH351.C4
Catfish, Channel
Diseases: SH179.C32
Fish culture: SH167.C44
Catfishes
Angling: SH691.C35
Aquarium fishes: SF458.C38
Cathaya argyrophylla
Forest trees: SD397.C37
Cats
Animal culture: SF441+
Diseases: SF985+
Laboratory animals: SF407.C37
Veterinary anatomy: SF767.C29
Cats, Feral: SF450
Cats, Longhair
Cat breeds: SF449.L65
Cats, Working: SF447.8
Cattle
Animal culture: SF191+
Diseases: SF961+
Veterinary anatomy: SF767.C3
Veterinary physiology: SF768.2.C3
Cattle, Beef
Animal culture: SF207
Cattle brands
Animal culture: SF101+
Cattle, Dairy
Animal culture: SF208
Cattle dog, Australian
Dog breeds: SF429.A77
Cattle dogs: SF428.6
Cattle, Draft
Animal culture: SF209+
Cattle, Dual purpose
Animal culture: SF211
Cattle egret
Agricultural zoology: SB996.C3
Cattle farm catalogs: SF217
Cattle, General care of: SF197
Cattle ranching
Animal culture: SF191+
Cattle sale catalogs: SF219
Cattle shows: SF215+
Cattleyas
Flowers and flower culture: SB409.8.C38
Caucasian fir
Forest trees: SD397.C38
Caucasian mountain dog
Dog breeds: SF429.C355
Caucasus goat's rue
Legumes: SB205.C37
Cauliflower
Plant pests and diseases: SB608.C35
Vegetable culture: SB333
Cavalier King Charles spaniels
Dog breeds: SF429.C36
Cavies
Pets: SF459.G9
Ceanothus
Forage and feed crops: SB207.C35
Ornamental plants: SB413.C4
Cedar
Forest trees: SD397.C4
Plant pests and diseases: SB608.C38
Cedar, Atlantic white
Forest trees: SD397.A76
Cedar, Incense
Forest trees: SD397.I53
Plant pests and diseases: SB608.I63
Cedar, Mulanje
Forest trees: SD397.M84
Cedar of Lebanon
Forest trees: SD397.C434
Cedar, Port Orford
Forest trees: SD397.P87

D

Enzymes
  Animal nutrition: SF98.E58
  Soil chemistry: S592.6.E57
Ephedra
  Medicinal plants: SB295.E63
Epidemiology, Veterinary: SF780.9
Epigonus telescopus
  Fisheries: SH351.E65
Epilachna
  Economic entomology: SB945.E65
Epilepsy
  Diseases of dogs: SF992.E57
Epiphytes
  Ornamental plants: SB427.8
Epizootic catarrh
  Cattle diseases: SF967.E65
Epizootiology, Veterinary: SF780.9
Epsom Derby
  Horse racing: SF357.E67
Equine encephalomyelitis
  Veterinary medicine: SF809.E7
Equine infectious anemia
  Horse diseases: SF959.A6
Equine viral arteritis
  Horse diseases: SF959.A76
Equipment
  Angling: SH447+
  Fish culture: SH155
  Fishery processing plant
    management: SH335.5.E65
  Flower arrangement. Floral
    decorations: SB449.2
  Horses: SF285.4
  Hunting sports: SK273+
  Trapping and snaring: SK283.2
Equipment, Aeronautical
  Forest fires and wildfires: SD421.43+
Equipment and supplies
  Animal culture: SF92
  Cats: SF447.3+
  Container gardening of flowers:
    SB418.4
  Dogs: SF427.15
  Forest fires and wildfires: SD421.38
  Gardens and gardening: SB454.8
  Lawns and turf: SB433.2
  Pets: SF413.5
Equipment and supplies
  Shrubs and ornamental trees:
    SB435.2
  Swine: SF396.4
  Vegetable culture under glass:
    SB352.7
Equipment, Dusting
  Farm machinery: S694
Equipment, Fertilizer: S693.5
Equipment, Riding
  Horsemanship: SF309.9
Equipment, Seed: SB118.45
Equipment, Spraying
  Farm machinery: S694
Eremophila
  Ornamental plants: SB413.E68
Ergot
  Plant pathology: SB741.E7
Ericaceae
  Ornamental plants: SB413.E7
Ericas
  Ornamental plants: SB413.E72
Ermine
  Diseases: SF997.5.E74
  Hunting: SK341.E74
  Predatory animals: SF810.7.E74
Erosion, Soil
  Forestry: SD390.4+
Erysipelas
  Swine diseases: SF977.E7
Erythrina edulis
  Oil-bearing and wax plants:
    SB299.E78
Escarole
  Vegetable culture: SB351.E58
Escherichia coli infections
  Swine diseases: SF977.E83
  Veterinary medicine: SF809.E82
Eskimo, American
  Dog breeds: SF429.A69
Eskimo dogs
  Dog breeds: SF429.E8
Esparto: SB201.E8
Essex
  Swine breeds: SF393.E7
Estates, Small
  Landscape architecture: SB473

Esthetics, Forestry
  Landscape architecture: SB476
Estimates
  Landscaping industry: SB472.565
Estimating
  Agriculture: S494.5.E8
Estrela mountain dog: SF429.E87
Ethical aspects
  Forestry: SD387.E78
  Hunting sports: SK14.3
Ethics, Professional
  Forestry: SD387.E78
Ethics, Veterinary: SF756.39
Ethology, Veterinary: SF756.7
Eucalyptus
  Forest trees: SD397.E8
  Ornamental plants: SB413.E92
  Plant pests and diseases: SB608.E82
Eucalyptus camaldulensis
  Forest trees: SD397.E814
  Plant pests and diseases: SB608.E83
Eucalyptus diversicolor
  Sylviculture: SD397.K27
Eucalyptus globulus
  Forest trees: SD397.E818
Eucalyptus grandis
  Forest trees: SD397.E82
Eucalyptus marginata
  Forest trees: SD397.J36
Eucalyptus regnans
  Forest trees: SD397.E824
Eucalyptus saligna
  Forest trees: SD397.E825
Eucheuma
  Aquaculture: SH391.E93
Euphorbia
  Ornamental plants: SB413.E95
Eurasian watermilfoil
  Weeds, parasitic plants, etc.:
    SB615.E87
Eurommia ulmoides
  Gum and resin plants: SB291.E8
European ash
  Forest trees: SD397.E827
European aspen
  Forest trees: SD397.E828
European beech
  Forest trees: SD397.E83
  Plant pests and diseases: SB608.E87
European chafer
  Economic entomology: SB945.E73
European corn borer
  Economic entomology: SB945.E75
European dace
  Fisheries: SH351.D3
European fan palm
  Textile and fiber plants: SB261.E87
European foulbrood
  Bee diseases and pests:
    SF538.5.E87
European gardens: SB457.63
European hornbeam
  Forest trees: SD397.E834
European larch
  Forest trees: SD397.E836
European perch
  Fish culture: SH167.P4
European pine shoot moth
  Economic entomology: SB945.E78
European pollack
  Fisheries: SH351.E85
European seabass
  Angling: SH691.E87
  Fisheries: SH351.E87
European Turkey oak
  Forest trees: SD397.E84
European white birch
  Forest trees: SD397.E845
European wildcats
  Pets: SF459.E95
Eurygaster integriceps
  Economic entomology: SB945.E845
Eurytrema
  Veterinary parasitology: SF810.E8
Euterpe edulis
  Food crops: SB177.E88
Euthanasia
  Veterinary medicine: SF756.394
Evaluation
  Agriculture: S540.E92
  Fishery management: SH329.E93
  Pesticides: SB964
  Rangelands: SF85.6.E82

Evapotranspiration
Agricultural meteorology: S600.7.E93
Eventing
Horse shows: SF295.7
Events, Competitive
Dogs: SF425+
Evergreen plants
Ornamental plants: SB428+
Evergreens
Forest trees: SD397.E85
Everlasting flowers
Ornamental plants: SB428.5
Evolution
Plant culture: SB106.O74
Examination of blood
Veterinary clinical chemistry: SF772.67
Examination of feces
Veterinary clinical chemistry: SF772.7
Examination of urine
Veterinary clinical chemistry: SF773
Examinations, Post-mortem
Veterinary medicine: SF769+
Exanthema, Vesicular
Swine diseases: SF977.V3
Excellence, Standards of
Poultry exhibitions: SF485
Stock shows: SF121
Exchange, Land
Forest reserves (U.S.): SD427.L3
Exercise
Dogs: SF427.45
Exercises
Cats: SF446.7
Exhibiting
Stock shows: SF118
Exhibitions
Agriculture (General): S550+
Animal culture: SF114+
Fisheries: SH338+
Forestry education: SD358.A1+
Grape culture: SB387.67
Landscape architecture: SB469.75+
Orchids: SB409.35+
Ornamental plants: SB441+
Poultry: SF483+
Roses: SB411.34+
Exhibits, Classification and preparation of
Fishery museums and exhibitions: SH338
Exmoor
Pony breeds: SF315.2.E92
Exotic animals
Diseases: SF997.5.E95
Exotic forests and forestry: SD387.E85
Exotic shorthair
Cat breeds: SF449.E93
Experiment stations
Forestry: SD356+
Experiment stations, Agricultural: S539.5+
Experimental forests
Forestry education: SD358.5+
Experimental ranges
Animal culture: SF84.86+
Experimentation
Forestry: SD356+
Experimentation, Agricultural: S539.5+
Experiments
Animal nutrition: SF97
Fertilizers and improvement of the soil: S639
Forestry research and experimentation: SD356.6.E94
Gardens and gardening: SB454.3.E95, SB454.3.E95
Plant pesticides: SB960
Soils: S593
Tobacco: SB276
Experiments, Field
Grape culture: SB387.65
Exploitation and utilization
Forestry: SD430+
Exploratory fishing: SH343.5
Explosions, Underwater
Effect on fish culture: SH177.P7
Explosives
Use in clearing land: S679+
Extension, Forestry: SD355.7+
Extension work, Agricultural: S544+
Eye diseases
Cats: SF986.E93
Dogs: SF992.E92

Florists' catalogs: SB445
Florists' designs: SB445
Flounder
  Fisheries: SH351.F5
Flour moth, Mediterranean
  Economic entomology: SB945.M5
Flower arrangement: SB449+
Flower arrangement, American: SB450.67
Flower arrangement, Chinese: SB450.7
Flower arrangement, French: SB450.73
Flower arrangement, Indonesian: SB450.78
Flower arrangement, Japanese: SB450+
Flower arrangement, Korean: SB450.8
Flower arrangement, Miniature: SB449.5.M56
Flower arrangement shows: SB449.15
Flower arrangement, Thai: SB450.87
Flower culture: SB403+
Flower shows: SB441+
Flowering
  Flowers and flower culture: SB406.87
  Plant culture: SB126.8
Flowering cherries
  Ornamental plants: SB413.C5
Flowering crabapples
  Ornamental plants: SB413.C644
Flowering plums
  Ornamental plants: SB413.P57
Flowering time
  Agricultural meteorology: S600.7.F56
Flowers
  Plant culture: SB403+
  Plant pests and diseases: SB608.O7
  Preservation and reproduction: SB447
Flowers, Cut
  Care and preparation for market: SB442.5
  Flower arrangements: SB449+
Flowers, Everlasting
  Ornamental plants: SB428.5
Flowers, Pressed
  Floral decorations: SB449.3.P7
Flowers, tropical
  Floral decorations: SB449.3.T76
Flowers, Wild
  Floral decorations: SB449.3.W5
  Ornamental plants: SB439+
Fluorides
  Plant pathology: SB747.F58
Fluorine
  Soil chemistry: S592.6.F58
Fluorine compounds
  Plant pesticides: SB952.F55
Fluorosis
  Cattle diseases: SF967.F55
Fluvisols: S592.17.F55
Fly casting
  Angling: SH454.2+
Fly fishing: SH456+
Fly fishing, Saltwater: SH456.2
Fly fishing, Streamer: SH456.25
Fly fishing, Tenkara: SH456.27
Fly, Fruit
  Economic entomology: SB945.F8
Fly, Olive
  Economic entomology: SB945.O4
Fly tying
  Angling: SH451
Fly, Wheat bulb
  Economic entomology: SB945.W56
Flyball
  Dog shows: SF425.85.F56
Flying
  Hunting sports: SK36.3
Flyingfish, Fourwing
  Fisheries: SH351.F68
Fodder trees
  Animal nutrition: SF99.F64
Fold, Scottish
  Cat breeds: SF449.S35
Foliage
  Care and preparation for market: SB442.5
  Floral decorations: SB449.3.F6
Foliage plants
  Ornamental plants: SB431
  Plant pests and diseases: SB608.F59
Foliar feeding: S662.5

Friesian
  Cattle breeds: SF199.F73
  Horse breeds: SF293.F9
Friesian, East
  Sheep breeds: SF373.E3
Fritillaria
  Medicinal plants: SB295.F74
  Ornamental plants: SB413.F74
Frog culture: SH185
Frogs
  Diseases: SF997.5.F76
  Laboratory animal culture: SF407.F74
  Pets: SF459.F83
Frost time
  Agricultural meteorology: S600.7.F76
Frosts, Damage from
  Plant pathology: SB781
Frozen ground
  Sylviculture: SD410.4
Fruit
  Fertilizers: S667.F8
  Plant pests and diseases: SB608.F8
  Soils: S597.F75
Fruit culture: SB354+
Fruit culture under glass: SB358
Fruit fly
  Economic entomology: SB945.F8
Fruit fly, Mediterranean
  Economic entomology: SB945.M54
Fruit fly, Oriental
  Economic entomology: SB945.O63
Fruit growers
  Directories: SB362
Fruit, Passion
  Fruit culture: SB379.P3
Fruit plant catalogs: SB362.3
Fruit seed catalogs: SB362.3
Fruit, Stone
  Fruit culture: SB378
  Plant pests and diseases: SB608.S83
Fruit trees, Dwarf
  Fruit culture: SB357.5
Fruits
  Floral decorations: SB449.3.F7
  Preservation and reproduction: SB447
Fruits, Choice, for culture
  Illustration and description of: SB361
Fruits, Citrus
  Fruit culture: SB369+
  Plant pests and diseases: SB608.C5
Fruits, Small
  Fruit culture: SB381+
Fryers
  Poultry: SF498.8
Fuchsia
  Ornamental plants: SB413.F8
Fuel consumption
  Farm machinery and farm engineering: S675.4
Fuelwood
  Forest exploitation and utilization: SD536.5+
Fuelwood crops
  Forest exploitation and utilization: SD536.5+
Fugu
  Angling: SH691.F83
Fulani, Sudanese
  Cattle breeds: SF199.S83
Fuller's teasel
  Economic plants: SB317.F85
Fumes
  Plant pathology: SB745
Fumigation
  Plant protection: SB973.3
Fumigation of plants and plant products: SB955
Funeral decorations
  Flower arrangement: SB449.5.F84
Fungi
  Animal nutrition: SF99.F8
  Biological pest control agents: SB976.F85
  Effect on fish culture: SH177.F8
Fungi, Edible
  Vegetable culture under glass: SB352.85+
Fungicides
  Plant pest control: SB951.3
Fungus diseases
  Plant pathology: SB733

Garlic mustard
Weeds, parasitic plants, etc.: SB615.G23
Garter snakes
Animal culture: SF515.5.G37
Gas bubble disease
Effect on fish culture: SH177.G3
Gastrodia elata
Medicinal plants: SB295.G37
Gastroenteritis
Diseases and pests of cats: SF986.G37
Gastroenteritis, Transmissible
Swine diseases: SF977.T7
Gastrointestinal diseases
Diseases and pests of dogs: SF992.G38
Gastropoda
Agricultural zoology: SB998.G37
Gates
Agricultural structures: S790+
Gathering, Seafood: SH400+
Gathering, Shellfish: SH400.4+
Gazehounds
Dog breeds: SF429.S68
Gazelles
Zoo and captive wild animal culture: SF408.6.G37
Gear
Fisheries: SH344+
Gear selectivity
Fisheries: SH344.15
Geckos
Animal culture: SF515.5.G43
Pets: SF459.G35
Geese
Diseases: SF995.2
Poultry: SF504.7+
Gelbvieh
Cattle breeds: SF199.G44
Gelidium sesquipedale
Aquaculture: SH391.G44
General cultural practices
Vegetables: SB321+
General quarantine
Veterinary medicine: SF740+
Generative organ diseases
Dogs: SF992.U75
Horses: SF959.U73
Genetic disorders
Dogs: SF992.G45
Genetic engineering
Agriculture: S494.5.G44
Grain and cereals: SB189.53
Plant propagation: SB123.57
Genetics
Plant culture: SB106.G46
Genetics, Forest
Sylviculture: SD399.5
Genetics, Veterinary: SF756.5+
Genome mapping
Veterinary genetics: SF756.65
Gentian
Ornamental plants: SB413.G3
Gentianella scopulorum
Plant pests and diseases: SB608.G38
Genypterus blacodes
Fisheries: SH351.G46
Geographic information systems
Fisheries: SH331.5.G46
Geography
Agriculture: S494.5.G46
Georgian gardens: SB457.68
Geraniums
Flowers and flower culture: SB413.G35
Tannin plants: SB315.G4
Geraniums, Scented
Aromatic plants: SB303.S34
Gerbera
Ornamental plants: SB413.G36
Plant pests and diseases: SB608.G4
Gerbils
Pets: SF459.G4
Geriatrics, Veterinary: SF768.5
German coach-horse
Horse breeds: SF293.G3
German hunt terrier
Dog breeds: SF429.G36
German pinscher
Dog breeds: SF429.G367
German shepherd
Dog breeds: SF429.G37

Greenhouse plants
  Fertilizers: S667.G74
  Plant pests and diseases: SB608.G82
Greenhouses: SB414.6+
Greenhouses, Window: SB416.3
Greens
  Vegetable culture: SB339
Greens, Salad
  Vegetable culture: SB351.S25
Grevillea: SB413.G73
Grevillea robusta
  Economic plants: SB317.G74
Grey Tirolean
  Cattle breeds: SF199.G74
Greyhound, Italian
  Dog breeds: SF429.I89
Greyhound, Racing: SF440
  Dog breeds: SF429.G8
Greyhounds
  Dog breeds: SF429.G8
Griffon, Brussels
  Dog breeds: SF429.B79
Grooming
  Cats: SF447.65
  Dogs: SF427.5+
  Horses: SF285.7
Grooming industry, Dog: SF427.55
Ground cover fires
  Forestry: SD421.47+
Ground cover plants
  Ornamental plants: SB432
Groundfish
  Fisheries: SH351.G76
Groundnut, Bambara
  Vegetable culture: SB351.B35
Grounds, Home
  Landscape architecture: SB473
Groupers
  Fish culture: SH167.G86
Grouse
  Bird hunting: SK325.G7
  Diseases: SF994.4.G7
Growers of fruit
  Directories: SB362
Growing media, Plant: S589.8+
Growing of seeds: SB117+
Growing, Seed
  Sylviculture: SD401.6+
Growing timber
  Costs: SD393
Growth
  Forest trees: SD396
Growth regulators
  Plant culture: SB128
Grunts
  Fisheries: SH351.G78
Guaaiacum
  Forest trees: SD397.L5
Guano
  Fertilizers and improvement of the
    soil: S649
Guar
  Economic plants: SB317.G75
Guarana
  Medicinal plants: SB295.G8
  Plant pests and diseases: SB608.G9
Guava
  Fruit culture: SB379.G8
Guayule
  Gum and resin plants: SB291.G8
  Plant pests and diseases: SB608.G93
Guazuma ulmifolia
  Economic plants: SB317.G77
Guernsey
  Cattle breeds: SF199.G8
Guerrilla gardens: SB454.3.G84
Guidebooks
  Horsemanship: SF309.254+
Guidebooks for traveling with dogs:
  SF427.457+
Guinea fowl
  Poultry: SF506
Guinea grass: SB201.G8
Guinea pigs
  Animal culture: SF401.G85
  Diseases: SF997.5.G84
  Laboratory animal culture:
    SF407.G85
Guinea pigs (Cavies)
  Pets: SF459.G9
Gujarati
  Sheep breeds: SF373.G84

Horses
  Veterinary physiology: SF768.2.H67
Horses, Claiming
  Horse racing: SF356
Horses, Coach: SF312
Horses, Competition
  Horse sports: SF294.3+
Horses, Draft: SF311+
Horses, Dressage: SF309.65+
Horses, Driving: SF305.75
Horses, Feral: SF360+
Horse's foot
  Veterinary medicine: SF907+
Horses, Racing, Illustration of: SF337
Horses, Show: SF295.185+
Horses, Western: SF309.34
Horses, Wild: SF360+
Horseshoeing
  Veterinary medicine: SF907+
Horseshoes
  Veterinary medicine: SF909
Horsetail, Marsh
  Weeds, parasitic plants, etc.:
    SB615.M3
Horsewomen: SF284.4+
Horticultural crops: SB317.5+
  Fertilizers: S667.A2
  Pests and diseases: SB608.H83
Horticultural machinery: S678.7
Horticultural service industry: SB446+
Horticultural voyages: SB39
Horticulture: SB317.5+
Hospitals, Veterinary: SF604.4+
Hosta
  Ornamental plants: SB413.H73
Hotels, Fishing: SH405
Houbara
  Game birds: SF510.H68
Houdan
  Poultry breeds: SF489.H7
Hound, Ibizan
  Dog breeds: SF429.I24
Hound, Pharaoh
  Dog breeds: SF429.P43
Hounds
  Dog breeds: SF429.H6
Hounds, Basset
  Dog breeds: SF429.B2
House plant industry: SB419.3
House plants
  Marketing: SB419.3
  Ornamental plants: SB419+
  Plant pests and diseases: SB608.H84
House plants in interior decoration:
  SB419.25
Houseplant industry: SB419.3
Houseplants
  Marketing: SB419.3
  Ornamental plants: SB419+
Houseplants in interior decoration:
  SB419.25
Housing
  Animal culture: SF91
  Birds: SF461.7
  Canaries: SF463.4
  Cattle: SF206
  Dogs: SF427.43
  Ducks and geese: SF505.55
  Goats: SF384
  Horses: SF285.35
  Laboratory animals: SF406.3
  Pets: SF414.2
  Poultry: SF494.5
  Rabbits and hares: SF453.8
  Sheep: SF375.8
  Swine: SF396.3
  Zoo and captive wild animals:
    SF408.45
Housing and environmental control
  Dogs: SF427.43
Hovawart
  Dog breeds: SF429.H66
Huckleberries
  Fruit culture: SB386.H83
Hucul horse
  Horse breeds: SF293.H78
Hummingbirds
  Pet and captive birds: SF473.H84
Humpback whale: SH384.H84
Humus: S592.8+
Hungarian
  Horse breeds: SF293.H79

I

Korat cat
  Cat breeds: SF449.K67
Korean flower arrangement: SB450.8
Korean gardens: SB458.2
Koryū Sokenryū
  Japanese flower arrangement:
    SB450.5.K68
Kōshū school
  Japanese flower arrangement:
    SB450.5.K69
Krill
  Fisheries: SH380.7+
  Fishery processing: SH336.5.K75
Kromfohrländer
  Dog breeds: SF429.K76
Kudzu
  Legumes: SB205.K8
  Weeds, parasitic plants, etc.:
    SB615.K83
Kuhland
  Cattle breeds: SF199.K9
Kuvasz
  Dog breeds: SF429.K88

L

Labor productivity
  Agriculture (General): S564
  Fishery processing plant
    management: SH335.5.L3
  Forestry: SD387.L3
Laboratories
  Forest exploitation and utilization:
    SD433
  Forestry education: SD356.7+
  Seeds: SB113.85
  Veterinary medicine: SF756.3+
Laboratories, Agricultural: S539.5+
Laboratories, Agricultural chemistry:
  S587.3+
Laboratory animals
  Animal culture: SF405.5+
  Diseases: SF996.5
Laboratory diagnosis
  Veterinary medicine: SF772.6+
Laboratory manuals
  Agricultural education: S495
Laboratory manuals
  Plant pathology: SB732.56
Laboratory rabbits
  Diseases: SF996.5
Laboratory rodents
  Diseases: SF996.5
Labradoodle
  Dog breeds: SF429.L29
Labrador retriever
  Dog breeds: SF429.L3
Labyrinth fishes
  Aquarium fishes: SF458.L26
Labyrinths
  Landscape architecture: SB475
Lac-insects
  Animal culture: SF561
Lacewings
  Insect culture: SF562.L33
Lady Dudley Challenge Cup
  Horse racing: SF359.7.L33
Ladybugs
  Insect culture: SF562.L34
  Pets: SF459.L33
Lafoensia glyptocarpa
  Forest trees: SD397.L25
Lagerstroemia
  Ornamental plants: SB413.L34
Lagorosiphon major
  Weeds, parasitic plants, etc.:
    SB615.L24
Laika, East Siberian
  Dog breeds: SF429.E3
Lake renewal
  Fish culture: SH157.85.L34
Lake sturgeon
  Fisheries: SH351.L33
Lake trout
  Angling: SH689.7
Lake whitefish
  Angling: SH691.L35
Lakeland terriers
  Dog breeds: SF429.L35
Lama (Genus)
  Animal culture: SF401.L35
  Diseases: SF997.5.L35
Lambs
  Animal culture: SF376.5

Lameness
Cattle diseases: SF967.L3
Horse diseases: SF959.L25
Lamiaceae
Vegetable culture: SB351.L36
Laminaria digitata
Aquaculture: SH391.L33
Laminaria hyperborea
Aquaculture: SH391.L35
Laminaria saccharina
Aquaculture: SH391.L38
Laminitis
Horse diseases: SF959.L3
Lampreys
Effect on fish culture: SH177.L3
Fisheries: SH351.L35
Land birds
Bird hunting: SK323+
Land, Clearing of
Use of explosives: S679+
Land conservation: S950+
Land exchange
Forest reserves (U.S.): SD427.L3
Land hermit crabs
Pets: SF459.H47
Land reclamation
Plants for: S621.5.P59
Landowners
Forestry: SD387.L33
Landrace
Swine breeds: SF393.L3
Landrace, Danish
Swine breeds: SF393.D34
Lands, Alkali: S595
Landscape architects: SB469.37+
Landscape architects, Women: SB469.375
Landscape architecture: SB469+
as a profession: SB469.37+
Landscape architecture, Desert: SB475.9.D47
Landscape architecture, Hillside: SB475.9.H54
Landscape architecture, Urban: SB472.7
Landscape contracting: SB472.55
Landscape design: SB472.45
Landscape design, Forest
Landscape architecture: SB475.9.F67
Landscape design, Wetland: SB475.9.W48
Landscape gardening: SB469+
Landscape irrigation: SB475.82
Landscape management
Forestry: SD387.L35
Landscape plants
Plant pests and diseases: SB608.L27
Landscapes, Tray
Ornamental plants: SB447.5
Landscaping, Edible
Landscape architecture: SB475.9.E35
Landscaping industry: SB472.5+
Landscaping, Interior
Ornamental plants: SB419.25
Landscaping, Natural
Ornamental plants: SB439+
Landscaping with native plants
Ornamental plants: SB439+
Landslides
Forestry: SD424
Language
Horticulture: SB318.36
Lannea coromandelica
Gum and resin plants: SB291.L35
Lantana camara
Weeds, parasitic plants, etc.: SB615.L35
Larch
Plant pests and diseases: SB608.L3
Larch, Dahurian
Forest trees: SD397.D3
Larch, European
Forest trees: SD397.E836
Larch, Japanese
Forest trees: SD397.J34
Larch, Polish
Plant pests and diseases: SB608.P774
Larch, Siberian
Forest trees: SD397.S515
Plant pests and diseases: SB608.S46
Larch, Western
Forest trees: SD397.W454

Mathematical models
Agricultural meteorology: S600.43.M37
Agriculture: S540.M38
Animal culture: SF140.M35
Fisheries: SH331.5.M48
Forest fires and wildfires: SD421.45.M37
Forestry: SD387.M33
Soil conservation and protection: S627.M36
Mathematics
Forestry: SD387.M33
Mathematics, Agricultural: S565.97+
Matwork plants: SB281+
Maure
Cattle breeds: SF199.M38
Mauritia flexuosa
Economic plants: SB317.M38
Maus, Egyptian
Cat breeds: SF449.E39
Mayhaws
Fruit culture: SB386.M39
Mazes
Landscape architecture: SB475
MCPA
Plant pesticides: SB952.M15
Meadow fescue: SB201.M4
Meadowlark
Agricultural zoology: SB996.M5
Meadows, Formation and care of: SB199
Meagre
Fisheries: SH351.M4
Meal, Soybean
Animal nutrition: SF99.S72
Measurement
Forest exploitation and utilization: SD555+
Irrigation water: S618.4
Mechanics, Agricultural: S674.4+, S675.3
Meconopsis
Ornamental plants: SB413.M42
Medicago
Legumes: SB205.M4
Medication
Animal nutrition: SF98.M4
Medicinal plants: SB293+
Plant pests and diseases: SB608.M38
Medicine, Preventive
Veterinary medicine: SF740+
Medicine, Veterinary: SF600+
Medieval gardens: SB458.35
Mediterranean climate
Gardens and gardening: SB454.3.M43
Mediterranean flour moth
Economic entomology: SB945.M5
Mediterranean fruit fly
Economic entomology: SB945.M54
Medusahead wildrye
Weeds, parasitic plants, etc.: SB615.M38
Melaleuca
Oil-bearing and wax plants: SB299.M44
Melaleuca quinquenervia
Weeds, parasitic plants, etc.: SB615.M39
Melbourne Cup
Horse racing: SF357.M4
Melioration
Lands: S604.8+
Melipona
Bee culture: SF539.8.M44
Meloidogyne
Agricultural zoology: SB998.M45
Melon-flies
Economic entomology: SB945.M56
Melons
Fruit culture: SB379.M44
Implements and machinery for: S715.M44
Plant pests and diseases: SB608.M4
Menhaden
Fisheries: SH351.M5
Meningitis
Horse diseases: SF959.M4
Veterinary medicine: SF799
Menippe mercenaria
Fisheries: SH380.47.M46

N

O

Oak
  Forest trees: SD397.O12
  Ornamental plants: SB413.O34
  Plant pests and diseases: SB608.O115
Oak, California black
  Forest trees: SD397.C33
Oak, Durmast
  Forest trees: SD397.D87
Oak, Emory
  Forest trees: SD397.E46
Oak, English
  Forest trees: SD397.E54
Oak, European Turkey
  Forest trees: SD397.E84
Oak, Live
  Forest trees: SD397.L64
Oak tasar silkworm
  Sericulture: SF560.O18
Oak, Valonia
  Forest trees: SD397.V3
Oat, Wild
  Grains and cereals: SB191.W53
  Weeds, parasitic plants, etc.: SB615.W54
Oats
  Animal nutrition: SF99.O28
  Grain and cereals: SB191.O2
  Plant pests and diseases: SB608.O2
Obedience classes
  Dog shows: SF425.7
Obedience trials
  Dog shows: SF425.7
Obstetrics
  Veterinary medicine: SF887
Oceanography, Fishery: SH343.2
Ocelots
  Pets: SF459.O2
Ocicat
  Cat breeds: SF449.O35
Ocimum
  Economic plants: SB317.B25
Ocotea rodiaei
  Forest trees: SD397.O36
Octopuses
  Fisheries: SH374+
Odor
  Animal nutrition: SF97.7
Ohara school
  Japanese flower arrangement: SB450.5.O4
Ohia lehua
  Plant pests and diseases: SB608.O25
Oil
  Plant pesticides: SB952.O4
Oil-bearing plants: SB298+
Oil cake
  Animal nutrition: SF99.O4
Oil, Cod liver
  Animal nutrition: SF99.C58
Oil palm
  Implements and machinery for: S715.O37
  Plant pests and diseases: SB608.O27
  Soils: S597.O35
Oil-polluted lands
  Melioration of lands: S621.5.O33
Oil pollution
  Effect on fish culture: SH177.O53
Oil sands
  Melioration of lands: S621.5.O34
Oil sands wastewater
  Effect on fish culture: SH177.O54
Oils
  Animal nutrition: SF98.O34
Oilseed plants
  Plant pests and diseases: SB608.O3
Oiticica tree
  Oil-bearing and wax plants: SB299.O38
Okra
  Vegetable culture: SB351.O5
Old English Game
  Poultry: SF502.8+
Old English sheepdog
  Dog breeds: SF429.O4
Old growth forest conservation: SD387.O43
Old growth forests: SD387.O43

P

People with disabilities
  Parks and public reservations:
    SB486.H35
Pepper
  Plant pests and diseases: SB608.P5
Pepper, Black
  Spice and condiment plants:
    SB307.P5
Pepper weevil
  Economic entomology: SB945.P48
Peppermint
  Medicinal plants: SB295.P4
Peppers
  Fertilizers: S667.P45
  Spice and condiment plants:
    SB307.P4
  Vegetable culture: SB351.P4
Perch
  Angling: SH691.P4
  Fish culture: SH167.P4
Perch, Pacific ocean
  Fisheries: SH351.P27
Perch, Pike
  Fish culture: SH167.P6
Percheron
  Horse breeds: SF293.P4
Perchlorates
  Animal nutrition: SF98.P44
Perennial veldt grass: SB201.V44
Perennials
  Ornamental plants: SB434
Periodical cicada
  Economic entomology: SB945.C55
Permaculture: S494.5.P47
Permit
  Angling: SH691.P45
Perosis
  Avian diseases: SF995.6.P4
Perro de presa canario: SF429.P35
Persian
  Cat breeds: SF449.P4
Persian gardens: SB458.5
Persimmon
  Forest trees: SD397.P47
  Fruit culture: SB379.P4
Personnel management
  Agriculture (General): S563.6
Peruvian paso horse
  Horse breeds: SF293.P45
Pest control
  Plant culture: SB950+
Pest introduction
  Plant pest control: SB990+
Pest resistance
  Plant pathology: SB750
Peste des petits ruminants
  Sheep and goats: SF969.P47
Pesticidal plants: SB292.A2+
Pesticide effects
  Plant pathology: SB744+
Pesticide residues
  Animal nutrition: SF98.P46
Pesticide toxicology
  Bee diseases and pests:
    SF538.5.P65
Pesticides
  Contaminant of milk and cream:
    SF254.P4
  Effect on fish culture: SH177.P44
  Plant pest control: SB950.9+
  Soil chemistry: S592.6.P43
Pesticides, Biodegradable
  Plant pest control: SB951.145.B54
Pesticides, Botanical
  Plant pest control: SB951.145.B68
Pesticides, Controlled release
  Plant pest control: SB951.145.C65
Pesticides, Light-activated
  Plant pest control: SB951.145.L54
Pesticides, Microbial
  Biological pest control agents:
    SB976.M55
Pesticides, Natural
  Plant pest control: SB951.145.N37
Pesticides policy, Plant: SB970+
Pesticides, Resistance to
  Plant pesticides: SB957
Pesticides, Soil
  Plant pest control: SB951.145.S65
Pesticides, Systemic
  Plant pest control: SB951.145.S97
Pests
  Bee culture: SF538+
  Cattle: SF967.P3

Riding schools
Horsemanship: SF310.A1+
Riding, Show
Horse shows: SF295.2
Riding, Trail
Horse shows: SF296.T7
Horsemanship: SF309.28
Riding, Trick
Horse shows: SF296.T75
Riding, Western
Horsemanship: SF309.3+
Rifle hunting: SK38
Rifles
Hunting sports: SK274.2+
Rigs
Angling: SH452.9.R5
Rikyū Koryū
Japanese flower arrangement: SB450.5.R54
Rinderpest
Cattle diseases: SF966
Ring-necked pheasant
Diseases: SF994.4.R5
Ring seines: SH344.6.R56
Ringworm
Veterinary medicine: SF809.R55
Ripening
Apple: SB363.4
Fruit: SB360.5
River sardine
Fisheries: SH351.R58
Roach
Angling: SH691.R6
Fisheries: SH351.R6
Roads, Forest: SD389
Roadside marketing: S571.5
Robinia
Forest trees: SD397.R62
Robotics
Farm machinery and farm engineering: S678.65
Rock-garden plants
Ornamental plants: SB421
Rock gardens: SB459
Rock lobsters
Fisheries: SH380+
Rock-rose
Ornamental plants: SB413.R7
Rocky Mountain goat
Big game hunting: SK305.R62
Rocky Mountain horse
Horse breeds: SF293.R63
Rocky Mountain locust
Economic entomology: SB945.R7
Rod wrapping
Angling: SH452.2
Rodenticides
Plant pest control: SB951.8
Rodents
Agricultural zoology: SB994.R6
Diseases: SF997.5.R64
Laboratory animal culture: SF407.R6
Pets: SF459.R63
Rodents, Laboratory
Diseases: SF996.5
Rods
Angling: SH452+
Roe's abalone
Fisheries: SH371.54.R63
Rohdea
Ornamental plants: SB413.R8
Roller
Canary breeds: SF463.7.R64
Roman gardens: SB458.55
Romanov
Sheep breeds: SF373.R6
Romans
History of agriculture: S431
Roof gardening
Ornamental plants: SB419.5
Roosevelt expedition, 1909-1910: SK252
Root crops: SB209+
Plant pests and diseases: SB608.R7
Vegetable culture: SB351.R65
Root diseases
Plant pathology: SB732.87
Root-knot nematodes
Agricultural zoology: SB998.M45
Root rot, Armillaria
Plant pathology: SB741.A7
Root rots
Plant pathology: SB741.R75

Satellites, Artificial
Agricultural meteorology: S600.7.R46
Satin moth
Economic entomology: SB945.S25
Saucer scallop
Fisheries: SH372.3.S28
Saury, Pacific
Fisheries: SH351.P3
Savannah
Cat breeds: SF449.S28
Sawflies
Economic entomology: SB945.S3
Saxifraga
Ornamental plants: SB413.S28
Saxon merino
Sheep breeds: SF373.S3
Scabies
Cattle diseases: SF967.S3
Sheep and goats: SF969.S2
Scabies, Psoroptic
Sheep and goats: SF969.P74
Scalare
Aquarium fishes: SF458.S34
Scale, Florida wax
Economic entomology: SB945.F64
Scale, Hemispherical
Economic entomology: SB945.H29
Scale insects
Economic entomology: SB939
Scale, San Jose
Economic entomology: SB945.S2
Scaling
Forest exploitation and utilization: SD555+
Scallops
Fisheries: SH372+
Scarabaeidae
Economic entomology: SB945.S35
Scarecrows
Agricultural zoology: SB995.25
Scatophagus argus
Fish culture: SH167.S26
Scented geraniums
Aromatic plants: SB303.S34
Scheduling of irrigation: S619.S33
Schipperke
Dog breeds: SF429.S36
Schnauzer, Giant
Dog breeds: SF429.G5
Schnauzer, Miniature
Dog breeds: SF429.M58
Schnauzers
Dog breeds: SF429.S37
Schnoodle
Dog breeds: SF429.S378
School farms: SB55+
School gardens: SB55+
School riding
Horsemanship: SF309.48+
Schools
Veterinary medicine: SF756.3+
Schools of Japanese flower arrangement: SB450.5.A+
Schools, Riding
Horsemanship: SF310.A1+
Schutzhund
Dog shows: SF425.85.S35
Schutzhund dogs: SF428.78
Sclerocarya birrea
Fruit culture: SB379.S35
Scleroderris canker
Plant pathology: SB741.S38
Scombridae
Fishery processing: SH336.5.S36
Scootering
Dogs: SF425.85.S38
Score books
Angling: SH455
Scorpionfishes
Aquarium fishes: SF458.S37
Scorpions
Pets: SF459.S35
Scots pine
Forest trees: SD397.P614
Plant pests and diseases: SB608.S44
Scottish deerhound
Dog breeds: SF429.S39
Scottish fold
Cat breeds: SF449.S35
Scottish terrier
Dog breeds: SF429.S4
Scrap, Fish
Fertilizers: S659

Soybean meal
  Animal nutrition: SF99.S72
Space mutation breeding
  Agriculture: S494.33
Spaniel, American water
  Dog breeds: SF429.A735
Spaniel, Clumber
  Dog breeds: SF429.C53
Spaniel, Cocker
  Dog breeds: SF429.C55
Spaniel, English cocker
  Dog breeds: SF429.E47
Spaniel, English toy
  Dog breeds: SF429.E73
Spaniel, Field
  Dog breeds: SF429.F36
Spaniel, Tibetan
  Dog breeds: SF429.T5
Spaniel, Welsh springer
  Dog breeds: SF429.W37
Spaniels
  Dog breeds: SF429.S7
Spaniels, Brittany
  Dog breeds: SF429.B78
Spaniels, Cavalier King Charles
  Dog breeds: SF429.C36
Spaniels, English springer
  Dog breeds: SF429.E7
Spaniels, Irish water
  Dog breeds: SF429.I83
Spaniels, Japanese
  Dog breeds: SF429.J3
Spanish broom
  Economic plants: SB317.S7
Spanish merino
  Sheep breeds: SF373.S75
Spanish moss
  Textile and fiber plants: SB261.S63
Spanish water dog
  Dog breeds: SF429.S72
Sparrow
  Agricultural zoology: SB996.S7
Spartina
  Weeds, parasitic plants, etc.:
    SB615.S63
Spavin
  Horse diseases: SF959.S6
Spawning, Artificial
  Fish culture: SH155.6
Spawning, Induced
  Fish culture: SH155.7
Spear fishing: SH458
Spears
  Hunting sports: SK274.85
Specialities
  Veterinary medicine: SF760.S64
Specialization, Veterinary medicine:
  SF760.S64
Specifications
  Landscaping industry: SB472.56
Spectacled caiman
  Big game hunting: SK305.S64
Spectroscopy, Nuclear magnetic
  resonance
  Agriculture: S540.N82
Sperm whale: SH384.S66
Spey casting: SH454.25
Sphaeraspis salisburiensis
  Economic entomology: SB945.S645
Sphynx
  Cat breeds: SF449.S68
Spice plants: SB305+
Spider, Red
  Economic entomology: SB945.R45
Spiders
  Economic entomology: SB945.S647
  Pets: SF459.S64
Spin-cast fishing: SH456.5
Spin casting
  Angling: SH454.6
Spin fishing: SH456.5
Spinach
  Vegetable culture: SB351.S7
Spinal cord disease
  Horse diseases: SF959.S65
Spinal osteophytosis
  Cattle diseases: SF967.S6
Spindle tree
  Gum and resin plants: SB291.S6
Spinning reels
  Angling: SH452.6
Spinone
  Dog breeds: SF429.S74

U

Ucuhuba
Oil-bearing and wax plants: SB299.U4
Udder diseases
Cattle diseases: SF967.U3
Udo
Vegetable culture: SB351.U3
Ultisols: S592.17.U48
Ultrasonography
Veterinary medicine: SF772.58
Umbelliferae
Plant pests and diseases: SB608.U42
Umbelliferae (General)
Vegetable culture: SB351.U54
Underwater explosions
Effect on fish culture: SH177.P7
Ungulata
Diseases: SF997.5.U5
Ungulates
Zoo and captive wild animal culture: SF408.6.U54
Upland game birds
Diseases: SF994.4.U6
Urban agriculture: S494.5.U72
Urban aquaculture: SH141
Urban forestry: SB436
Urban landscape architecture: SB472.7
Urban livestock production systems
Animal culture: SF140.L65
Urban pests
Economic entomology: SB938
Plant culture: SB603.3+
Urban soils: S592.17.U73
Urban vegetation management: SB472.7
Urchins, Sea
Fisheries: SH399.S32
Urea
Animal nutrition: SF98.U7
Fertilizers and improvement of the soil: S650.8+
Ureas, Benzoylphenyl
Plant pesticides: SB952.B43
Urease inhibitors
Fertilizers and improvement of the soil: S652.3
Urena lobata
Textile and fiber plants: SB261.U7
Urinary diseases
Cats: SF986.U74
Dogs: SF992.U75
Horses: SF959.U73
Urinary organs
Veterinary medicine: SF871+
Urine examination
Veterinary clinical chemistry: SF773
Urochloa trichopus
Grasses: SB201.U75
Urogenital organs
Veterinary medicine: SF871+
Utensils
Japanese flower arrangement: SB450.6
Uterine diseases
Cattle diseases: SF967.U8
Utilization
Forestry: SD541
Landscape architects: SB469.38
Veterinarians: SF756.46+
Utilization of algae: SH389.6
Utilization of marine algae: SH390.7

V

Vacation guides
Horsemanship: SF309.254+
Vacation guides for traveling with dogs: SF427.457+
Vaccines
Veterinary pharmacology: SF918.V32
Vaccinium vitis-idaea
Fruit culture: SB386.V3
Vaginitis, Granular
Cattle diseases: SF967.G65
Valeriana
Medicinal plants: SB295.V34
Valley oak
Forest trees: SD397.V27
Vallhund, Swedish
Dog breeds: SF429.S94

Valonia oak
  Forest trees: SD397.V3
Valuation
  Forest exploitation and utilization: SD551+
  Shrubs and ornamental trees: SB437.6+
Vanadium
  Effect on fish culture: SH177.V35
Vanda
  Flowers and flower culture: SB409.8.V36
Vandalism
  Parks and public reservations: SB486.V35
Vanilla
  Spice and condiment plants: SB307.V2
Variation, Wood
  Forest exploitation and utilization: SD535.7
Variegated plants
  Ornamental plants: SB438.8
Varieties
  Apple: SB363.3.A1+
  Field crops: SB185.75
  Fruit: SB357.33
  Grain and cereals: SB189.47
  Grape culture: SB398.28
  Orchids: SB409.7
  Roses: SB411.6+
  Vegetables: SB324.73
Varieties, Protected
  Plant breeding, crossing, selection, etc.: SB123.5
Variety testing
  Plant breeding, crossing, selection, etc.: SB123.45
Varmint hunting: SK336
Varroa disease
  Bee diseases and pests: SF538.5.V37
Varroa jacobsoni
  Bee diseases and pests: SF538.5.V37
Vaulting
  Horse shows: SF296.V37
Vegetable culture under glass: SB351.7+
Vegetable fertilizers and amendments: S661+
Vegetable oils
  Agricultural chemistry: S587.73.V44
Vegetable plant catalogs: SB320.27
Vegetable seed catalogs: SB320.27
Vegetables
  Fertilizers: S667.V5
  Floral decorations: SB449.3.F7
  Implements and machinery for: S715.V4
  Plant culture: SB320+
  Plant pests and diseases: SB608.V4
  Soils: S597.V4
Vegetables, Chinese
  Vegetable culture: SB351.C54
Vegetables, Japanese
  Vegetable culture: SB351.C54
Vegetables, Leafy
  Vegetable culture: SB339
Vegetables, Tropical: SB324.56
Vegetation management
  Plant culture: SB106.V43
Vegetation management, Urban: SB472.7
Vegetative propagation
  Fruit culture: SB359.45
Veld grass
  Forage crops: SB201.V44
  Plant pests and diseases: SB608.V44
  Weeds, parasitic plants, etc.: SB615.V44
Veld plants
  Economic plants: SB317.V44
Veldt grass, Perennial: SB201.V44, SB201.V46
Vernacular gardens: SB457.52
Vernonia
  Vegetable culture: SB351.V47
Vertebrates
  Agricultural zoology: SB993.4+
Vertical gardening: SB463.5
Verticillium
  Plant pathology: SB741.V45

Worms
Pets: SF459.W66
Worms, Marine
Fisheries: SH399.W65
Wormseed
Oil-bearing and wax plants: SB299.C45
Wounds
Veterinary medicine: SF914.3+
Wrapping, Rod
Angling: SH452.2
Wrasses
Aquarium fishes: SF458.W73
Wreaths
Floral decorations: SB449.5.W74
Wreckfish
Fisheries: SH351.W73
Württemberg
Sheep breeds: SF373.W9
Wyandotte
Poultry breeds: SF489.W9

X

Xanathates
Effect on fish culture: SH177.X35
Xanthomonas
Plant pathology: SB741.X35
Xanthorrhoea
Ornamental plants: SB413.X36
Xeriscaping
Landscape architecture: SB475.83
Xerophytes
Ornamental plants: SB439.8
Xiphophorus
Aquarium fishes: SF458.X58
Xoloitzcuintli
Dog breeds: SF429.X6
Xyleborus destruens
Economic entomology: SB945.X94

Y

Yabbies
Fisheries: SH380.94.Y32
Yak
Animal culture: SF401.Y3
Yam
Root and tuber crops: SB211.Y3
Yamamai
Sericulture: SF560.Y34
Yeast
Animal nutrition: SF99.Y4
Yellow-bellied sapsucker
Agricultural zoology: SB996.Y4
Yellow birch
Forest trees: SD397.Y44
Yellow buckeye
Forest trees: SD397.Y442
Yellow perch
Fish culture: SH167.P4
Yellow pines
Forest trees: SD397.P75
Yellowfin tuna
Fisheries: SH351.Y43
Yellowhead
Pet and captive birds: SF473.Y44
Yellowtail
Fisheries: SH351.Y44
Yersinia enterocolitica infections
Veterinary medicine: SF809.Y47
Yew
Forest trees: SD397.Y46
Yield
Animal culture: SF111+
Forest exploitation and utilization: SD553
Yogurt
Dairy products: SF275.Y6
Yomud
Horse breeds: SF293.Y7
Yorkie poo
Dog breeds: SF429.Y57
Yorkshire
Canary breeds: SF463.7.Y67
Swine breeds: SF393.Y6
Yorkshire terrier
Dog breeds: SF429.Y6
Yucca
Economic plants: SB317.Y82

Z

Zambezi teak
  Forest trees: SD397.Z35
Zander
  Angling: SH691.Z35
Zante currants
  Fruit culture: SB399
Zebra danio
  Laboratory animal culture: SF407.Z42
Zebra finch
  Pet and captive birds: SF473.Z42
Zebus
  Cattle breeds: SF199.Z4
Zeiraphera rufimitrana
  Economic entomology: SB945.Z43
Zinc
  Agricultural chemistry: S587.5.Z55
  Effect on fish culture: SH177.Z5
  Fertilizers and improvement of the soil: S653.5.Z56
  Plant nutrition disorders and deficiency diseases: SB743.Z55
  Soil chemistry: S592.6.Z55
Zinnia
  Ornamental plants: SB413.Z54
Zizania latifolia
  Economic plants: SB317.Z49
Zoo animals
  Animal culture: SF408+
  Diseases: SF995.84+
Zoo veterinarians: SF995.84+
Zoology, Agricultural: SB992+
Zoology, Economic: SF84+
Zoology, Economic, applied to crops: SB992+
Zoonosis control
  Veterinary medicine: SF740+
Zoysia japonica: SB201.Z6, SB202.A+

GPO U.S. GOVERNMENT PRINTING OFFICE: 2012–372–396/40014